Psychology
FOR
DUMMIES®

Psychology FOR DUMMIES®

by Adam Cash, PsyD

Hungry Minds™

Best-Selling Books • Digital Downloads • e-Books • Answer Networks • e-Newsletters • Branded Web Sites • e-Learning

New York, NY ◆ Cleveland, OH ◆ Indianapolis, IN

Psychology For Dummies®

Published by:
Hungry Minds, Inc.
909 Third Avenue
New York, NY 10022
www.hungryminds.com
www.dummies.com

Library of Congress Control Number: 2002103273

ISBN: 0-7645-5434-4

Printed in the United States of America

10 9 8 7 6 5 4 3 2 1

1B/QZ/QV/QS/IN

Distributed in the United States by Hungry Minds, Inc.

Distributed by CDG Books Canada Inc. for Canada; by Transworld Publishers Limited in the United Kingdom; by IDG Norge Books for Norway; by IDG Sweden Books for Sweden; by IDG Books Australia Publishing Corporation Pty. Ltd. for Australia and New Zealand; by TransQuest Publishers Pte Ltd. for Singapore, Malaysia, Thailand, Indonesia, and Hong Kong; by Gotop Information Inc. for Taiwan; by ICG Muse, Inc. for Japan; by Intersoft for South Africa; by Eyrolles for France; by International Thomson Publishing for Germany, Austria and Switzerland; by Distribuidora Cuspide for Argentina; by LR International for Brazil; by Galileo Libros for Chile; by Ediciones ZETA S.C.R. Ltda. for Peru; by WS Computer Publishing Corporation, Inc., for the Philippines; by Contemporanea de Ediciones for Venezuela; by Express Computer Distributors for the Caribbean and West Indies; by Micronesia Media Distributor, Inc. for Micronesia; by Chips Computadoras S.A. de C.V. for Mexico; by Editorial Norma de Panama S.A. for Panama; by American Bookshops for Finland.

For general information on Hungry Minds' products and services please contact our Customer Care department; within the U.S. at 800-762-2974, outside the U.S. at 317-572-3993 or fax 317-572-4002.

For sales inquiries and resellers information, including discounts, premium and bulk quantity sales and foreign language translations please contact our Customer Care department at 800-434-3422, fax 317-572-4002 or write to Hungry Minds, Inc., Attn: Customer Care department, 10475 Crosspoint Boulevard, Indianapolis, IN 46256.

For information on licensing foreign or domestic rights, please contact our Sub-Rights Customer Care department at 212-884-5000.

For information on using Hungry Minds' products and services in the classroom or for ordering examination copies, please contact our Educational Sales department at 800-434-2086 or fax 317-572-4005.

Please contact our Public Relations department at 212-884-5163 for press review copies or 212-884-5000 for author interviews and other publicity information or fax 212-884-5400.

For authorization to photocopy items for corporate, personal, or educational use, please contact Copyright Clearance Center, 222 Rosewood Drive, Danvers, MA 01923, or fax 978-750-4470.

Hungry Minds™ is a trademark of Hungry Minds, Inc.

About the Author

Dr. Adam Cash is a graduate of Loma Linda University. He teaches psychology at both the community college and university level. He has worked as a clinical psychologist in a wide variety of settings and currently works as a forensic psychologist with mentally disordered criminal offenders. He is also in private practice in Pomona, California, specializing in chronic mental illness, stress and coping, and men's issues.

Dedication

To my beautiful wife Liyona. Thank you for the inspiration. Also to my family, friends, and colleagues.

Publisher's Acknowledgments

We're proud of this book; please send us your comments through our Hungry Minds Online Registration Form located at www.dummies.com.

Some of the people who helped bring this book to market include the following:

Acquisitions, Editorial, and Media Development

Project Editor: Tonya Maddox Cupp

Acquisitions Editor: Greg Tubach

Copy Editor: Mike Baker

Acquisitions Coordinator: Joyce Pepple

Technical Editors: Jay Brand PsyD, Robert Sawicky MD

Editorial Manager: Jennifer Ehrlich

Media Development Manager: Laura VanWinkle

Editorial Assistant: Carol Strickland

Cover Photos: PHX-Hagerstown

Production

Project Coordinator: Ryan Steffen

Layout and Graphics: Stephanie D. Jumper, Tiffany Muth, Barry Offringa, Betty Schulte, Julie Trippetti, Mary J. Virgin, Jeremey Unger, Erin Zeltner

Proofreaders: Laura Albert, Andy Hollandbeck, Susan Moritz, TECHBOOKS Production Services

Indexer: TECHBOOKS Production Services

General and Administrative

Hungry Minds Consumer Reference Group

Business: Kathleen Nebenhaus, Vice President and Publisher; Kevin Thornton, Acquisitions Manager

Cooking/Gardening: Jennifer Feldman, Associate Vice President and Publisher; Anne Ficklen, Executive Editor; Kristi Hart, Managing Editor

Education/Reference: Diane Graves Steele, Vice President and Publisher

Lifestyles: Kathleen Nebenhaus, Vice President and Publisher; Tracy Boggier, Managing Editor

Pets: Kathleen Nebenhaus, Vice President and Publisher; Tracy Boggier, Managing Editor

Travel: Michael Spring, Vice President and Publisher; Brice Gosnell, Publishing Director; Suzanne Jannetta, Editorial Director

Hungry Minds Consumer Editorial Services: Kathleen Nebenhaus, Vice President and Publisher; Kristin A. Cocks, Editorial Director; Cindy Kitchel, Editorial Director

Hungry Minds Consumer Production: Debbie Stailey, Production Director

Contents at a Glance

Cartoons at a Glance

By Rich Tennant

page 325

page 23

page 91

page 207

page 245

page 113

page 7

page 57

Cartoon Information:
Fax: 978-546-7747

E-Mail: richtennant@the5thwave.com
World Wide Web: www.the5thwave.com

Table of Contents

Introduction

. . . .

So you've bought *Psychology For Dummies*. How does that make you feel? Hopefully, you're feeling pretty good. And why shouldn't you be? You're going to discover all kinds of interesting information about the basics of human behavior and mental processes.

Everybody is interested in psychology. People are fascinating, and that includes you! We often defy explanation and evade predication. Figuring people out can be pretty hard. Just when you think that you've figured someone out, bang, he surprises you. Now I know that some of you may be thinking, "Actually, I'm a pretty good judge of people. I've got a handle on things." If that's the case, that's great! Some folks do seem to have a more intuitive understanding of people than others. For the rest of us though, there's psychology.

About This Book

Psychology For Dummies is an introduction to the field of psychology. I tried to write this book using plain English and everyday examples with the hope that it will be real and applicable to everyday life. I've always felt that tackling a new subject is more enjoyable when it has real-world importance. Psychology is full of jargon, so much jargon that it even has its own dictionary, aptly named *The Dictionary of Psychology* (Penguin Reference Books). This book is for those of you who are interested in what people do, think, say, and feel, but want the information presented in a clear and easily understandable manner.

The information in this reference is not intended to substitute for expert medical advice or treatment; it is designed to help you make informed choices. Because each individual is unique, a physician must diagnose conditions and supervise treatments for each individual health problem. If an individual is under a doctor's care and receives advice contrary to information provided in this reference, the doctor's advice should be followed, as it is based on the unique characteristics of that individual.

Conventions Used in This Book

Conventional language for psychologists can sound like gibberish to someone who has never had a psychology class. As I state earlier in this chapter, I try to stay away from jargon and technical language in this book. You may come across an attempt at a joke or two. I tend to take a lighter approach to life, but sometimes people don't get my sense of humor. If I try to crack a joke in the text and it bombs, please don't be too harsh. I'm a psychologist after all, and I don't think we're known for our sense of humor. I hope I don't come across as insensitive or cavalier either — that is certainly not my intention.

Sometimes, talking about psychology can be pretty dry, so I try to liven things up with examples and personal stories. I make no references to any patients I've ever had in therapy. If there appears to be a resemblance, it's purely coincidental. In fact, I took great care in preserving the privacy and confidentiality of the people I have worked with.

Foolish Assumptions

You can find a lot of psychology books out there. Most of them are either too technical and specialized or cover too narrow an area of psychology. Here are some of the reasons why I think *Psychology For Dummies* is the book for you:

- ✔ You've got a lot of questions about people.
- ✔ You've got a lot of questions about yourself.
- ✔ You're thinking about going into the field of psychology.
- ✔ You're currently studying psychology or a related discipline, such as social work or counseling.
- ✔ You're interested in psychology but don't have the time or the money to take a psychology course.
- ✔ You've got people all figured out, and you want to see if I'm on track.

How This Book Is Organized

Psychology For Dummies is divided into eight separate sections; each is intended to cover one of the broad areas or topics of psychology. A nice thing about *For Dummies* books is that they're designed to be user friendly. You don't have to read the entire book from cover to cover to find what you're looking for. Just flip to the section that interests you and have at it!

Part 1: Behaving Yourself

Part I provides a definition of psychology and an overview of the field. I cover armchair psychologists and introduce the concept that we're all "acting" psychologists, analyzing and assessing human behavior everyday.

This part also contains a brief outline of the professional practice of psychology. I introduce the scientific nature of psychology and the different approaches psychologists use to investigate and understand people. Finally, I briefly touch on the different applicable areas of psychological knowledge from treatment to applied psychology.

Part 11: Picking Your Brain

In Part II, I discuss the basic structures of the nervous system and the important role that biology plays in psychological knowledge. After introducing you to the brain and its parts, "Nice to meet you," I introduce the concept of conscious awareness and its important role in psychology. Finally, I explain the faculties that permit us to stay in contact with the world around us — our senses.

Part 111: Thinking and Feeling

Part III covers human thought, which psychologists call cognition. I discuss both the content of thought and the thought process here. I include a discussion of the concept of intelligence and the different theories of "being smart." I also cover emotion and motivation in this part. Definitely check this part out if you're interested in love. Or, if you'd rather read about being angry, there's something here for you as well.

Part 1V: Barking Up the Right Learning Tree

In Part IV, I introduce you to the extremely important contributions that Ivan Pavlov, the "father" of classical conditioning, has made to the field of psychology. I briefly discuss his classic experiments and provide some good examples (at least I think they're good) designed to illustrate the basic principles of how humans learn. After talking about Pavlov and his dogs for a while, I introduce the second coming of learning theory, operant conditioning. I provide some basic definitions that cover the concept and some more edge-of-your-seat examples. Well, maybe they're not that exciting, but they're still pretty good.

Part V: Getting Personal with Social Psychology

Part V introduces psychoanalysis and the work of Sigmund Freud. I begin with the basic structure of the psyche and follow that up with Freud's theory of psychosexual development, along with a discussion on the famous defense mechanisms, such as denial and repression. I also introduce you to the second generation of psychoanalysts, Anna Freud, Erik Erikson, and others.

Next, I introduce you to personality theory and the most common personality types. This part goes on to cover topics such as knowing yourself, developing identities, forming relationships, and communicating — social stuff, as the title of Part V implies. I also discuss the influence that others have on our behavior and the different ways that individuals behave in groups. Finally, I take a look at developmental psychology and briefly trace development from conception to adolescence.

Part VI: Knowing Whether You're a Nut

Modern *psychopathology* (the study of mental illness and abnormal behavior and mental processes) basically began in the early twentieth century with the theories of Eugene Bleuler and Sigmund Freud. Part VI covers contemporary approaches to abnormal psychology, including neuropsychological and cognitive explanations for psychological problems. I discuss some of the major and most infamous psychological disorders, including anxiety disorders, depression, schizophrenia, and posttraumatic stress disorder. I also discuss forensic psychology, or criminal psychology. Topics related to this subject include the areas of criminal responsibility and criminal profiling, major theories of criminal behavior, and theories on treatment and correction.

Part VII: Helping You Heal

Part VII starts out by introducing you to psychological testing and assessment. (Yes, this is where that famous instrument, the Rorschach inkblot test, is discussed.) Within this discussion, I deal with the most common areas of psychological assessment, such as intelligence and personality. Next, I introduce you to the traditional "talk" psychotherapies — psychoanalysis, behavior therapy, cognitive therapy, and other popular forms of psychological treatment. I give you the lowdown on the different approaches and goals of each of these therapies, and I provide a look at how each of these therapy encounters unfolds. Finally, I talk about stress and the relationship between psychological and physical health.

Part VIII: The Part of Tens

In this part, I first introduce you to a new orientation in psychology called "positive" psychology. The focus here is on psychological *health* instead of the traditional focus on *sickness*. Within this discussion, I provide some practical advice on maintaining your psychological health. After that it's time to go to the movies!

Icons Used In This Book

Throughout this book, you'll find icons in the margins. They're there to help you easily find certain types of information. Here's a list of the icons you'll see:

When you see this one, I'm asking you to engage in a little psychological experimentation. In other words, you're the guinea pig when you run across this icon. What would psychology be without its guinea pigs? Don't worry — the experiments are harmless. No shocks, I promise.

When you see this icon, I'm trying to emphasize a bit of information that may come in handy some day.

With this creative piece of art, I'm trying to alert you to information that is a "must know" if you're going to learn psychology.

Don't forget it. When you see this icon I am reminding you of the highlights from that section. It flags the "If you learn just one thing from this chapter" type of stuff, so pay attention.

Where to Go from Here

Psychology is a broad field. I think you'll find that the organization of this book lets you check out what you're interested in and leave the rest of the stuff behind, if you want. You don't have to read it cover to cover. Kind of like a cafeteria — take what you like and leave the rest. But hey, if I can write an entire book on psychology, I think you can read an entire book on this stuff. Besides, I think you'll like it. Psychology is a great subject. Enjoy!

Part I
Behaving Yourself

The 5th Wave — By Rich Tennant

"DON'T TOUCH ANYTHING. DON'T PICK ANYTHING OFF THE FLOOR AND EAT IT. DON'T PLAY WITH YOUR EARS. DON'T FOOL AROUND WITH BILLY MAGUIRE'S RETAINER. DON'T GRAB ANYONE'S HAIR. DON'T FORGET TO SAY PLEASE AND THANK YOU. DON'T PICK YOUR NOSE, TALK LOUD, OR PLAY WITH TOO MANY TOYS. AND HAVE A WONDERFUL TIME."

In this part . . .

Part I provides a definition of psychology and an overview of the field. I cover armchair psychologists and introduce the concept that we're all "acting" psychologists, analyzing and assessing human behavior every day.

This part also contains a brief outline of the professional practice of psychology. I introduce the scientific nature of psychology and the different approaches psychologists use to investigate and understand people. Finally, I briefly touch on the different applicable areas of psychological knowledge from treatment to applied psychology.

Chapter 1

Why Do People Do What They Do?

*M*ost people I know have a certain idea in mind when they think about psychology. I'm a psychologist. But what's that? Obviously, it's someone who knows psychology. But is that all there is to it? When I get together with family and friends during the holidays, it seems like they still don't know exactly what it is I do for a living. Some of my patients have said, "All you do is talk. Can't you prescribe some medicine for me?" Still others grant me seemingly supernatural powers of knowledge and healing. I wrote *Psychology For Dummies* to clear things up about psychology.

So what are some of those ideas that come to mind when people think about the topic of psychology? That all depends on who you ask. Sometimes, I imagine myself as a guest on a television talk show, like *Oprah*. I'm bombarded by questions from the audience that I can't answer. My heart starts to pound. I start to sweat. I start to stand up so that I can run off the set, but then, something comes to me that keeps me in my seat. I'll ask the audience what it thinks psychology is and why it thinks a psychologist can answer questions about psychology.

Before I provide a definition of psychology, I want you to take a few minutes to jot down some of your ideas on what psychology is. Why did this book catch your eye? Looking for answers? Looking for advice? What's the question that you want answered?

"Why do we do what we do?" is the question that lies beneath a lot of the other questions that people ask of psychologists. Whether you're a professional psychologist, a researcher, or a layperson, this one simple question seems to be the root issue.

Why did that shooting happen?

Why can't I stop feeling sad?

Why did she break up with me?

Why are people so mean?

These are examples of the motivating questions that drive the discipline of psychology. At a very basic level, psychology is a branch of knowledge. But this explanation just scratches the surface. The main topic of psychology is *people,* either as individuals or in groups. That's why the title of this chapter isn't "Why Do Elephant Seals Do What They Do?" However, some psychologists do actually study animal behavior and so they might actually be asking this question.

To this point in the chapter, psychology is a discipline concerned with why people do what they do. Another fundamental question of psychology is the "how" question:

How can I get a better grade on my final?

How can I get my 2-year-old to stop throwing tantrums?

How does the mind work?

Still another question is the "what" question:

What are emotions?

What is mental illness?

What is intelligence?

These why, how, and what questions comprise the intellectual and philosophical core of psychology. Therefore, *psychology* can be defined as the scientific study of human behavior and mental processes. Psychology attempts to uncover what we do and why and how we do it.

Playing Armchair Psychologist

In a way, each of us is an amateur psychologist of sorts. Professional psychologists aren't the only ones who try to figure people out. When I started taking psychology courses, I had my own ideas about people. Sometimes, I agreed with the theories of Freud and others, and sometimes, I disagreed wholeheartedly. I'm sure that I'm not alone. Most of us seem to have our own ideas about what makes others tick.

One of the neatest things about psychology is that it covers a topic that we all have experience with — people. It's pretty hard to say the same thing about chemistry and astronomy. Of course, we all encounter chemicals every day, but I can't remember the last time I asked, "How do they get that mouthwash to taste like mint?"

One of the best places to catch armchair psychologists in action is the local coffeehouse. The tables are filled with people sitting around and talking about the whys and the wherefores of other people's behavior. "And then I said. . . ." "You should have told him. . . ." It's like being in a big group therapy session sometimes. We're all hard at work figuring people out.

Psychologists sometimes call this armchair psychologizing *folk psychology* — a framework of principles used by ordinary people to understand, explain, and predict their own and other people's behavior and mental states. In practice, we use a variety of psychological notions or concepts to explain individuals' mental states, personalities, or circumstances. Two concepts that a lot of us use for this purpose are *beliefs* and *desires.* We all believe that people have beliefs and that they act on those beliefs. Why do people do what they do? Because of their beliefs.

When we practice folk psychology, we assume that people do what they do because of their thoughts and mental processes — their beliefs and desires. Folk psychology isn't the only tool that armchair psychologists use. It's not unusual for people to explain other's behavior in terms of luck, curses, blessings, karma, fate, destiny, or any other number of non-psychological terms. I don't want to make these explanations sound like a bad thing. It's pretty hard to explain why someone wins the lottery from a psychological perspective. Explaining why someone continues to buy tickets even when they keep losing? Now that can be explained using psychology.

One Among the Sciences

A number of scholarly fields attempt to use their own perspectives to answer the same core questions that psychology attempts to answer. In one way or another, physics, biology, chemistry, history, economics, political science, sociology, medicine, and anthropology all concern themselves with people. The psychological perspective is just one voice among this chorus of disciplines that strives for validity based on the acceptance of the scientific method as the most valid and useful approach to understanding reality.

Psychology exists among and interacts with other disciplines. Just as each of us lives in a community, psychology is part of a community of knowledge, and it provides a unique contribution to that community. It's a tool for understanding people. Sometimes, its theories and research are the right tools, and sometimes, they're not. Not everything is reducible to a psychological understanding, but we need tools for understanding the chaos of human behavior and mental processes.

Over the years, hundreds of thousands of psychologists have come up with a basic set of *metatheories* or "grand theories" to guide our work. These theories are used to cast a framework on the whirling and buzzing world of human behavior and mental processes in order to begin to understand it. One comment I get from students from time to time is, "What makes you think that psychology has all the answers?" My answer, "Psychologists are just trying to provide a piece of the puzzle, not all the answers."

Framing with Metatheories

Each of the following grand theories provides an overarching framework within which most psychological research is conducted. (There are other perspectives that represent hybridized approaches, such as neuropsychology and cognitive science. But for now I'm just sticking with the basics.) Each of these metatheories has a different point of emphasis when approaching the core psychological questions of why, how, and what. A lot of research and theory is based on one or more of these grand theories. When a psychologist finds a behavior or mental process she's interested in researching, she typically begins to work from within one of these theories.

- ✔ **Biological:** Focuses on the biological underpinnings of behavior and the effects of evolution and genetics. The premise is that behavior and mental processes can be explained by understanding human physiology and anatomy. Biological psychologists focus mostly on the brain and the nervous system. (For more on biological psychology, see Chapter 3.)

  We've all seen people act differently when they're under the influence of alcohol. Holiday office parties are good laboratories for applying the biological perspective. Imagine walking into a party and seeing Bob, the relatively quiet guy from accounting, burning up the cubicles like some kind of disco inferno that could make John Travolta sweat. He's the lady's man. He's funny. He's drunk. Do you think Bob will remember?

- ✔ **Psychoanalytic:** Emphasizes the importance of unconscious mental processes and early child-development issues as they relate to childish impulses, childish wishes, immature desires, and the demands of the reality that we live in. Sigmund Freud founded psychoanalysis, and since then, hundreds of theorists have added to his work. The newer theories are typically labeled *psychodynamic* because they emphasize the dynamic interplay between various components of personality. (For more on psychoanalysis, see Chapters 10, 11, and 19.)

I once read an article about the significance of a child beating his or her parent at either a game or a sports activity. Should parents let their children win? Psychoanalysts largely believe that competition is inherent between parent and child and that the eventual acceptance of that competition is essential to the child's healthy psychological adjustment in life.

✔ **Behaviorism:** Emphasizes the role of previous learning experiences in shaping behavior. Behaviorists don't traditionally focus on mental processes because they believe that mental processes are too difficult to observe and measure objectively.

One of the most powerful behavioral influences on our behavior comes from watching other people. Monkey see — monkey do! Psychologists call this process *observational learning.* In recent years, a lot of controversy has arisen about the influence of television and videogame violence on children. The research has been pretty consistent. Children who view violent television and play violent videogames are more likely to engage in violent behavior.

✔ **Cognitive:** Focuses on the mental processing of information, including the specific functions of reasoning, problem solving, and memory. Cognitive psychologists are interested in the mental plans and thoughts that guide and cause behavior.

Whenever someone tells me to look at the bright side, they're coming from a cognitive perspective. When something bad happens to me, I can feel better if the problem gets solved or the issue is resolved. But how should I feel if nothing changes? If my circumstances don't change, do I have to feel bad forever? Of course not — I can change the way I think about the situation. I can look on the bright side!

✔ **Humanistic and existential:** Emphasizes the uniqueness of each individual person and our ability and responsibility to make choices in our lives. I'm not a victim of circumstance! I have choices in my life. Humanists believe that a person's free choice, free will, and understanding of the meaning of events and his or her life are the most important things to study.

Have you ever felt like just another nameless face in the crowd? Has your life ever seemed as if it were controlled by the winds of chance? How did it feel? Probably not very good. Feeling like we have choices and making good choices give us a sense of true being and affirm our existence.

✔ **Sociocultural:** Focuses on the social and cultural factors that affect our behavior.

Never underestimate the power of groups or culture in investigating the why, how, and what of behavior and mental processes. The tattoo phenomenon of the 1990s is a good example of this power. Before the '90s, people who got ink were seen as acting outside of the status quo, so "status quo" people weren't lined up outside the tattoo parlor. Nowadays, tattoos are widely accepted, and even Mr. Status Quo may have a tat or two or three.

✔ **Feminism:** Focuses on the political, economic, and social rights of women and how these forces influence both men's and women's behavior. The feminist perspective originated in the women's movement of the 1960s.

One issue in particular has caught the attention of feminist researchers and clinicians — eating disorders. From their perspective, eating disorders in young women are largely the consequence of excessive pressures to be thin that mass media and culture place upon girls. Feminists draw our attention to the fashion magazines and female role models in popular culture.

✔ **Postmodernism:** Questions the very core of psychological science, challenging its approach to truth and its focus on the individual. Postmodernists propose, for example, that in order to understand human thinking and reason, we need to look at the social and communal processes involved in thinking and reason.

They make the argument that people in powerful positions have too much to say about what is "real" and "true" in psychology. They advocate a *social constructionist* view of reality, which states that the concepts of "reality" and "truth" are defined, or constructed, by society. These concepts have no meaning, apart from the meanings that society and its "experts" assign to them.

The Biopsychosocial Model

How does one begin to sort through and choose among the metatheories listed above? There is a more simple way to go about figuring people out. Over the years, each of these metatheories has enjoyed its day in the sun, only to be put on the shelf by the next big thing. One way of dealing with this revolving door of explanatory frameworks is to adopt an integrationist approach. The *biopsychosocial model* of psychology represents a popular attempt at integration.

The basic idea behind this model is that human behavior and mental processes are the products of biological, psychological, and social influences and how these influences interact. Any explanation of behavior and mental processes that doesn't consider all three factors is relatively incomplete.

The role of the body

We are material beings. We're made of flesh and bones. Any discussion of thoughts, feelings, or any other psychological concept that doesn't consider the body, especially the brain and nervous system, ignores the facts of our existence. Take the "mind" for example. Most of us think we have a "mind" and that others (well, most others) have one too. But where does this "mind" exist? These days, psychologists accept that the "mind" exists in, or is synonymous with, the brain — that lump of flesh inside our skulls. The biological metatheory is integrated into the biopsychosocial model because of this component.

The role of the mind

I think that most people have this aspect of the biopsychosocial model in mind (no pun intended) when they think of psychology. Thoughts, feelings, desires, beliefs, and numerous other mental concepts are addressed through this aspect of the model, the role of the mind. What if this book was about botany? Would the biopsychosocial model still be useful? Only if you believed that plants had minds, and the "social" component of the model referred more to the ecological niche that plants exist within. In other words, it'd be a stretch!

This is a good illustration of the uniqueness of the biopsychosocial model of psychology. The mind is central to understanding human behavior and mental processes. Behaviorists neglect the mind. Biological psychologists study the mind as the brain. And social psychologists primarily focus on the third aspect of the biopsychosocial model.

The role of people

Our brains and minds would be pretty lonely without the third component of the model, the social aspect of human behavior and mental processes. Brains don't work, and minds don't think in a vacuum. Behavior and mental processes are embedded within a context that includes other people and the material environment around us. The social aspect of the model also includes non-human aspects of our environment, such as nature and technology.

It's important not to underestimate the power of other people in shaping and determining our behavior and mental processes. Most of us are aware of the detrimental effects that negative social events or experiences, such as physical or sexual abuse, can have on us. To neglect the social is to neglect reality.

Don't forget about culture

Do behaviors and mental processes vary across cultures? Let me put the question to you this way: If I only conducted research with white, middle-class, college students, could I state that my results apply to all people? Definitely not. This subject has been a hot topic in psychology over the last 30 years or so. As technological advances help make our world a smaller place and different cultures come into contact with each other more often, understanding the role of culture in psychology becomes increasingly important.

Cultural influence needs to be addressed in psychology for at least two reasons, one is scientific, and the other is humanistic. Science seeks objectivity and truth. All us are vulnerable to cultural bias; therefore, psychology should try to understand the influence of culture in order to provide the most objective and complete picture of reality as possible. If not, all we'll have is a bunch of "regional psychologies" that are useless and inaccurate outside of the cultures they were developed in.

Finally, from a humanistic perspective, many people generally agree that it's wrong to impose their culture's brand of truth onto other cultures. What if my American research shows that using baby talk to communicate with infants stunts the growth of mature speech, and I go to another culture and design a public education program based on these findings? Although they hold true for the United States, these research results may not be applicable to the other culture. My education program would be imposing a "truth" that's not really a "truth" onto that culture. We should always be careful to respect the relativity of truth across cultural boundaries.

Branching Off

There are three main types of psychologists:

- ✔ **Experimental psychologists** spend the majority of their time conducting research, and they often work in academic settings. Experimental psychology covers a wide range of topics, but individual researchers typically have a specialty.

- ✔ **Applied psychologists** directly apply research findings and psychological theory to everyday settings and problems. Applied psychologists work in a wide variety of settings, such as business, government, education, and even sports.

- ✔ **Clinical psychologists** study, diagnosis, and treat psychological problems. The American Psychological Association states that in order for an individual to be considered a psychologist, he or she must possess a doctoral degree (a PhD, PsyD, or EdD, for example). And nearly all states in the United States require the individual to obtain a license to practice psychology, which typically involves taking an intensive licensing exam.

Chapter 2

Making Theories out of Chaos

• •

In This Chapter

▶ Getting scientific

▶ Coming up with a hypothesis

▶ Performing research

• •

*1*t seems that I've always been looking for *the* truth. When I was in college, I frequented a little bookstore near campus that specialized in spiritual, philosophical, and popular-psychology books. At least once a week, I would peruse the shelves looking for something interesting. The books were arranged by topic: metaphysics, Eastern wisdom, Western wisdom, Buddhism, Taoism, Judaism, Islam, Christianity, new age, channeling, and so on. I read books from every section. I was searching for some kind of ultimate truth, some kind of answer.

One day, I realized that I had sampled works from every section in this bookstore, but I still wasn't satisfied. Then, I had a strange thought — this bookstore was full of opinions! How was I supposed to find the "answers" or the "truth" when I was only getting opinions? Many of these books contained testimonials, logical arguments, and stories but very little, if any, evidence or proof. I simply had to take everyone's word for it. How could they all be right? Some of the authors even contradicted or criticized the others. Who was right?

I guess I'm just one of those people who needs proof. It would be an exaggeration to say that I found all the answers in psychology, but I can confidently say that I found a field that makes a serious effort to establish the truth of its claims with proof, which is referred to as empirical evidence. The *empirical method* is an approach to truth that uses observation and experiment. Psychology, as the scientific study of human behavior and mental processes, uses the empirical method. It relies on research in an attempt to substantiate its claims. How do we know that psychologists' claims about behavior and mental processes are true or accurate, right or wrong? Why is it worth paying for a psychologist's services in treating depression or a phobia, for example?

What makes her the expert? Experts and professionals are expected to possess a specific knowledge and truth about their respective subjects. The authority of these experts is maintained through the ways in which they know and investigate their subject matter.

Words like *knowledge* and *truth* can be a little tricky sometimes. Understanding where psychologists' knowledge comes from is an important first step in learning about psychology. In this chapter I explore the different ways, such as scientific research and theory, that psychologists attempt to substantiate the truth of their claims and knowledge and establish their expertise in human behavior and mental processes.

Applying the Scientific Method without a Bunsen Burner

We all have an opinion about the behavior and mental processes of others and ourselves. "She left you because you're emotionally unavailable." "If you don't express yourself, it just stays bottled up inside." We're full of answers to the why, how, and what questions regarding people. But how do we really know that not talking about feelings leads to bottling them up? I may think that not expressing feelings allows them to drift away like clouds on a windy day. Who's right? You may be thinking that it doesn't matter, but we've got this whole group of psychologists that claim to be experts on these matters. But on what grounds can they make this claim to expertise?

Psychologists strive to maintain their expertise and knowledge through the use of three forms of knowledge acquisition or ways of knowing:

- **Authority:** Utilized to transmit information, usually in a therapy setting or the education and training process. Patients and students don't have time to go out and research everything that they're told. They have to take someone's word for it at some point.

- **Rationalism/logic:** Used to create theories and hypotheses. If things don't make logical sense, they probably won't make sense when researchers use the scientific method to investigate them.

- **Scientific method:** Used as the preferred method of obtaining information and investigating behavior and mental processes. Psychologists implement the scientific method through a variety of different techniques.

Let me be perfectly clear: Not everything that psychologists do, talk about, and believe is based on scientific research! A lot of stuff is based on the authority of well-known personalities in the field. Other knowledge is based on clinical experience without any systematic investigation. Finally, a good-sized chunk of information that's out there is purely theoretical, but it makes sense on rational/logical grounds.

The vast majority of psychologists prefer to use the scientific method when seeking truth because it's seen as a fair and impartial process. When I do a research study, I'm expected to outline exactly what I'm doing and what it is that I claim to be looking for. That way, if people want to try to prove me wrong, they can repeat my work, step by step, and see if they get the same results. If knowledge is based on authority alone, I can never be sure that the information I receive is unbiased and trustworthy. When the scientific method is in place, a theory that doesn't match the empirical results "experienced" in a research study is labeled inaccurate. Time for a new theory! Scientists should never change their experimental data to match their original theory — that's cheating!

Developing a Good Theory

Because a fair amount of psychological knowledge is based on theory, it may by helpful to know what a theory is exactly. If you already have a handle on what a theory is, indulge me for a moment. A *theory* is a set of related statements about a set of objects or events (the ones being studied) that explains how these objects or events are related.

Theories and hypotheses are similar but not exactly the same thing. Psychologists test theories by studying their logical implications. Hypotheses are specific predictions based on these implications. We can add new information to theories, and we can use existing theories to generate new ones.

Not every theory is a good theory. In order for a theory to be good, it must meet three criteria:

- **Parsimony:** It must be the simplest explanation possible that still explains the available observation.
- **Precision:** It must make precise, not overly large or vague, statements about reality.
- **Testability:** It must lend itself to scientific investigation.

Researching for the Truth

Psychologists use two broad categories of research when they want to scientifically evaluate a theory:

- ✔ **Descriptive research:** Consists of observation and the collection of data without trying to manipulate any of the conditions or circumstances being observed. It's a passive observation of the topics being investigated. Descriptive studies are good for developing new theories and hypotheses and are often the first step for a researcher investigating things that haven't been studied much. However, they don't help much if you're interested in cause and effect relationships.

  If I'm only interested in the content of bus-stop conversations, I may videotape people talking to each other at a bus stop and analyze the video. But, if I want to know what causes people to talk about certain subjects at bus stops, I should conduct an experiment.

- ✔ **Experimental research:** Involves the control and manipulation of the objects and events being investigated in order to get a better idea of the cause and effect relationships between the objects or events.

  Say I have a theory of bus-stop conversations called the "five-minute or more rule" that states, "Strangers will engage in conversation with each other only after having been in each other's presence for five or more minutes." My hypothesis would be, "After five minutes, apparent strangers will engage in a conversation beyond the simple pleasantries and greetings afforded to strangers." That is, I am hypothesizing that once strangers at a bus stop have been there for five minutes, they will start having a conversation. How can I test my hypothesis?

  I could just hang out at a bus stop and watch to see if it happens. But how could I know that my five-minute-or-more rule is behind my observations? I couldn't! It could be any number of things. This is a problematic issue in research I like to call the z-factor. A *z-factor* is something affecting the hypothesis that I am unaware of or not accounting for; it is an extraneous variable that I need to control in order to have confidence in my theory. Some possible z-factors in the bus stop study might be culture, age, and time of day. Good research studies try to eliminate z-factors or extraneous variables by controlling for their influence and factoring it out of the explanation.

  A descriptive or observational study won't account for z-factors, so instead I set up an experiment in which I approach people at bus stops and try a variety of things to test my hypothesis. I might go up and try to talk to someone after two minutes. I might wait for ten minutes. I might conduct studies during a thunderstorm or while dressed in particular ways, and I would try to prove my hypothesis wrong! I would seek to find that people have conversations at bus stops before five minutes. If this is the case, then the five-minute rule would be inaccurate. The more often I failed to prove my five-minute-or-more rule wrong, the more it would deserve my confidence.

Is this confusing you? Why would I try to disprove my hypothesis instead of just proving it right? In any scientific investigation, I can never really prove a hypothesis true. Instead, I set out to disprove the opposite of my hypothesis. For example, we once thought the earth was flat. Everything we observed at that time was consistent with this idea. However, someone came along and provided evidence that disputed this idea, which showed the flaw in this thinking. If I have a hypothesis and I keep finding evidence for it, I can be more and more confident in my hypothesis but never really know for sure. But if I can find just one example that contradicts my hypothesis, then this casts doubt on my hypothesis. If I say all swans are white, what happens when I find one black swan? The notion that all swans are white is false!

The rest of this book introduces you to various theories and research. There's a lot of stuff in here! Because psychology is about people, some people might argue that everything about people is "psychology." I couldn't write a book about everything. This is not *Everything About People For Dummies*. I established a way to decide what to put in the book and what not to so I used scientific research and theory as my measuring rod. The information you find in this book is considered part of legitimate psychological science and theory. Are you ready? Here we go.

Part II
Picking Your Brain

The 5th Wave — By Rich Tennant

In this part . . .

In Part II, I discuss the basic structures of the nervous system and the important role that biology plays in psychological knowledge. After introducing you to the brain and its parts ("Nice to meet you,"), I introduce the concept of conscious awareness and its important role in psychology. Finally, I explain the faculties that permit us to stay in contact with the world around us — our senses.

Chapter 3

Hardware, Software, and Wetware

Sometimes psychology can be pretty abstract, seemingly having more in common with philosophy than biology. In this book, I introduce you to all kinds of "psychological" concepts, such as thoughts, feelings, beliefs, and personalities. But have you ever wondered where all of these things exist? If I wanted to find a thought or feeling, where would I look?

One place that seems logical to look for these psychological concepts is inside the human mind. But where can I find a mind? That's easy — it's inside my skull, in my brain. So if you take a flashlight and look in someone's ear, you can see all kinds of thoughts, feelings, and other psychological stuff floating around inside, right? If you've ever tried this procedure, you know that it's a pretty poor investigative technique. But what if you opened up someone's skull and exposed her brain? Would you find all those psychological concepts then?

I think you'd be pretty disappointed. When you open up someone's skull to see her brain, all you're going to see is a wrinkled and convoluted mass of grayish-pinkish-whitish tissue. There's no visible thoughts, feelings, or beliefs. Where are they then? We all know that they exist because we experience them every day.

The question of where the mind, the home of psychological concepts, exists is an age-old philosophical question. Is the mind in the brain? Is the mind somewhere other than the brain? Are the brain and the mind the same thing? Most scientists today hold the position that the mind and the brain are one in the same. Scientists taking this position, known as *monism,* believe that the key to understanding the human mind, with all of its psychological concepts, lies in understanding the body, specifically the nervous system. Carlson states, "What we call the 'mind' is a consequence of the functioning of the human body and its interactions with the environment." This is a powerful idea — the key to unlocking the mysteries of such psychological concepts as thinking and feeling is in the development of a thorough understanding of biology.

The idea that all of human psychology can be reduced to biology is known as *reductionism.* I've had a lot of students protest this idea over the years. It seems to insult our sense of free will, self-awareness, and consciousness. How can all this complex stuff going on inside our minds be reduced to a hunk of flesh resting between our ears? If you feel this way, maybe you're not a *monist,* a believer in monism. For the sake of this chapter, however, I'm going to be a monist. I focus on understanding human biology as the key to understanding human psychology.

Believing in Biology

We didn't always believe that human behavior and mental processes were the consequences of biology. In the times of the ancient Greeks and Romans, human behavior was seen as the consequence of supernatural forces, namely the whims and passions of the gods. But somewhere along the line, we started suspecting that maybe our bodies had something to do with it. Where would we get such an idea, that our behavior and mental processes are the consequences of our biology?

The history of research in this area is long, and I won't bore you with all the details. But, at the core of all of this research lies a very simple observation. Changes in our biology result in changes in our behavior and mental processes.

Let's take alcohol consumption, for example. People obviously act differently when under the influence of alcohol. They may flirt, dance like a wild man, get emotional and sentimental, or even become angry. Alcohol has a chemical effect on the brain; it alters the biology of the drinker's brain. It goes something like this:

Alcohol consumption → Chemical effect on brain → Thinks he's Don Juan

What about more serious changes in our biology like brain damage? People who suffer from brain damage can exhibit drastic changes in their personality and thinking. They may go from being very organized to very messy. Or, they may have been a very laid-back, easygoing person, but now they fly into a rage at the slightest frustration.

I think most of us have an intuitive understanding that what goes on within our bodies has an effect on our behavior and mental processes. *Biological psychologists* are a group of psychologists who have extended this intuitive belief and these casual observations, using the techniques and methods of modern science to investigate the idea that changes in biology lead to changes in psychology.

Although a lot of this seems logical, you may be thinking, "I still think there's more me than just biology." That's just the dualist in you acting up. My suggestion is to try and not struggle with it too much, at least while you read this chapter. Even if I think that we're all more than just cells and molecules, I can still benefit from the research of biological psychology.

Remember the *biosychosocial model* from Chapter 1? (If not, you may want to check it out. Trust me — it's a good chapter.) It helps to think of human psychology as a function of these three levels of understanding, the biological level, the psychological level, and the social level. Each level is important. This chapter focuses on the biological level, and the remainder of the book focuses on the other two. In order to respect the contributions of each level to our understanding of behavior and mental processes, we have to propose a way in which they interact. That is, we have to come up with a way to conceptualize how the biology influences psychology, how the psychology influences the biology, and so on.

A useful metaphor for understanding how these different levels interact is the modern computer. Most of us know that a computer has at least two functional components: the hardware and the software. The hardware consists of the actual physical components of the computer, like the processor, the hard drive, the wires, the CD-ROM, and the various other components. The software consists of the operating system, the word-processing software, and the various other programs that we use when we actually work on a computer.

In this metaphor, the hardware of a computer represents the biological level of understanding. This is our actual physical body, specifically our nervous system. The software represents the psychological level, and the interface between the user and the software represents the social level. The hardware is useless without software, and vice versa. So, even if you're not a monist, you can still respect the role that our physiology (hardware) plays in psychology (software).

The word "wetware" in the title of this chapter represents the actual physical substance of the brain. We don't have "hard" ware in our brains (wires, plastic, silicon, and so on); instead, we have "wet" ware (neurons, tissue, and chemicals, for example). In order to be consistent with my metaphor, I really focus on the wetware level of psychology in this chapter.

In this chapter, I introduce you to the wetware of the human nervous system and the endocrine system. These two areas of interest in physiological psychology represent the two most important for explaining psychological experience.

Running Like a Well-Oiled Machine: Body Systems

The human nervous system consists of two large divisions: the *central nervous system (CNS)* and the *peripheral nervous system (PNS)*. The basic building blocks of the nervous system are nerves, neurons, and neurotransmitters and glial cells. The CNS includes our brain and spinal cord. The PNS includes the nerves outside the CNS; they are in the periphery of the body.

Keep in mind that the nervous system is a living part of our bodies and, therefore, has the same basic needs as any other part of our body (like fuel and immune protection). The components of the nervous system are kept alive and healthy by the circulatory system and other regulatory body functions. The specifics of the support systems for each division of the nervous system are discussed in more detail within each division's corresponding section in this chapter.

If you remember a little physics, chemistry, or biology, you may remember that the building blocks of life begin with atoms (operating under the laws of physics); atoms grouped in particular ways to make up molecules, that then form compounds, move on up to molecules, then form compounds, then cells, then tissue, then me! So if we really wanted to be reductionistic we'd just study physics and do away with all other branches of science. Or, we could look at human behavior and mental processes from a molecular level. This is the focus of the field of *neurobiology*.

Typically, however, biological psychology begins at the cellular level of understanding. Two types of cells appear in the nervous system, *supporting cells* and *neurons*.

Tiptoeing into the periphery

Of the two divisions of the body's nervous system, think of the peripheral nervous system (PNS) as a system of connections that make it possible for the brain and spinal cord to communicate with the rest of the body. Two sets of nerves are involved:

- ✔ **Spinal nerves:** These nerves travel from the spinal cord to the muscles and other body parts, carrying neural signals both to and from the spinal cord.

- ✔ **Cranial nerves:** These nerves are involved in the muscular and sensory processes of the head and neck.

In addition to these two sets of nerves, the PNS also contains a subsystem of the overall nervous system known as the *autonomic nervous system (ANS)*. The autonomic nervous system helps regulate two specific types of muscles (smooth and cardiac) and the glands in our body. The ANS is involved in "automatic" or involuntary action. Bodily organs, reflexive muscle contractions, and even the dilation of our pupils are all automatic behaviors governed by the ANS. There are two very important divisions of the ANS:

- ✔ **Sympathetic nervous system:** The sympathetic branch of the ANS is involved in the energetic activation of the body when we need excess energy. For example, then I am confronted with a life-threatening situation, my sympathetic nervous system kicks in and gives me the energy to either take on the challenge or flee the situation.

- ✔ **Parasympathetic nervous system:** The parasympathetic branch of the ANS deactivates the SNS after it has been engaged. This action is sometimes called the *relaxation response* because the activity of the SNS is relaxed, or shut off, and we return to normal functioning.

Feeling nervous?

The CNS consists of both the brain and the spinal cord. There are three main divisions of the brain: *forebrain, midbrain,* and *hindbrain.* Each of these divisions consists of many substructures that are involved in various behaviors and activity.

An important thing to keep in mind about the brain is that it is a complex, integrated system. All of its components work together to produce the complexity of behaviors that each of us is capable of. The concept of *localization* refers to the idea that there are specific parts of the brain for specific components of behaviors. Various parts of the brain work together to produce vision, hearing, speech etc. These divisions have been discovered and established through the use of different neurological techniques such as postmortem brain examination, CT (co-axial tomography) scans, MRI (magnetic resonance imaging) scans, and PET (positron-emission tomography) scans.

Forebrain

The human forebrain consists of these different subdivisions.

- **Cerebral cortex:** If you think of the brain as a mushroom, with a top and a stalk, the cerebral cortex is the top of the mushroom. It's divided into two halves, called *cerebral hemispheres* (the left and the right — pretty creative). These halves are connected by a bundle of nerve fibers known as the *corpus collosum*. Without the corpus collosum, the halves wouldn't be able to communicate with each other.

  The four major divisions of the cerebral cortex are shown in Figure 3-1 and listed below with their corresponding functions:

  - **Frontal lobe:** Planning, organizing, coordinating and controlling movements, reasoning, and overall monitoring of the thinking process

  - **Parietal lobe:** Sensation

  - **Temporal lobe:** Hearing, speaking, and other verbal activity

  - **Occipital lobe:** Vision

- **Limbic system:** Located on the underside of the mushroom top (the cerebral cortex), the limbic system is involved in learning, memory, emotional behavior, and mating or reproduction (see Figure 3-2).

- **Basal ganglia:** This subdivision is involved in the control of movement.

- **Thalamus:** This "neural switchboard" is a relay station for the different parts of the brain.

- **Hypothalamus:** The hypothalamus takes part in the control of the endocrine system and works with the limbic system to control behaviors such as aggression, eating, protection, and mating.

Midbrain and hindbrain

The midbrain consists of the following divisions and their respective areas of responsibility:

- **Tectum:** Auditory and visual systems
- **Tegmentum:** Sleep, arousal, attention, muscle tone, and reflexes

The hindbrain also consists of two divisions with their own assigned duties:

- **Cerebellum:** Motor movement and its coordination
- **Medulla:** Vital functions of the body such as the cardiovascular system, breathing, and the movement of skeletal muscles

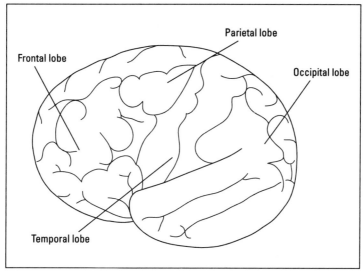

Figure 3-1:
Look at
the lobes.

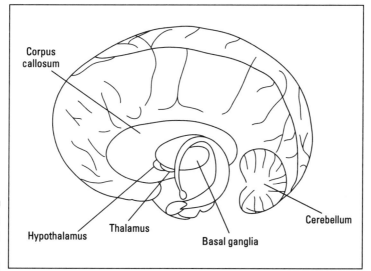

Figure 3-2:
Do the
limbo.

Damaging the brain

As you can see from preceding lists of brain divisions, there's a whole lot
going on. Essentially, everything we do involves our brains. What happens,
though, when some part of the brain gets damaged? The behavior and mental
processes associated with the damaged portion of the brain are adversely

affected, which also has an impact on related functions. Clinical neuropsychologists are particularly interested in the behavioral and mental consequences of receiving a brain injury.

Our brains can be damaged in numerous ways:

- ✔ **Closed-head injuries:** These injuries occur when someone sustains a blow to the head without anything penetrating the skull. A common form of closed-head injury is a *contrecoup* injury — the injury occurs to the part of the brain opposite from where the individual was struck. If I'm hit in the back of the head, I may sustain damage to my frontal lobe, thus affecting my organizational and planning abilities.

- ✔ **Open-head injuries:** These injuries occur when the skull is either penetrated or fractured and can often lead to serious brain injury.

- ✔ **Other brain disorders:** Degenerative diseases such as Alzheimer's can produce brain damage in the form of atrophied brain tissue and cellular death. Strokes and other vascular accidents also can result in brain damage by denying the brain blood and oxygen, causing cellular death.

Enter the Endocrine System

The endocrine system is responsible for the hormonal functions of the body. You may have experienced the power of hormones in influencing behavior during those wonderful years we call puberty. We go to bed a boy or a girl; we wake up a maniac. Drastic changes in the balance of hormones can often have drastic effects on our behavior. So it goes for even minor changes such as the fluctuations of the menstrual cycle.

Specific glands throughout the body secrete hormones that influence our behavior and bodily functions. Ovaries and testes influence a great deal of sexual behavior. Sex hormones can influence when and how fast a child enters puberty, for example. Hormones secreted by the adrenal gland influence aggressive behavior. The pituitary gland plays a role in our stress levels.

Superkalafragalistic Psychopharmacology

The use of medications in the treatment of mental illness has gained prominence over the last 50 or so years. Hundreds of drugs have been developed that are used to target the specific symptoms of a particular mental disorder with amelioration of their expression, alleviation of suffering, and improvement of overall functioning as primary goals of *pharmacotherapy*.

Many brain systems involved in the symptoms of mental illness involve one particular neurotransmitter. The sleep difficulties and appetite disturbance often seen in major depressive disorder are thought to be related to the limbic system for example. Drugs used for the treatment of mental illness are designed to affect the functioning of the specific neurotransmitters in that brain region. For these particular symptoms, the neurotransmitter serotonin is targeted.

Theoretically, different disorders, or more specifically, different symptoms implicate different neurotransmitters. Drugs designed to treat these symptoms are selective for their effects on the particular neurotransmitter involved.

Easing depression

Medications that are used to treat depression are called *antidepressants.* Most antidepressants affect one or both of two neurotransmitters: *norepinephrine* and *serotonin.* Basically, there are two different classes of antidepressant medications differentiated by their mechanism of action.

Tricyclic antidepressants, for example, block the presynaptic neuron's re-absorption of mostly norepinephrine (NE). This allows for a functional "increase" in the level of NE in the synapse and prolongs the activation of the postsynaptic neuron when stimulated by NE.

Selective serotonin reuptake inhibitors (SSRIs) block the re-absorption of serotonin rather than NE and have the similar effect of prolonging activation. Some of the more popular brands of SSRIs are Prozac, Paxil, and Zoloft.

Hearing voices

The experience of auditory hallucinations or feeling like someone is out to get you can be extremely troubling. These are common symptoms of the mental disorder schizophrenia. One of the most powerful treatments for some of the symptoms of schizophrenia is the use of *antipsychotic medications.*

Antipsychotic medications have a specific effect on the neurotransmitter dopamine. The *dopamine dysregulation hypothesis* of schizophrenia holds that the symptoms of psychosis result from disruptions in the action of dopamine in the brain. Antipsychotic medications block the postsynaptic receptor sites of dopamine. This blockage keeps dopamine from being able to activate the postsynaptic neuron and has been found to reduce the presence of psychotic symptoms substantially.

Unfortunately for antipsychotic medications, as for all medications, they don't just affect the neurotransmitters in the brain areas theorized to be implicated in the disorder. They also affect other brain areas and can often lead to very unpleasant side effects. The experience of these side effects often leads people to stop taking their medication, which can have serious negative consequences. This situation keeps drug researchers searching for more selective drugs.

Relaxing

Anxiety disorders are the most common mental disorder in the United States. Millions of people suffer from intolerable worry, panic attacks, and disabling phobias. The good news is that medications can help with these symptoms.

Anxiolytic medications are drugs designed to relieve the symptoms of anxiety disorders. Psychiatrists and family physicians prescribe one class of anxiolytics, *benzodiazapines,* quite often. Benzodiazepines affect the neurotransmitter GABA, which has a suppressing effect on the central nervous system. In other words, it slows things down in the brain.

Benzodiazepines are very effective in reducing anxiety. Unfortunately they are also highly addictive. They have a near-immediate effect and often produce sedation and an overall feeling of calmness. These feelings are highly pleasurable, and patients sometimes don't want to stop taking these medications even after their anxiety disorder has been successfully medicated. Table 3-1 gives an overview of some frequently prescribed medications.

Table 3-1: Major Medication Groups

Medication	Problem	Common Example
Antidepressants	Depression	Prozac
	Panic disorder	Zoloft
	Obsessive-compulsive disorder	Paxil
	Bulimia	
	Social phobia	
Antianxiety/Anxiolytics	Insomnia	Benzodiazepines
	Situational anxiety	
	Generalized anxiety disorder	
	Panic disorder	

Medication	Problem	Common Example
Antipsychotics	Schizophrenia	Haldol
	Mania	Zyprexa
	Psychotic depression	
Mood stabilizers	Mania	Lithium
	Bipolar disorder	Depakote
Stimulants	ADHD	Ritalin

Chapter 4

Conscious Beings

• •

• •

*P*erhaps since the beginning of time, human beings have been trying to alter their consciousness. For some, it may seem like a way to get in touch with a reality greater than themselves. For others, it may simply be a way to escape the harsh realities of a bad home or a meaningless job. Wallace and Goldstein defined *consciousness* as our current state of awareness of external and internal stimuli. A *stimulus* is anything in our world (an event, situation, or object) that triggers a psychological response.

Being conscious is like having a light on in our brain. When the light is out, we're unconscious. Consciousness allows us to monitor ourselves and our environment, giving us greater control over our actions and behaviors. But, if you've stood on a busy street corner in a large city, you've realized that there's a heck of a lot going on around us at any given time. We only have so much awareness to go around. Consciousness has its limits. The quantity or amount of material in our awareness, along with the content of that material, defines the level of consciousness we find ourselves in at any one moment.

Exploring the Horizons of Awareness

Consciousness is an elusive concept. We know it's there, but it's hard to put our finger on it. My consciousness exists in my inner voice and my awareness of myself, my surroundings, and my experience. But, I'm typically not aware of numerous mental processes, bodily sensations, and things going on in my mind. For example, I don't usually hear my heart beating as I'm walking down the street, but I can hear it when I try to hear it. When I become consciousness of something that I was unconscious of, I become aware of it.

Planes with faces; pets with agendas

Believe it or not, children's cartoons represent a challenge of sorts to our concepts of consciousness. How? Everything in a cartoon is a conscious being, from toasters to trees to animals. One of my favorite cartoons was about a family of airplanes, Poppa Plane, Momma Plane, and so on. Each of the planes had its own little personality. The attribution of human consciousness and traits to inanimate objects is called *animism*. Most of us are pretty sure that machines and plants don't possess consciousness, but what about animals? I know plenty of pet owners that swear that their little buddy has deep thoughts of his or her own. They get pretty upset when I suggest that little Scruffy is just a bundle of routines and reflexes, acting without conscious deliberation. "Should I bury this bone here or over by the garage?"

One of the best ways to think about the psychology of consciousness is to think about absence of consciousness. A coma is a state of extreme unawareness or lack of consciousness. A person in a coma is essentially disconnected from the world around her. She may be aware of her own mind and body, and she may even know that she's in a coma, but as far as outside observers are concerned, she's unconscious.

I once heard that the entire idea of vampires and the undead came from medieval observations of dead bodies. I don't exactly know why people were digging up dead bodies, but when they did, they found that their hair and fingernails had continued to grow. Sometimes, the bodies would utter a deep groan when someone moved them. What was going on? Scientifically speaking, hair and nails continue to grow for a short period of time after death, and the groaning sound could have been caused by leftover air in the body's chest cavity passing over the vocal chords when the chest was compressed. But medieval grave robbers attributed life to the bodies based on these observations. They attributed the cause of these phenomena to conscious action and deliberation of the dead person, not reflexive byproducts of physiology and anatomy.

Consciousness, as elusive as it is, can be pinned down in at least three ways:

- ✔ **My subjective experience of my own awareness.** Have you ever had a dream in which you knew you were dreaming? Really, you were aware that you were asleep. Being aware of my own awareness involves realizing or being aware that you are either awake or asleep.

- ✔ **Other's observations of my deliberate actions.** One of the most important features of consciousness is that it mediates our behavior. Sometimes we act impulsively and reflexively; we don't think about what we're doing, we just do it. Other times, there's a step of conscious deliberation, an act of will, before acting. In that case, you are consciously analyzing what you are going to do. Willful acts are a signal of conscious awareness. We attribute consciousness to acts of deliberation and intention. When someone does something willfully, we assume that he is conscious.

✔ **Electrical measurement of my brain's electrical activity.** Consciousness can be observed physiologically, in addition to behaviorally, through the measurement of brain activity. Different EEG (electroencephalogram — a special machine that measures the "brain waves" or electrophysiological activity of the brain) measurements of electrical activity in the brain correspond to different levels of observable consciousness.

Altering Your Consciousness

People have been trying to deliberately alter their consciousness since the beginning of human history. Human beings have used meditation, religious rituals, sleep deprivation, and numerous other means to alter their levels of everyday awareness.

Stanley Krippner identified over 20 states of altered consciousness. One of the more common states is dreaming (see the "Arriving at Work Naked: Dreams" section later in this chapter). Some of the more intriguing altered states of consciousness identified by Krippner are

✔ **Rapture:** An intense feeling of overpowering emotion, experienced as pleasurable and positive. People have reported experiencing rapture after sex, ritualistic dancing, religious rituals, and the use of psychoactive substances.

✔ **Meditative states:** Minimal mental activity that includes reductions in mental imagery (the pictures "inside" your head) brought on by meditation, yoga, or even prayer.

✔ **Trance states:** An alert but very suggestible state. An individual in a trance is focused on a single stimulus and oblivious to much of everything else going on around him or her. People in trances sometimes report that they feel "at one" with the world. Religious rituals, chanting, hypnosis, brainwashing, and even music can induce trance states.

✔ **Daydreaming:** Rapid thinking unrelated to an individual's current environment. Daydreaming can often result from boredom, sensory deprivation, and sleep deprivation.

✔ **Expanded consciousness:** Increased awareness not typical of everyday experience and awareness. People try all kinds of ways to "expand" their consciousness from using drugs to sensory deprivation. There are four levels of expanded consciousness:

- **Sensory:** An altered experience of space, time, and other sensory phenomena.

- **Recollective-analytic:** An experience in which individuals develop novel ideas and revelations about themselves, the world, and their role within the world.

- **Symbolic:** Identification with a historical figure or famous person accompanied by mystical symbols such as having a vision of a crucifix or an angel.

- **Integral:** A religious and/or mystical experience usually involving God or some other supernatural being or force. The person usually feels merged with or at one with the universe. This state has sometimes been called *cosmic consciousness.* Krippner and other experts believe that very few people are actually capable of attaining this level of consciousness.

Getting high on conscious life

Perhaps one of the most common methods for altering consciousness is the use of drugs. Drug use is both a historical as well as a contemporary phenomena. Archeologists have even found traces of cocaine in mummified bodies from ancient Egypt. Some people claim that one of the purposes of taking drugs is to gain added insight into the concept of consciousness itself. Most people who have used drugs report that they do so in order to get "high" or intoxicated.

The state of being "high" actually represents a change in consciousness, perhaps going from a level of awareness that induces negative feelings to a different level of awareness where an individual no longer feels "bad." The idea that drugs are an escape rings true, if you consider that many mind- and mood-altering drugs create an "escape" from one state of consciousness to another.

Not all drugs necessarily have an impact on consciousness. I don't recall feeling "altered" the last time I took an aspirin or antibiotic. Drugs whose main effect is the alteration of consciousness are called *psychoactive drugs.* Common psychoactive drugs and substances include LSD, PCP, marijuana, cocaine, amphetamines, barbiturates, ecstasy, and alcohol.

Although many people see drug use for the claimed purpose of expanding their consciousness as a good thing, as a health professional I feel compelled to warn you of many of the negative effects of psychoactive substance use and abuse. Addiction, brain damage, mental illness, psychological distress, and social and legal problems are common consequences of psychoactive drug use. With these in mind, I strongly caution anyone considering the use of drugs and would strongly argue for seeking higher states of consciousness without the use of substances.

TIP

A natural high

Stanley Krippner defines an altered state of consciousness as a mental state that is subjectively experienced as representing a difference in psychological functioning from an individual's normal, alert, waking state. The importance of the subjectively experienced difference can be illustrated by a story told by Baba Ram Das in his book *Be Here Now* (Crown Publishing Group). Baba Ram Das's original name was Richard Alpert. Alpert was a psychology professor at Harvard in the 1960s, where he and Timothy Leary conducted experiments with LSD. They both were eventually fired. Ram Das traveled to India to seek the path of Hindu wisdom and to find out if anyone could explain why LSD seemed to have such a profound effect on consciousness.

One day, Ram Das encountered a very wise and respected guru. Ram Das asked the guru if he could explain the effects of LSD. The guru asked for some LSD, and Ram Das complied. The guru took more LSD than Ram Das had ever seen a human being take, but the guru seemed completely unaffected! He didn't have an "acid trip" at all. There was no change in his current state of consciousness — he didn't experience an altered state of consciousness when he took the LSD. Does that mean that the guru was already on some sort of "reality trip" or "spiritual LSD?"

Your eyes are getting very heavy. . . .

Close your eyes and relax. You are soooooo relaxed. Your breathing is slow. You're beginning to feel sleepy. You are soooooo relaxed.

Well, did it work? Hello? Are you under my hypnotic spell? Probably not. I'm not even trained in hypnosis. It's a special skill, and not all therapists or psychologists are trained in it. *Hypnosis* is a procedure in which a person called a *hypnotist* suggests changes in sensations, feelings, thoughts, or behaviors to a subject. Some psychologists think hypnosis is simply an increase in suggestibility that allows the hypnotist to "control" the subject's behavior. Other psychologists propose that hypnosis is actually an altered state of consciousness in which a person *dissociates* (separates) from her normal or regular state of consciousness.

The key to understanding the mechanism of hypnosis is *suggestion*. A *suggestion* is a directive given to the subject to act, feel, or think in a particular way. A hypnotist begins the process with some pleasant suggestions and progresses to more sophisticated requests. This process is called *hypnotic induction,* and it's considered a light hypnotic trance.

False memories?

As for recovering memories from childhood, one subject participating in a study by Fromm spontaneously began speaking the forgotten language of her childhood under hypnosis. There have been hundreds, if not thousands, of claims of recovered memories from childhood, including many memories of sexual or physical abuse. Things get a little sensitive at this point. Elizabeth Loftus has argued vehemently that such memories are questionable at best and that a therapist should be very careful when conducting this type of work. Research has shown that patients under hypnosis can be easily persuaded to believe that they've experienced abuse when they may in fact have not. Again, the question of verifiability is a difficult one. The long and the short of it is that we still don't know enough about the memory-enhancing effects of hypnosis to provide a definitive answer.

Hypnosis has been used for many different purposes ranging from entertainment to helping people stop smoking. The more controversial applications of hypnosis involve past-life regression and the recovery of repressed memories. There is little scientific evidence supporting the legitimacy of past-life regression through hypnosis. It's virtually impossible to prove. Why? Anything that someone reports can only be verified through historical records, and if I can look it up for verification, the individual in question could have looked it up to fake a regression.

Catching some zzzzs

Sleep represents a change in consciousness. When we're asleep, we're unconscious. Sleep is characterized by a change in our *electrophysiological activity* — our "brain wave" activity. Sleep, as a level of consciousness, can be distinguished from other levels of consciousness by measuring this electrophysiological energy of the brain with an EEG. When we're awake and alert, our brains emit a wave with a frequency of 13 to 30 hertz (Hz), called *beta activity*. When we're awake but relaxed, just kickin' it, our brains show *alpha activity* — a frequency of 8 to 12 Hz.

Carlson has distinguished four stages of sleep with one substage, which is characterized by brain activity one would expect from an awake and alert brain.

✔ **Stage 1:** When a prospective sleeper closes her eyes and begins to relax, getting into sleep mode, her brain waves are at an alpha frequency. As she drifts deeper into Stage 1, her brain waves become less regular, and they have a higher amplitude. This is *theta activity,* 3.5 to 7.5 Hz. Carlson identifies this stage as a transition period between being awake and asleep, and it lasts approximately 10 minutes.

In case you're wondering why higher amplitude waves are associated with smaller hertz measurements, it's because hertz is a measure of frequency. Amplitude is a measure of wave height. If a wave is really high, it takes longer to get somewhere and thus has a lower frequency.

✔ **Stage 2:** During Stage 2 sleep, brain wave activity is irregular and contains spikes of very low-amplitude EEG waves called *K-complexes.* There are also short bursts of 12 to 14 Hz waves called *spindles.* We're soundly asleep at this stage, but we may think that we're not actually sleeping. My wife wakes me up while I'm sleeping in front of the television set all the time to tell me that I'm snoring, but I always tell her I wasn't sleeping. I must have been snoring while awake. I don't know which is worse — snoring while asleep or awake.

✔ **Stage 3:** In Stage 3, we emit high-amplitude waves (3.5 Hz), which are an EEG signal of *delta activity.* We spend about an hour and a half in Stage 3.

✔ **Stage 4:** This stage is signaled by the presence of more theta waves interrupting the smooth waves of delta. During Stage 4, our eyes begin to move back and forth very rapidly, which is called *rapid eye movement (REM).* Now, we're in *REM sleep,* characterized by the presence of beta activity. REM sleep is the substage in which the brain is active, but we're asleep.

We dream during REM sleep. After we reach REM sleep, about an hour and a half into the whole sleep process, the rest of the night is characterized by alternating periods of REM sleep and non-REM sleep (activity seen in Stages 1, 2, and 3).

Why do we sleep? I don't necessarily know why other people sleep, but I usually sleep because I'm tired. For the most part, researchers still don't know why we sleep, but some believe that sleep has a *restorative* function. Research that looks at the effects of a lack of sleep, or sleep deprivation, suggests that we engage in sleep so that our body can restore what was lost or damaged during our waking hours.

Arriving at Work Naked: Dreams

Sigmund Freud is credited with saying that dreams are the "royal road to our unconscious." I think that if you ask most people, they would tell you that they believe that dreams have either symbolic or prophetic importance. Dreams represent another altered state of consciousness.

Based on the restorative theory of sleep (see the "Catching some zzzzs" section earlier in this chapter), dreams are the by-product of the brain reorganizing and storing the information gathered over the course of a waking day. This explanation actually allows for the possibility that dreams can be interpreted because they relate to real events and situations; therefore, they can have meaning.

Psychoanalysis has probably provided us with the most comprehensive look at the psychological importance of dreams and dreaming. Freud and other psychoanalysts make a simple point: Dreams have deeper meanings than their surface content suggests. If I have a dream about getting a new car, it means more than I just want a new car. It could mean any number of things, but the meaning is something unique to my psychological makeup, something idiosyncratic. The car may represent a repressed desire to be free, and the car is a symbol of movement.

Psychoanalysts believe that the contents and processes of our dreams represent deep, unconscious conflicts, desires, and issues. Dreams are hard to decipher; they're often convoluted, and they don't make much sense. In *The Interpretation of Dreams,* Freud states that dreams often represent our attempts to fulfill wishes that we're not consciously aware of. Through the technique of dream interpretation, a psychoanalyst helps a patient to get to the bottom of the meaning of his or her dreams.

Again, like many of the other topics in this chapter, the "true" meaning of a dream is extremely difficult, if not impossible, to discover. Dreams and their meanings are very personal and subjective phenomena. Even if dreams and their symbolic meanings are difficult to analyze scientifically, it shouldn't take away from anyone's belief that their dreams have some deeper meaning. The process of discovering the meaning of dreams in therapy, whether factually correct or not, can be an exciting and often helpful experience.

Chapter 5

Go Ahead, Be a Little Sensitive

Seeing is believing! I have no idea where that phrase came from, but it tells us something important about ourselves. We have an easier time understanding or comprehending things if we can see them, touch them, hear them, and so on. Why doesn't everyone believe in ghosts, UFOs, or any number of things that most people have not experienced? That's precisely the point, and most people haven't experienced these phenomena with their own senses, so they don't believe in them. How do we know if something is part of the world we live in or not and — whether it's real?

A branch of philosophy known as *ontology* deals with the question, "What is real?" Psychologists also have searched for the answer to this question by following their own philosophy known as *materialism,* the belief that everything in the world is made of matter, of material stuff. Before I start going too far down the philosophical trail and putting you to sleep, let me tell you why this subject is important in a book about psychology.

As you can see by looking at the table of contents of this book, the subject of psychology is made up of a bunch of different areas of study that all point to the ultimate questions of why and how we humans do what we do. This chapter is about the why and how of something that we all do: sense and perceive the world around us. They're as obvious as the nose on our faces, but we often don't realize how important our senses are to us. We see, hear, taste, touch, feel, and so on. Psychology as the study of behavior and mental processes includes taking a look at how our senses actually work.

We're not just little brains floating around inside of a body with no contact with the outside world. Quite the contrary; we are typically in full contact with the world around us, taking in the information that the world provides us, processing it, and using that information to navigate our way through a wide ocean of possibilities. So why is understanding materialism important? Because the way we actually maintain contact with that information is through the physical materials that it consists of.

Sensation is the basic process of receiving raw energy/information from our environment. *Perception* is the process of organizing and making sense of this raw energy. In the following sections, I take a closer look at the ways we sense and perceive our world.

Building Blocks: Our Senses

Physicists and chemists have long pointed out that our world is made up of material stuff: particles, atoms, molecules, and various forms of energy. Basically, the universe is one big ball of energy. Everything consists of a particular configuration of energy. A working definition of *sensation* is the process by which we mentally acquire information about the world through the reception of its various forms of energy.

The forms of energy in the world that humans are most commonly in contact with are: light (electromagnetic energy), sound (acoustic energy, or sound waves), heat (thermal energy), pressure (mechanical or physical energy), and chemical energy. Some organisms are in touch with the same kinds of energy as humans, but they're sensitive to different ranges of them. Sharks can smell chemical particles (of blood, for example) in far smaller quantities than we can, and dogs can hear much higher frequencies of sounds.

For each form of energy that we sense, a specific organ system or "device" is used to receive it. Humans have five basic senses, each receptive to a specific form of energy:

- ✔ **Sight:** Receives light energy
- ✔ **Hearing:** Receives sound energy or sound waves
- ✔ **Touch:** Receives mechanical energy
- ✔ **Smell:** Receives airborne chemical energy
- ✔ **Taste:** Receives chemical energy

The sensing process

When light travels from a light bulb or sound waves travel from a radio speaker, our sensing devices, or *accessory structures,* intercept them. Our eyes, ears, skin, noses, and mouths are called *accessory structures* because they provide us "access" to our environment. After the energy reaches our sensory structures, it has to get inside our brains somehow. We don't have light, sound waves, and heat waves bouncing around inside of our heads. Well, at least I don't. So, how do they get inside?

First, keep in mind that our brains use their own form of energy. In Chapter 3, I discuss the specific type of energy in our brains called *electrochemical energy.* This energy is how our neurons communicate with each other and operate. So, in order for our brains to understand the various forms of energy that our sense organs receive, each form of energy has to undergo a transformation process called *transduction* that turns it into electrochemical, or *neural,* energy. This process is called *transduction.*

The presence of specific types of cells, *receptors,* in each of the sensory systems makes transduction possible. Each sensory system has its own type of receptor cell. After the receptor cells *transduce,* or convert, the environmental energy, a neural signal travels along a *sensory nerve,* taking the information to the part of the brain that is involved in processing and analyzing the information.

Does the music we listen to or human voices have only one tone? Does the light we see only come in one color? Of course not! Each of these sensory experiences, or *stimuli,* is made up of a complex array of wavelengths of light, frequencies of sound, intensities of smells and tastes, and so on. Never fear however, our sensory systems are on the job. Through the process of *coding and representation* our brains are able to capture the complexity of the environmental stimuli that we encounter.

The complexity of a stimulus is captured by the translation of its different features into a specific pattern of neural activity. The theory of *specific nerve energies* states that each sensory system provides information for only one sense, no matter how nerves are stimulated. In other words, there are specific parts of the brain that will always label the stimulation they receive as light or sound.

Psychologists have worked with neurosurgeons to conduct experiments with patients who for other reasons needed a portion of their skulls removed, exposing their brains. Then, they took an electrode and zapped specific parts of these exposed brains with a little jolt of electricity. When they applied this shock, a weird thing happened. The people in the experiment said, "I can hear chickens squawking." If they zapped the part of the brain involving taste, a person might have said, "I can taste tomato soup. Mmm, that's good!" How is this possible? When a particular part of the brain is stimulated, the brain thinks that it's receiving sound or taste information from the sense organ, even if it's not. So, specific sensory systems are wired into specific brain regions permitting the brain to know the difference between hearing a sound and seeing a light.

Different aspects of a stimulus are coded in the brain depending on which neurons are activated and the pattern of neuron activation. If neurons in the visual system are activated, the brain senses light. If the pattern of neural activation differs, the brain senses different wavelengths or intensities of light such as sunlight versus candlelight. The end of the sensory trail leads to a neural *representation* of the sensation in a specific region of the brain where we finally hear the music or see the colors.

Sight

Sight is one of the most important senses that we have. Although the other senses are also important, our ability to see is extremely critical for getting along in our world. In this section, I chronicle a little journey — the journey light takes through the eye and on into the brain, completing our sensation of light.

Our journey begins with *electromagnetic radiation,* more commonly known as light. Visible light occupies wavelengths between 400 and 750 nanometers. I remember from physics class that light travels in waves. The intensity of light is calculated by measuring the size of the waves, and its frequency is measured by how many peaks of a wave pass a particular point within a specific period of time. Wavelength is important because different wavelengths allow us to experience different colors.

1. Light enters our eye through the *cornea.*

2. Light passes through the *pupil.*

3. The *lens* focuses the light onto the *retina.*

4. Light energy is converted into neural energy — light *transduction.*

In order to understand the process of light transduction, a closer look at the retina is necessary. The retina is located on the back lining of the eyeball and contains some special cells called *photoreceptors* that are responsible for transduction. These cells contain chemicals called *photopigments* that are broken apart when the photons of light traveling in the lightwave make contact with them. This event starts a chemical reaction that tells the cell to fire a signal to the *optic nerve.* The signal then travels to the *visual cortex* of the brain, the part of the brain responsible for analyzing visual stimuli.

Synesthesia

Some people claim to hear light and see sounds. Other people report that they can feel colors. *Synesthesia* is the name of an ability that certain people have to sense one (or more) forms of energy with a sensory system other than the one typically used. This phenomenon is estimated to affect about one in every 2,000 people. Scientists have suspected that this experience is a product of some of the brain's wiring being crossed. Baron-Cohen have hypothesized that this is made possible by the presence of extra connections in the brain that allow for otherwise separate sensory systems in the brain to interact. Whatever the cause, it sounds kind of cool! I'd love to be able to see the music when I dance because I sure can't feel it!

So, light is transformed into neural energy by literally breaking up chemicals in the retina, which then has the effect of causing a neural signal to occur. Next, I have to introduce an important "wrinkle" in this whole process. It's all about two types of photoreceptors, *rods* and *cones.*

- ✔ Rods contain a chemical called *rhodopsin,* which is very light-sensitive. This chemical reacts to very low-intensity light and helps with our peripheral vision.

- ✔ Cones contain a different chemical called *iodopsin,* which responds to different wavelengths of light and is involved in seeing color.

Seeing colors

Some people are colorblind to particular shades of blues, greens, and reds. This condition means that they have a hard time sensing the specific wavelengths of light associated with those colors. They lack a photo pigment that is sensitive to those wavelengths. Fortunately most of us aren't colorblind. We get to see the world in all its rainbow-colored glory.

There are two basic theories of color vision, the *trichromatic theory* and the *opponent-process theory.*

- ✔ The trichromatic theory is really basic. The idea is that the retina contains three different types of cones (photoreceptors) that each respond to different wavelengths of light, and these provide our experience of different colors. *Short-wavelength* cones respond to light around 440 nanometers, or blue light. *Medium-wavelength* cones respond to light around 530 nanometers, or green light. *Long-wavelength* cones respond to light around 560 nanometers, or red light. When each cone system is partially activated, we see variations of these three basic colors that give us colors like aquamarine and orange. But the main idea is that our experience of all colors originates from these three basic cone inputs.

✔ The opponent-process theory of color vision states that the brain contains different types of neurons that respond differently to different colors. The idea is that these cells will fire more — when compared to their baseline, or background, level of firing — and when stimulated by one type of light and fire less when stimulated by another. If I'm looking at red, the specialized red cells will increase their firing rate. When I'm looking at green, those red cells will slow down their firing rate, while the rate of the green cells increases. There are other "cell sets" for yellow and blue as well.

This theory explains something called the *negative-afterimage effect* images in your "mind's eye" that are different colors than the actual image. The most popular example uses a U.S. flag that is colored black where the white stars are, green where the red stripes are, and yellow where the blue background is. After looking at the image for a while, someone can close their eyes and see the flag in its real colors. That's because the cells being stimulated by black, green, and yellow light are now recovering from that stimulation and are "seeing" white, red, and blue light instead. Try it. Stare at a 1-x-1-inch yellow square for about 30 seconds and then look at a white sheet of paper. You should see a blue square.

Figuring distances

How can we tell how far something is away from us just by looking at it? Some people are good at eyeballing distances. Personally, I need a tape measure, ruler, land-surveyor, and a global positioning satellite to figure distances. Depth and distance are calculated by our visual systems using two inputs: *monocular cues* and *binocular cues*.

✔ Monocular cues are simple; we know that some things are bigger than other things. Dogs are bigger than mice. Cars are bigger than dogs. Houses are bigger than cars. Because we know these things from experience, whenever we see a mouse's image on our retina that is bigger than the image of the dog in the same scene, we know that the mouse is closer to us than the dog. If we see a dog that's bigger than a car, the dog is closer. The rule is that things that cast bigger images on our retinas are assumed to be closer. Artists use this rule all the time when they want to depict a three-dimensional scene on a two-dimensional canvas.

✔ Binocular cues are interesting and also a little weird. Remember the Cyclops from the Sinbad movies? He only had one eye, and according to binocular vision rules, he would have had a hard time figuring out distances. Binocular distance cues depend on having two eyes to provide information to the brain.

• *Convergence* is one such binocular cue and refers to information provided by the muscles of the eyes to the brain to help calculate distances. When your eyes are pointing inward, toward the nose, the brain knows that you're looking at something close to you. When your eyes are pointing outward, the brain knows that you're looking at an object that is farther away.

- *Stereoscopic* vision is the second type of binocular cue. Try this real quickly. Make a viewing frame with your hands by joining your thumbs at the tips and extending your index fingers up, while keeping the rest of your fingers folded. Then, close one eye and focus on an object around you. Frame the object in the middle of the box. Now, close that eye and open the other. What happened? The object should have moved. This happens because of stereoscopic vision. Each of our eyes gives us a slightly different angle on the same image because they are set apart. Our brains judge distance using these different angles by calculating the difference between the two images.

Hearing

Sound travels in waves and is measured by its *amplitude* or *wave size* and *frequency* or *number of waves per unit time.* Each of these translates into a psychological experience: Amplitude determines loudness (my neighbor's rock band), and frequency provides pitch or tone (the screeching lead singer of my neighbor's rock band). The structures of the ear are specifically designed to transduce, or convert, sound-wave energy into neural energy.

A sound first enters the ear as it is funneled in by the *pinna.* Our crumpled-up outer ear is designed as a "sound scoop." As the wave passes through the ear canal, it eventually reaches the eardrum, or the *tympanic membrane.* The vibrating eardrum shakes three little bones *(malleus, incus,* and *stapes,* Latin words for *hammer, anvil, and stirrup),* which amplifies the vibration.

After the sound wave reaches the inner ear, the *cochlea,* auditory transduction occurs. The cochlea contains the hardware for the transduction process. The cochlea is filled with fluid, and its floor is lined with the *basilar membrane. Hair cells* (they actually look like hairs) are attached to the basilar membrane. The sound waves coming into the inner ear change the pressure of the fluid inside the cochlea and create fluid waves that move the basilar membrane. Movement of the basilar membrane causes the hair cells to bend, which starts the transduction ball rolling. When the hair cells bend, their chemical properties are altered, thus changing their electrical polarity. As I discuss in Chapter 3, when a cell's polarity is altered, it is in a position to fire and send a neural signal. The sound waves, now turned into neural electrochemical energy, travel to the *auditory cortex* (the part of the brain responsible for hearing) for perceptual processing.

Touch

The sense of touch includes sensing pressure, temperature, and pain. Specialized cells in the skin sense touch, which send a signal to the spinal chord and then on to the brain. In this case, transduction in touch is a physical or mechanical process; it's much more straightforward than the chemical transduction in the eye for vision. When heat, cold, or weight stimulates touch receptors in the skin, this sends a neural signal toward the brain, much the same way that the hair cells of the inner ear operate. The pressure leads directly to a neural signal.

Pain is a special case for the sense of touch because it would be hard to avoid harm and survive in this world without our sense of pain. How do I know fire can damage my flesh and possibly lead to death? Because it hurts when I touch it. Pain is an important signal that something is harming, damaging, or destroying the body.

A-delta fibers and *C fibers,* two specific nerve fibers located throughout our skin, signal pain to the brain. A-delta fibers carry sharp sensations and work rapidly, sending swift signals to the brain. C fibers send signals of chronic and dull pain and burning sensations.

I've played sports most of my life, and one thing is for sure — pain tolerance is always an issue. "No pain, no gain!" I'd hear in practice every day. I've had to play through many an injury, and it really hurt! Some people seem to have a really high threshold for pain. The *gate-control theory of pain* states that pain signals must pass through a gate in the spinal cord that "decides" which signals will get through to the brain and which ones will not. If another sense is using the pain pathways, the pain signal may not reach the brain. Also, there might be competing signals coming from another body part toward the gate, thus inhibiting the pain signal from traveling up to the brain. If you've ever rubbed your thigh while your ankle aches, it seems to help. That's because the rubbing signal (pressure) from the thigh is competing for access through the gate with the pain signal from the ankle. That's amazing! I'm always blown away by the complexity of the human body.

Smell and taste

Our sense of smell is called *olfaction.* Sometimes I can smell my neighbor's barbecue on the weekend. I have that experience because little particles from the cooking food, *volatile chemical particles,* have become airborne and traveled over to the smell receptors in my nose. Inside my nose are thousands of olfactory receptors that can sense tens of thousands of different odors.

The molecules from the volatile chemicals cause a chemical change in the receptors in my nose, which sets the transduction process in motion. The chemical energy is then converted into neural energy by the receptor cells, and a signal is sent to the *olfactory bulb* in my brain where the signal is processed. The olfactory bulb also connects with the part of my brain that involves emotion. Some researchers think that this connection is why smells can activate emotional memories from time to time.

There's been a lot of talk about *pheromones* scents that animals send out as signals to other animals, during mating season, for example. Some companies have marketed pheromone products for humans, especially for those men out there desperate to find a date. Do humans really produce pheromones? The research jury is still out, but a few recent findings seem to suggest that we do. One thing is for sure though: Pheromones or no pheromones, the perfume and cologne industries seem to be on to something!

Gustation refers to our sense of taste. Taste is a chemical sense made possible by the chemical receptors on our tongues known as *taste buds.* All tastes are variations on four themes: sweet, sour, bitter, and salty. We have approximately 10,000 taste buds. The taste buds react to the molecules of the food, which again converts chemical energy into neural energy and sends that information to the area of the brain involved in analyzing taste information.

Finishing the Product: Perception

Obviously, the world we're in touch with through our senses is a lot more complex than just a bunch of singular sounds, smells, tastes, and other sensations. We hear symphonies, not just notes. We see fireworks, not just single photons of light. We indulge our taste buds with scrumptious meals, not just salty, sour, bitter, and sweet tastes. We can thank the ability of perception for all of these pleasures.

Perception is the process of organizing, analyzing, and providing meaning to the various sensations that we are bombarded with on a daily basis. If sensation provides us with the raw material, perception is the final product.

There are two popular views of this complex process:

✔ **Ecological view:** This idea states that our environment provides us with all of the information that we need to sense the world; very little interpretation or construction is needed. For example, when I perceive a tree, it's not because I've constructed a perception of it in my mind. I perceive the tree because the tree has provided me with all of the necessary information to perceive it as it is.

✔ **Constructionist view:** In this view, the process of perception relies on previous knowledge and information to construct reality from fragments of sensation. We are not just passive recipients of sensory information. We are actively constructing what we see, hear, taste, and so on.

Regardless of whether you're an ecologist or a constructionist, there are some basics to the process of perceiving. If sensation is the process of detecting specific types of energy in our environments, how do we know which information is worth detecting and which is just background noise? After all, we couldn't possibly respond to every bit of sensory energy around us. We'd easily be overwhelmed with all the roaring traffic, howling wind, bustling pedestrians, and other stuff around us. The good news is that our perceptual systems have a built-in system for determining what information should be or is actually detectable.

The concept of an *absolute threshold* refers to the minimum amount of energy in the environment that a sensory system can detect. Each sensory system has an absolute threshold below which energy does not warrant or garner perceptual attention.

Another determinant of whether a stimulus is detected or not comes from *Weber's law,* which gives the idea of the *just-noticeable difference (JND).* Each sensory system determines a constant fraction of intensity for each form of energy that represents the smallest detectable difference between energy intensities. The idea is that a stimulus has to exceed the JND in order for it to be detectable; otherwise, it will go unnoticed because the difference is too small.

Yet, another theory known as *signal-detection theory* takes a slightly more complicated look at the problem. An overwhelming amount of the environmental energy around us is considered background noise. When we encounter a stimulus, called the *signal,* it's analyzed based on our individual *sensitivity* and *response criterion.* Based on the sensitivity and response criterion of their individual sensory systems, people can either correctly detect a stimulus *(hit),* fail to detect a signal when there is one *(miss),* detect a signal when there isn't one *(false alarm),* or report no signal when there isn't one *(correct rejection).*

Our individual biases and motivations determine our response criterion and play a role in whether we make an accurate detection or not. So, when people think I'm not listening to them, it's not my fault. I'm not detecting their signal because my response criterion is set not to respond to anyone talking to me at that moment. I'm an innocent victim of my perceptual processes.

Organizing by Principles

The perceptual system is not made up of a bunch of arbitrary rules and random processes. Psychologists and other researchers over the years have discovered a number of principles that guide the way our perceptual systems organize all the information that we receive from our sensory systems:

✔ **Figure-Ground:** Information is automatically divided into figure and ground, or immediate and background. The information that is figural is more obvious, and the ground is less meaningful.

If you focus on, or *make figural,* the white area, all you see is a shapely vase. If you focus on the black areas, making them figural, you can see two faces looking at each other.

✔ **Grouping:** This large category contains principles that are used to determine whether stimuli belong in a group with similar stimuli.

- **Proximity:** Stimuli that are close together in space are perceived to belong together.

- **Common fate:** Stimuli that move in the same direction and at the same rate are grouped together.

- **Continuity:** Stimuli that create a continuous form are grouped together.

- **Similarity:** Similar things are grouped together.

✔ **Closure:** This principle is the tendency to fill in missing information to complete a stimulus.

Most psychologists today are in the *constructionist* camp. (See the "Finishing the Product: Perception" section earlier in this chapter.) They view perception as a process of building the things we perceive of reality out of fragments of information. We are born with some of the rules for organizing information, but a few other factors can influence the way we perceive things.

Our experiences have a powerful impact on how we perceive things. The concept of *perceptual set* tries to capture this idea, an expectation of what I will perceive. We use cues from context and experience to help us understand what we are seeing. For example, if I am driving down the street and see someone in a police uniform standing next to someone's car window, I assume that he is making a traffic stop. I could actually be seeing a person in a police uniform asking for directions, but my experience tells me otherwise.

Illusions and magic

Perceptual illusions are a consequence of the organizing principles of our perceptual systems. We might see things that aren't really there or see things moving when they're motionless. Illusionists, such as magicians, use these perceptual organizing rules against us. They have a keen understanding of how our perceptual systems work, and they take advantage of this knowledge to carry out their tricks.

Another powerful influence on how we perceive things is the culture that we live in. A good example of the role cultural influences play in our perceptions involves figuring out a story line based on a series of pictures. Consider that I have five pictures, each containing a different piece of a puzzle that, when viewed in sequence, can tell a story. The story that I think the pictures are telling might be different if I'm from a different culture. For example, I'm looking at a series of pictures that show a woman carrying a bag, a picture of her crying, a man approaching her, and a picture with her bag missing. What's going on here? I might see a woman who is upset because she dropped her bag and a man who is coming to help her. Or, I might see a woman crying out of fear because a man is coming to steal her bag. Depending upon my culture or subculture, not to mention my experience, I could see two very different stories.

Part III
Thinking and Feeling

The 5th Wave® By Rich Tennant

"I don't know, Mona—sometimes I get the feeling you're afraid to get close."

In this part . . .

Part III covers human thought, which psychologists call cognition. I discuss both the content of thought and the thought process here. I include a discussion of the concept of intelligence and the different theories of "being smart." I also cover emotion and motivation in this part. Definitely check this part out if you're interested in love. Or, if you'd rather read about being angry, there's something here for you as well.

Chapter 6

Watching Yourself Think

● ●

In This Chapter

▶ Thinking about thinking

▶ Turning on your mind's computer

▶ Processing ideas

▶ Reasoning like Spock

● ●

*B*efore I talk about the complex psychological area of thinking, here's a little mental experiment. For background, imagine yourself lying in your bed having just awakened from a good night's sleep. You reach over to shut off your annoying alarm, toss the blankets to the side, and head for the bathroom. Now, here's the experimental part. When you get to the bathroom, you forget why you're in there. The answer may seem obvious because you just got out of bed and walked straight to the bathroom, but you've forgotten. You look around and can't figure out where you are. Nothing seems familiar, and you're surrounded by a strange world of shapes, figures, objects, sounds, and lights. You look into an object that reflects an image of some other thing back at you, but you don't know what it is. You're confused, disoriented, and basically lost. Your mind is completely blank. You can't even think of anything to say in order to cry out for help. You're stuck there. What are you going to do?

If the example seems a little strange, or at least a little abstract, it's for a reason. The situation would be pretty strange. What would it be like if you had no ability to think? The bathroom example might be what it's like. You couldn't recognize objects. You couldn't solve any problems. You couldn't communicate. You'd really be in trouble. You wouldn't even be able to figure out how to get out of the bathroom. Have you ever heard the saying, "You couldn't fight your way out of a wet paper bag?" In this case, you couldn't *think* your way out of a wet paper bag, or the bathroom either.

We rarely notice our thinking. It's like background music, always there but never obvious. Thinking seems so automatic and effortless. I used take my "mind" for granted, and I rarely paid any attention to it. The only time that I really sat up and took notice of my mind was when it went on vacation. I guess I didn't really know what I had until it was gone. But how would I know if my mind was gone, if I didn't have one anymore? That topic is better left for late night philosophy sessions at the local coffeehouse. For the purposes of this chapter, you can assume that we all have a mind, and that all of us possess the ability to think.

What's On Your Mind?

What exactly is thought? A bit later in this chapter, I ask you to analyze your own thought processes, so it would help if you knew what you were analyzing. In psychology, thought or thought processes are called *cognition* or *cognitive processes*, the mental processing of information including memorizing, reasoning, problem solving, conceptualizing, and imagining.

Studying thinking is pretty hard to do. Why? It's hard to see! If I opened up your skull and looked inside, would I see thinking? No, I'd see a wrinkly-looking, grayish-pink thing (in other words your brain). In the early years of psychological research on thinking, psychologists asked people participating in studies on thinking to engage in something called introspection. *Introspection* is the observation and reporting of one's own inner experience. Psychologists gave participants a simple math problem to solve and asked them to talk out loud as they performed the calculations. These exercises were intended to capture the steps involved in the thinking process.

Try it! Get a piece of blank paper and a pencil. Your instructions are to solve the following math problem and write down each step that you take, one by one:

47,876 + 23,989

The answer you came up with should have been 71,865. If not, don't worry about it; we've all got our weaknesses. Actually, if you got the wrong answer, the introspection technique may be able to show you what you did wrong. Take a second to go over each of the steps you went through to solve the problem.

You've just participated in a psychological experiment, and it didn't hurt a bit, did it? The introspection technique should have been able to capture your thought processes related to a relatively simple problem-solving task.

Now, imagine how hard it would be to use introspection to analyze all of your thoughts. It would be pretty difficult, if not impossible. Part of the reason psychologists don't use introspection anymore is that it is too simple. It can't capture the sophisticated thought processes. These days, psychologists use computer modeling and other complex means of researching thought. Another reason introspection fell out of favor is that some of the most important aspects of thinking — those that we tend to take for granted — are not readily available for our evaluation. No matter how far inside our mind we look, we still can't discover its building blocks; we only experience its final products.

Plugging Your Mug into a PC

With the advent of the modern computer, psychologists and related investigators began to look at the operations performed by computers, called *computing* or *computation,* as potential models for human thought. This was a significant breakthrough. Using the computer as a model for how thinking occurs is called the *computational model of mind* (and thinking). The idea is both profound and simplistic: The mind, and all of its complex processes, such as perceiving, thinking, problem solving and all the rest, are an information-processing procedure, a computation. The mind is an information processing machine.

Processing information

Your mind goes through four basic steps when processing information:

1. Stimulus information from our senses reaches the brain. (You see Michael Jackson moonwalking for the first time.)

2. The meaning of this information is analyzed. (Your brain thinks, "Wow. Those are phat dance moves.")

3. Different possible responses are generated. (Your brain tries to figure out how he's doing that dance.)

4. A response is executed and monitored for feedback. (You throw off your shoes and try it out on the kitchen floor.)

So, thinking is a process that involves the analyzing of information. But what is "information?" For starters, consider that thinking is always about some-*thing* or things. When I'm thinking, I'm thinking about something or some object a car, a person, an event, and so on. What kinds of "things" or objects does a computer use in its calculations? Consider a calculator, one of the most common types of information processors. What kinds of objects does a calculator use in its operations? Numbers or symbols, right? Thinking involves the processing of mental or thought symbols. Thought symbols are mental representations of objects in our world. The following paragraph illustrates this point.

Turing's challenge

Alan Turing came up with something called the *Turing test*. A popular parlor game at the time involved placing a man and a woman behind two different doors; guests had to communicate with them by typewritten notes. The point was to guess correctly who was the man and who was the woman based only on their answers to questions of your choosing. Turing proposed the comparison be changed to a computer and a human being — and if guests were unable to determine whether the computer or the human being were answering their questions, the computer would have to be considered intelligent.

Sit back for a second, get comfortable, and conjure up an image of a pink rose in your mind. Concentrate so that the image is clear, the green stem and leaves, the pink petals, the thorns, and so forth. Try to imagine the rose in detail. If someone comes into the room as you're doing this and asks if there is a rose in the room, what would you say? If there isn't actually a rose in the room, then you'd say "no." But consider the idea that there is actually a rose in the room, or at least it's in the room because there's one inside your mind, the rose that you're thinking of. So, if I cut open your skull and looked into your head, I'd see a pink rose, right? Of course not! The rose only "exists" in symbolic or representational form inside of your mind. When you read the word "door" on this page, you have an image of a door in your mind. You have the thought of "door." How is this possible? Symbolic representation! The word "door" is a linguistic mental symbol for that wooden (typically), rectangular thing attached to the front of your house.

Thinking consists of symbols that represent information about our world and the objects within it and the manipulation of those symbols. The mental manipulation of these symbols is based on combining, breaking down, and recombining symbols into more complex strings or systems of symbols that have meaning. Take the word "door" again. It consists of simpler parts called letters, and the specific combination of those letters gives rise to the specific word and image of the object called "door." The letters could be rearranged to spell the word "odor," which is an entirely different thing and thus an entirely different thought. Hopefully you can see that even a simple system like the alphabet can give rise to an almost infinite set of larger and more meaningful symbols or representations.

Where do all these symbols come from? The symbols are generated by sensing things in the world. When I see a rose, there's a corresponding symbolic representation of that rose in my mind as I think about it.

Conceptualizing

When was the last time you went out with a friend just to talk? Did you go to a coffeehouse? Did you talk about recent romances and frustrating relationships in your life? Did you talk about politics or the weather? It doesn't matter what you talked about, you were talking about a concept.

A _concept_ is a thought or idea that represents a set of related ideas. "Romance" is a concept. "Relationship" is a concept. "Politics" is a concept. "Weather" is a concept. Remember, these concepts are represented as symbols in your information processing systems of thought. How do they get there? We learn them. Concepts are derived and generated; they are formed. When objects share characteristics, they represent the same concept. Some concepts are well-defined, others are not.

Consider the following words:

> Tail, Fur, Teeth, Four legs

What do these words describe? It could be a cat, a dog, a lion, or a bear. The fact is, you really can't tell just from those four words. Some crucial detail is missing, some piece of information that clearly defines the concept and separates it from others.

Now, consider this list of words:

> Tail, Fur, Teeth, Four legs, Bark

What is being described now? This has to be a dog. Why? Cats, lions, and bears don't bark. The feature "bark" uniquely defines the concept of "dog." "Bark" is the concept's _defining feature_. It is an attribute that must be present in order for the object to be classified as an example of a particular concept. Consider the following words:

> Feathers, Beak, Eggs, Fly

What do these describe? A bird? Hold on a minute. Aren't there at least two birds that don't fly? What about penguins and ostriches? They don't fly, but they're still birds. So, flying is not a defining feature of being a bird because animals don't have to have that attribute in order to be considered a bird. However, most birds do fly, so "flying" is what we call a _characteristic feature_ or attribute. It is an attribute that most members of a concept group, but not all, possess.

Think about a chair. Try to imagine and picture a chair. Now, describe it. (Describe it to someone else or you'll look funny describing an imaginary chair to yourself.) Your imagined chair probably consists of wood, four legs, a rectangular or square seat, and a back constructed of two vertical supports on each side of the seat connected by a couple of horizontal slats.

This is a typical chair. It's common. In fact, it might be considered as a proto-typical chair. A *prototype* is the most typical example of an object or event within a particular category. It is the quintessential example of the concept being represented.

Early in our development, category attributes are combined in an incremental fashion, building on simple characteristics, combining them into larger units until your conceptual net of information about the objects in your world grows to an immense capacity. But we all know that our thinking is much more complex than a simple one-word understanding. After a while, we combine single word concepts into sentence-long concepts, sentence-long concepts into paragraph-long concepts, and so on. Check out this process, which continuously builds upon itself.

"War is hell" is an example of two concepts, "war" and "hell" being related.

✔ You build *mental models* by clustering many propositions to help you understand how things relate to each other. Here's an example:

> War is hell.
>
> World War II was a war.
>
> World War II was hell.

✔ *Schemas* are basic units of understanding that represent the world and are the result of organizing mental models into larger groups. An example might be, "Some of the soldiers who fought in WWII experienced psychological trauma. Some people believe that this was due to the extreme nature of war. Some people have even said that war is hell."

Attributes are combined into concepts. Concepts are combined into propositions. Multiple propositions are combined into mental models. Finally, mental models are combined into schemas, which are used as basic units of understanding and representing the world in our language of thought.

An example may be to consider the concept "book." Combine the concept of book with another concept, like reading. Then connect those concepts to another concept, like library. Now, you have three concepts related to each other: book, reading, and library. These three concepts may give rise to the proposition of studying (as opposed to reading for pleasure). Studying then can be imbedded into the larger divisions, or schema, of school or going to school.

Turning Those Gears

Human thinking depends upon a conceptual grasp and representation of the world we live in. So, after we've got all these concepts inside our minds, what do we do with them?

Consider this: Every two to three months, in every university across the country, something very strange happens. The event is as predictable as the tides, the cycles of the moon, or student debt. With each new course a student takes and a professor teaches, a predictable phenomenon occurs. John Smith, student, walks into the classroom or lecture hall, faces forward, takes out a notebook and a writing utensil, and waits for the professor to begin speaking about things that the student will take down as notes. This repeating process or sequence of events is a perfect example of a script, representing a type of schema that demonstrates a student's knowledge of the concepts of "being in class" or "being a student."

How does thinking employ concepts (like "being a student") to navigate our world and solve the problems that we face every day? If thinking is a form of computation, and our minds are very powerful computers, then how exactly are these calculations carried out? We know that the substance of our mental language consists of concepts, propositions, mental models, and schemas, but how do these chunks or organized sets of concepts actually guide our thinking and behavior?

Most of the time, thinking is organized and goal-directed. Some would even say it's logical and rational. Organized thinking is rule-determined and based on the goal of solving the numerous problems that each of us face every day. And the number one problem we face every day? Survival. Thinking has a point, and it directs our actions so that we reach our goals, the goals of staying alive!

Take a baby, for example. (Well, don't really take him. Just mull him over.) If I'm a baby and I'm getting hungry, I will instinctively and reflexively cry out. Finally, someone puts the remote control down long enough to come over and give me a bottle. At that point, my thinking becomes very important. Hopefully, I establish an understanding of a relationship between the behavior of crying and the consequence of being fed a bottle. Basically, I generate the thought, "When I cry, someone gives me a bottle." This is now a "rule" for me. It is based on simple logic: if A, then B; if A and B, then C.

A (crying) + B (someone gives me a bottle) = C (satisfied hunger)

In the sections that follow, I introduce you to the basic mechanisms of thinking, sometimes called the *architecture* of thought. These are the *rules of thought*. In addition to the representation of knowledge of the world in the form of concepts, thinking requires all the following basic components:

- ✔ **Input:** Sensory information coming in from our world or from within our own minds.

- ✔ **Memory:** System necessary for storage of knowledge. Information about the world is stored in our minds and memories. Birthdays, names, and other information are all stored in our memory.

- ✔ **Operations:** Rules that determine how the information in the memory system is utilized (reasoning, problem solving, and logical analysis). Take math as an example: If I have 100 numbers stored in my memory and am confronted with a mathematical problem, these operations determine how I solve that problem.

- ✔ **Output:** Action "programs" that involve telling the rest of the mind and body what to do after the thinking operations have been carried out.

Input

The input component of cognitive processing is not really part of the thinking process at all. Actually, what I'm talking about here is perception. The input stage is the place where the information about the world around us gets "put" into our brains. Basically, all of that information "out there" has to get into our minds so we can think about it. How does it get there? Our senses: vision, audition, touch, smell, and taste input all of the information. Our senses serve as the input to thinking. Everything we see, hear, touch, smell, and taste about the world then becomes part of our thought processes. You can read more about perception in Chapter 5.

They say it goes first: Memory

Thinking involves the manipulation of mental symbols that are stored as concepts, representations of the objects we encounter in our worlds. How are these mental symbols stored? Memory!

There are three separate storage systems in memory: *sensory memory, short-term memory, and long-term memory.*

A useful metaphor here makes understanding memory a little bit easier. Envision a bank, you know, that thing that we keep our money in. Anyway, think about your bank. Most of us have a checking account, but we all know that there are other types of accounts as well. Each of these accounts does something a little different with our money. Basically, the bank stores our money and keeps it safe in different ways using different accounts. Checking accounts are typically for everyday and short-term use. Savings are for longer-term storage. Our memories store information in different ways as well.

Sensory storage

Sensory memory is a split second memory system that stores information coming in through your senses. Have you ever looked at the sun and then closed your eyes and looked away? What happens? You can still see a type of sun in your mind.

Short-term memory

Short-term memory (STM) consists of the information that is active in your consciousness right now; the things you're aware of. The light on the book page, these words being read, the grumbling in your stomach, and the sound of traffic outside your window are all are parts of your conscious awareness and are all being stored in your STM. Things you are not aware of can be committed to longer-term storage or simply forgotten.

How much information can your STM store? The common consensus is that it can store seven items of information, plus or minus two items. This is sometimes called the "magical number seven" of STM capacity. Did you ever wonder why phone numbers are seven digits? The magical number seven is why!

Does that mean that I can only store seven words, seven numbers, or seven other simple items in my STM? No, thanks to a process called *chunking,* I can store a lot more information than that. A classic example of chunking is the use of *mnemonics,* where you take a big chunk of information and break it down into a little phrase, so it's easier to remember.

Here's an easy way to form a mnemonic. If you have a list of something you have to memorize, take the first letter of each word on the list and make a catchy phrase out of it. Here's one I've never forgotten, and I learned it in eighth grade: Kings play chess on fine green silk. Do you know what that stands for? It stands for the way biologists classify different organisms on the earth: Kingdom, Phylum, Class, Order, Family, Genus, and Species.

The duration of memory for the STM system is approximately 18 seconds. You can extend the length of time information can be kept in STM only by engaging in something called rehearsal. *Rehearsal* is the process of repeating something over and over again in your mind or out loud so that you don't forget it.

Long-term memory

If the information in STM is rehearsed long enough, it eventually ends up in your long-term memory storage system, the long-term memory. There are basically two different ways to deposit information into your long-term memory banks.

- ✔ **Maintenance rehearsal:** Transfers the information, from your STM, by repetition until it's committed to long-term storage.

- ✔ **Elaborative rehearsal:** Your mind elaborates on the information, integrating it with your existing memories. When information is meaningful and references something that we already know, it is easier to remember and harder to forget.

Our LTM is broken down into three basic divisions:

- ✔ **Episodic memory:** Events and situations unique to your experiences (marriages, birthdays, graduations, car accidents, and so on)

- ✔ **Semantic memory:** Factual information such as important holidays, the name of the first president of the United States, and your Social Security Number

- ✔ **Procedural memory:** Information on how to do things like riding a bike, solving a math problem, or tying your shoes

Theoretically, the size and time capacity of LTM is infinite because researchers haven't found a way to test its capacity. Just remember that it has enough capacity to get the job done. This sounds kind of strange, when you consider how much information we seem to forget. If the information is "in there" somewhere, why do we forget it?

Forgetting information stored in LTM is more of a process of not being able to access it rather than the information not being there. Two forms of access failure plague us when we fail to retrieve something from memory. Both of these access failures involve the inability to access a memory because other information gets in the way.

- ✔ **Retroactive interference:** Having a hard time remembering older information because newer information is getting in the way

- ✔ **Proactive interference:** Having a hard time remembering newer information because older information is getting in the way

The next time you watch a sitcom on television try to remember the details of the first 10 to 12 minutes, the middle 10 to 12 minutes, and the last 10 to12 minutes of the program. Or, listen to a lecture and try to remember what was said during the beginning, middle, and end of the presentation. You might notice something psychologists call the *serial position effect.* Information from the beginning and end of the show or lecture is easier to remember than the middle. Why is that?

FREE ASSOCIATION

The serial position effect occurs because the information at the beginning of the show or lecture is usually committed to long-term memory because of the amount of time that elapses. The information at the end of the show is being kept in your short-term memory because it's fresh in your mind. The middle stuff? It's just gone.

Playing Operation(s)

The third step in the thinking process involves the implementation of mental operations or activities. Two common types of mental activities are *problem solving* and *reasoning*.

Solving problems

Problem solving sounds pretty straightforward. You have a problem, and you solve it. Remember that television show *MacGyver?* MacGyver could solve just about any problem that came his way. He could turn a toothpick into a Jet Ski or a rocket launcher. I'd just sit back and watch in amazement, and then I'd get out my trusty toolbox and dismantle the toaster, trying to turn it into a satellite receiver — four hours later all I'd have was a pile of parts and no way to make toast. I guess MacGyver had better problem-solving skills than me.

Newell and Simon (1972) are like the godfathers of problem-solving psychology. Nearly every research study on the topic cites their study. They gave us these basic steps of the problem-solving process:

1. Recognizing a problem exists is kind of like the idea that you can't deal with an addiction or alcohol problem until you admit that one exists

2. Constructing a representation of the problem that includes the initial state and the eventual goal

3. Generating and evaluating the possible solutions

4. Selecting a possible solution

5. Executing the solution and determining if it actually worked

These steps are sometimes identified by the acronym IDEAL (Bransford and Stein, 1993):

"I" identify the problem

"D" define and represent the problem

"E" explore possible strategies

"A" action

"L" look back and evaluate the effects

As many problem-solving strategies probably are out there as there are problems, although most of us basically use the same ones over and over again. We all know how to use *trial and error* to solve a problem. I've seen young children use trial and error when trying to put shapes into their respective holes. First he'll pick up the circle and try it in every cut-out hole until it fits and so on. This strategy is pretty inefficient, but sometimes it's the only tool we have. Trial and error can be used if no clear definition of the problem exists and when part of the problem is figuring out what the problem is.

Here are a couple more common problem-solving techniques:

✔ **Means-ends analysis:** This strategy involves breaking the problem down into smaller sub-problems to solve to get to the end result.

✔ **Working backwards:** This way to solve a problem is like taking something apart and putting it back together again in order to figure out how the object (or problem) is built.

✔ **Brainstorming:** A technique that involves coming up with as many possible solutions to the problem without editing them in any way. It doesn't matter how implausible, unfeasible, idiotic, or ridiculous the solutions are; you just put them all out there and eliminate them after you can't think of any more possible solutions. Even my idea to have Superman use his super-cool breath to stop global warming is included in this technique.

✔ **Analogies and metaphors:** These strategies involve using a parallel or similar problem that has already been solved to solve a previously unrelated problem. The Cuban Missile Crisis was like a nuclear-powered game of chicken, and whoever flinched, blinked, or chickened out first was the loser. I guess President Kennedy was pretty good at chicken.

Reasoning and logic

Supposedly, reasoning and the ability to solve problems logically are two of the primary abilities that set humans apart from animals. In case you're wondering, humans can reason, animals can't. I know that this fact may be up for debate, especially for all of you pet owners out there who think that your dog Fido can solve math problems by barking the answers, but trust me. Remember Dr. Spock on *Star Trek?* He was always so logical, and Captain Kirk was always winning the day with his passionate and emotionally based solutions. So much for logic and reasoning. But remember that *Star Trek* was only a television show.

Reasoning can be defined as a thinking process that involves drawing *conclusions based* on the truth of the premises that precede the conclusion. Premises state some state of affairs, like "All fire trucks are red." Another premise might be, "My dad drives a fire truck at work." So a logical conclusion might be, "My dad drives a red truck at work." Reasoning can help us figure out if our conclusions are valid or if they make logical sense.

When our arguments make logical sense, our reasoning is good. It makes logical sense that my dad drives a fire truck at work because this follows from the premises. But what if it went like this: All fire trucks are red. My dad's truck is red. Therefore, my dad's truck is a fire truck. This is not logical! The first premise doesn't state that all trucks are red, only that fire trucks are red. So, other trucks can be red, including fire trucks. My dad might drive a red Toyota. Logic is like a measuring stick for verifying our reasoning.

All basic reasoning problems involve two basic components:

- **Premises:** These are statements about some object or event that are used to support a conclusion.

- **Conclusions:** These are the points derived from the premises. They are only valid if they can be logically or reasonably drawn from the premises.

There are two basic types of reasoning:

- **Inductive:** In inductive reasoning, you begin with making observations (the premises) in order to collect facts to support or disconfirm (validate) some hypothetically stated outcome or situation (the conclusion). Consider the following:

  Monday it rained.

  Tuesday it rained.

  Therefore, I conclude that Wednesday it is going to rain.

This is an example of inductive reasoning. Two observations or premises are used to predict a third outcome. I think my local weather person uses inductive logic to make his forecasts, not the million-dollar computer technology that the TV station advertises.

✔ **Deductive:** Deductive reasoning uses premises that claim to provide conclusive proof of truth for the conclusion. A conclusion based on deductive logic is by necessity true provided that it begins with true premises. Deduction often begins with generalizations and reasons to particulars. Consider the following example of deductive reasoning:

All men should be free.

I am a man.

Therefore, I should be free.

The conclusion follows logically from the two premises. It has to be that way based on what is stated in the premises. Here's an example of a false conclusion:

All chickens lay eggs.

My bird laid an egg.

Therefore, my bird must be a chicken.

Why is this false? Because the first premise refers to a subset of the larger category, birds. The second premise includes this larger category, and therefore refers to some events not covered by the first premise. If we turn the two premises around, we can create a logically valid syllogism:

All birds lay eggs,

My chicken laid an egg,

Therefore, my chicken must be a bird.

Output

So far thinking looks like this:

Input →→ Memory →→ Operations are performed

What's left? The output of the thinking process is the "action" phase or outcome. If I receive numbers to solve a math problem, I access my memory about subtraction, perform the operations mentally, and then my brain tells my hands to write the solution on the paper. This output is sometimes called a *motor program* because it involves movement of muscles (like those in my head). The solution of the subtraction problem is also output, but instead of being a muscle or motor program, it is "mental" output that might then be verbalized by using the muscles of my mouth. Then it becomes a motor program.

Thinking You're Pretty Smart

Psychologists have been trying to figure out what intelligence is for a long time. Plenty of examples of a lack of intelligence exist. Just take a look at those goofy home-video shows. The guy who forgets to turn the electricity off before trying to rewire a room. Or the lady who tries to feed to a polar bear and almost becomes dinner. Maybe we are entertained by this misfortune of others caught on videotape because these people couldn't have been any less intelligent. Another more controversial possibility is that we feel giddy because we did not suffer their fate.

We all differ in our abilities to solve problems, learn, think logically, use language well, understand and acquire concepts, deal with abstractions, integrate ideas, attain goals, and so on. This impressive list of abilities represents some of the ideas of what intelligence actually is, these things *are* intelligence.

For a more concrete definition, *intelligence* is a collection of abilities that allows a person to experience, learn, think, and adapt successfully to the world. Such a broad definition allows for such concepts as street smarts, something a lot of psychotherapy patients claim that therapists don't have.

Two-factor theory

Oh, if only it were that simple. Ever since psychologists started studying intelligence, they've relied heavily on psychological tests for their concepts. The first and still most popular form of intelligence is called the *two-factor theory.* In it there are (surprise) two factors:

- ✔ **g-factor:** Some psychologist comes up with a test of mental abilities and gives it to a lot of people. When a score is calculated and averaged across abilities, a general intelligence factor is established. This is factor one of the two-factor theory, commonly referred to as the *g-factor,* or the general intelligence factor. It is meant to represent how generally intelligent you are based on your performance on this type of intelligence test. This is often called the *psychometric theory* of intelligence. *Psycho* means psychological, and *metric* means measured by a test.

- ✔ **s-factor:** The individual scores on each of the individual subtests represent the s-factor. It represents a person's ability within one particular area. Put all the s-factors together, and you get the g-factor. Commonly measured s-factors of intelligence include memory, attention and concentration, verbal comprehension, vocabulary, spatial skills, and abstract reasoning.

So, intelligence in the psychometric theory is your score on an intelligence test. How can this be? Each test is made up of a group of little tests or subtests. Typically, people who score high on one test also will do well on the other tests. In other words, there is a relationship between each of the individual abilities measured by the subtests represented by the general intelligence concept underlies that relationship.

In a related theory, Thurston came up with a theory of intelligence called *primary mental abilities*. It's basically the same concept as the s-factor with a little more detail. For Thurston, intelligence is represented by an individual's different levels of performance in seven areas: verbal comprehension, word fluency, number, memory, space, perceptual speed, and reasoning. However, this theory has a couple of problems. It has received very little research support, and some psychologists have developed lists of over 100 primary mental abilities. Some people decided it was time for something a little simpler.

Sternberg's triarchic theory of intelligence

Robert Sternberg developed the *triarchic theory* of intelligence in part to address the street smarts controversy. An urban myth claims that Albert Einstein was extremely intelligent and gifted in mathematics and physics, but he couldn't even tie his own shoes. I don't know if this is true or not, but Sternberg seems to agree that an important aspect of being intelligent is to possess a good level of common sense or practical intelligence. The three intelligence components of his theory are

- ✔ **Componential:** *Componential intelligence* is basically the same factors measured by traditional intelligence tests (memory, verbal fluency, and so on). This is the book smarts aspect of intelligence. Sternberg emphasized that these abilities are often disconnected from ordinary life, issues, and problems. Einstein seemed to have possessed this component.

- ✔ **Experiential:** *Experiential intelligence* encompasses the ability to deal with two different types of problems: new problems and routine problems. It requires the ability to recognize new problems, as opposed to everyday problems; search for and generate solutions; and implement the solutions.

- ✔ **Contextual:** Sternberg's last component is a type of practical intelligence that allows people to go about their daily lives without walking in front of cars, telling police officers to get lost, or letting the trash pile up to the ceiling. This is the street smarts aspect of intelligence that we psychologists seem to lack in the eyes of our clients.

Multiple intelligences

Have you ever wondered what makes Michael Jordan such a good basketball player? What about Mozart? He wrote entire operas in one sitting without editing. That's pretty impressive! According to Howard Gardener (1983), each of these men possessed a specific-type of intelligence that is not usually considered intelligence at all. They are usually considered talents.

Gardener generated a theory known as *multiple intelligences* from observing extremely talented and gifted people. He came up with seven types of intelligence that are typically left out of most people's ideas of what intelligence actually is:

- ✔ **Bodily-kinesthetic ability:** Michael Jordan seems to possess a lot of this ability. People high in bodily-kinesthetic ability have superior hand-eye coordination, a great sense of balance, and a keen understanding of and control over their bodies while engaged in physical activities.

- ✔ **Musical ability:** If you can tap your foot and clap your hands in unison, then you've got a little musical intelligence, just a little. People high in musical intelligence possess the natural ability to read, write, and play music exceptionally well.

- ✔ **Spatial ability:** Have you ever gotten lost in your own backyard? If so, you probably don't have a very high level of spatial intelligence. This intelligence involves the ability to navigate and move around in space and to the ability to picture three-dimensional scenes in your mind.

- ✔ **Linguistic ability:** This is the traditional ability to read, write, and speak well. Articulate, well-spoken people, along with poets, writers, and gifted speakers, are high in this ability.

- ✔ **Logical-mathematical ability:** This intelligence includes basic and complex mathematical problem-solving ability.

- ✔ **Interpersonal ability:** The gift of gab and the used-car salesman act are good examples of interpersonal intelligence. A "people person" who has good conversational skills and knows how to interact and relate well with others is high in interpersonal ability.

- ✔ **Intrapersonal ability:** How well do you know yourself? Intrapersonal intelligence involves the ability to understand your motives, emotions, and other aspects of your personality.

Any one of us can have varying degrees of Gardener's intelligences. I might be one heck of a baseball playing, singing, math wiz but I might get lost in my own backyard, can't carry a conversation, and am the last one to realize if I have a feeling or not.

Chapter 7

How Does That Make You Feel?

*W*hy do people get up and go to work every day? Why did my teenage cousin get her bellybutton pierced? Why do people go to the gym? What fun would psychology be if we didn't get to ask all these interesting questions?

There isn't always a lot of mystery behind why people do the things they do. Most of us work to make a living. We eat to stay alive. We pay our taxes to avoid going to jail. These things make sense to most of us, and we don't usually give them much thought. But when someone does something extraordinary, extremely difficult, or horrific, we often find ourselves asking "Why?"

Traumatic experiences often leave us asking why, especially if the trauma is at the hands of another person. Trauma often leaves us feeling confused and in need of answers. Answers can help us come to terms with the way we feel. We often find ourselves asking why someone would do such a thing to another human being. But our quest for answers isn't always focused on the negative. Take Mother Teresa, for example. She dedicated the greater part of her life to working with the sick and the poor in India. She lived in abject poverty, sacrificing all comfort in order to help the poor and seemingly forgotten. Why would she do such a thing? Mother Teresa's dedication to her religious calling and duty was remarkable. She endured harsh conditions and stayed the course. Were her actions a result of love for the people she worked for? Whatever her motivations were, they were strong and unyielding.

In this chapter, I introduce the psychological approach to motivation. Simply knowing the nuts and bolts of an action leaves a gaping hole in our understanding, if we don't know why people do what they do, or at least why they think they do the things they do.

In addition to exploring the various theories of motivation, I also take a look at emotions, which some psychologists feel are the primary motivating factors for all of us. Psychologists make a big deal about emotions because of their central role in human behavior and mental processes. "Why we do what we do" has a lot to do with the way we feel.

The big joke about going to a psychologist is that she'll ask, "How does that make you feel?" What's the big deal about feelings and emotions? Being hungry or tired can be important. Wait a minute though. Is hunger a feeling? What about being tired? It seems like some people wouldn't know an emotion if it crash-landed on their doorstep. Other people seem to be a little too "in touch" with their emotions. Hunger and fatigue are not considered emotions. But just like food and sleep, emotions are just as important to our psychological survival.

Calling on Tony for Some Motivation

Tony Robbins has built a multimillion-dollar empire by helping people find their motivation. He's a motivational speaker. I'm not familiar with the specifics of his technique, and I'm not even sure his approach to motivation really works. He's got an army of celebrities endorsing him though. From a business standpoint, it doesn't really matter whether or not it really works. The point is that people want to be motivated. People need to be motivated. People are spending a lot of money to find out how to motivate themselves the Tony Robbins way.

It's hard to imagine life without motivation. Without motivation, I may just want to sit on the couch all day, eating chips and watching television. Not everyone wants to save the world or cure cancer! Whatever we do, psychologists who study motivation believe that some psychological process is responsible for our motivation.

Trusting your instincts

Does a plant grow toward sunlight because it wants to? Would a little rebellious plant, the black sheep of ferns, grow toward the shade just to be different? A plant couldn't perform this feat even if it wanted to. Plants grow toward the sunlight because they can't help themselves. They need sunlight in order to survive. That's an instinct.

Would you like some adrenaline with that bear?

We can thank evolution for any instincts we may possess. Over the course of human evolution, certain behaviors were naturally selected for (selected "to keep") because they contributed to the ultimate survivability of the species. Imagine that there's a group of people that live in a forest with wolves, bears, and various other dangerous beasts. Now, imagine that a group of three men and three women from this larger group encountered a bear. One man and one woman took off running the second they saw the bear, and they got away. Another man and woman stood there, frozen in their tracks. The final couple tried to fight the bear off with sticks and rocks. They lost.

If the man and woman who ran away decide to have a child, there's a good chance that their child will be a runner, when it comes to encounters with bears. The other couples (the freezers and the fighters) died, so they can't have children. This is a crude illustration of how evolution selects for traits that help us survive. Those who survive reproduce. We might assume that the couple that ran away had better instincts than the other two couples. Their instincts were better in the sense that they were able to stay alive. Instincts that help keep us alive stay in the gene pool.

An *instinct* is an automatic, involuntary, and unlearned behavior that occurs in response to a specific trigger, or *stimuli*. Numerous examples of what we consider human instincts can be found in phrases that we use every day: the maternal instinct, the survival instinct, the killer instinct, the gut instinct, and so on. Instincts motivate us in the sense that we do what we do because we have to do it. It's something we do automatically and involuntarily.

James McDougall came up with a way to classify some of our basic instincts. Instincts are purposeful, and they guide our behavior toward the meeting of specific goals — like survival! McDougall believed that an instinct could be identified by identifying its intended goal. He identified numerous instincts, including parenting, seeking food, and mating. So don't feel so bad about eating so many cheeseburgers, it's just your food-seeking curiosity instinct driving you.

A lot of instinct research has been done with animals. Geese fly south for the winter. Why? Maybe they like the poolside bars in Florida, or maybe it's instinct. Konrad Lorenz conducted extensive research exploring the instinctive behaviors of animals. Lorenz's specific approach is known as the *ethological* approach to motivation, and according to Petri, an ethologist, instinctive behaviors have *action specific energy* — the idea that a specific trigger sets an instinct into action. All instinctive behaviors have a specific trigger or triggers, called *key stimuli*. Driving by a nice coffee shop is a key stimulus for my coffee instinct. Caffeine must have helped my ancestors survive. Key stimuli come from the environment. Key stimuli that come from other members of an animal group are called *releasers*.

Key stimuli produce behaviors that are fixed and automatic. These behaviors are called *fixed action patterns*. One of the popular examples of a fixed action pattern is something Konrad Lorenz called *imprinting*. Imprinting is kind of like a bonding instinct between a young animal and its parents. Remember that cartoon where the baby duck hatches from its egg and starts following around the first animal that it sees, even though it's not a duck?

Feeling needy

Most of us can relate to being worried about money and our finances. I'm sure that even the computer software moguls of the world have spent one or two sleepless nights of their lives mentally counting their pennies. Some of us have learned to live on a budget. We set aside money for our mortgage, car payments, medical insurance, and household costs. We even keep a little money for entertainment if there's any left over. When I started living on a budget, something weird began to happen. When I went to a store and saw something that I liked, such as a new CD or a pair of shoes, I asked myself if I really needed that item. Part of developing a budget involves figuring out what we really need, and what our financial priorities are.

I first spend my money on what I need. My needs are a powerful determinant in what I do with my money. I might even say that I'm *driven* (or pushed) by my prioritized needs. Satisfying my needs is one of my top, if not the top, drive in my life. Needs drive my behavior; they motivate me.

Clark Hull came up with a theory of motivation that emphasized need satisfaction. Needs are generated from two things, *homeostasis* and *equilibrium restoration*. I experience homeostasis when my needs are met and I feel balanced. When my needs aren't being met, I find myself out of balance, and I'm then motivated to restore the equilibrium through the satisfaction of my needs.

Hull's theory is called *drive reduction theory* because I'm driven to satisfy my needs. *Drives* are motivations toward satisfaction and homeostasis. There are two kinds of drives:

✔ My biological needs necessary for survival are called *primary drives*. Hunger, fatigue, and thirst are all examples of primary drives. If you think about it, primary drives play a pretty big role in our everyday routine. A large part of our lives revolves around satisfying hunger and obtaining shelter.

✔ Any need other than a primary drive is called a *secondary drive.* A lot of these are learned from our families, social groups, and the larger culture that we live in. These secondary drives derive their importance as they become associated with primary drives. We're driven to go to school and get good grades in order to have a better life and to be able to provide for our future families and ourselves. Secondary drives have no inherent worth in and of themselves, they only matter as they relate to primary drives.

One of the limitations of drive reduction theory is that it leaves no room for needs that seem only peripherally related to our biological survival. Does going surfing restore my homeostatic balance? What basic need does surfing satisfy? I may be able to stretch it a little and say that if I don't go surfing, I'll get depressed, and then I won't be able to go to work, and then I won't be able to eat. That would make surfing a secondary drive at the bottom of a long chain of other secondary drives. Most of us probably don't reduce, consciously anyway, our every activity to the lowest common denominator of biological survival.

Although it's not technically an instinct theory, Abraham Maslow's motivational theory states that our motivations stem from a basic set of needs that we naturally strive to satisfy. Maslow believed that some needs are more basic than others. Eating is more basic than getting an A on your English final. They're both needs (for some people anyway), but one is just more fundamental than the other.

Maslow created a priority list of needs that he arranged into a triangle called the *hierarchy of needs:*

✔ At the lowest and most foundational level are our *basic physical needs* for food, water, and sleep. These needs direct our behavior until we satisfy them.

✔ The next level of the triangle contains our needs for *safety and security.* We need proper shelter and protection.

✔ *Love and belonging* is the next level of need.

✔ The fourth level of need is *self-esteem.* We strive toward situations that enhance our sense of self-worth.

✔ *Self-actualization* — the need to fulfill our top potential and to live at a high level of awareness of ourselves and our desire — is the top level. When we've reached the highest part of the triangle/hierarchy, we have a *peak experience,* or a feeling that signals our arrival at the highest level of motivation.

Arousing interest in prime rib

Optimal level of arousal theory is considered a more refined version of drive reduction theory. Instead of just being driven to satisfy our basic biological needs at a minimum level, we're motivated to reach the highest level of satisfaction possible. What do I mean by "highest level of satisfaction?" Think of this as the "prime rib theory" of arousal. When my body needs energy, I get hungry, and I develop a primary drive or motivation to eat something. Now, if this theory was the "hamburger theory" of arousal or the "minimal level of arousal theory," I'd just get a greasy cheeseburger and be done with it. But why would I eat hamburger if I can eat steak? I can satisfy my primary need of hunger and enjoy the flavor at the same time.

Another component of optimal level of arousal theory is that we're driven to seek the best (optimal) level of arousal in order to maximize our performance. In an example of how optimal level of arousal theory might work, Yerkes and Dodson found that we perform activities best when we're moderately aroused — not too relaxed, not too uptight. This is called the *Yerkes-Dodson law*. I guess that makes the optimal level of arousal theory more like the "chicken-fried steak theory" of arousal instead of the "prime rib theory."

Have you ever had to make a presentation in front of a large group or class? Were you nervous? How nervous? Throwing-up, passing-out nervous? Being that nervous constitutes an extreme level of arousal, and as those of you who've been there know, it doesn't contribute to a topnotch performance. If someone is too relaxed though, he may not put out enough effort to properly prepare for the presentation, and he may then give an equally bad performance. The best place to be is right in the middle.

Getting cheaper long distance is rewarding

At least once a week, I come home and find the red light on my answering machine flashing, and I wonder who called. Was it a friend I haven't talked to in a while? A long-lost relative? No, it was one of those annoying long-distance phone companies trying to get me to change my provider.

A lot of marketing efforts are based on a motivational theory called *expectancy theory*. Expectancy theory holds that our motivations are the product of an analysis of the potential rewards associated with a particular behavior and how likely we are to achieve those rewards. Long-distance carriers count on me associating a switch with an expectation of a reward. This is a straight-forward but powerful means of motivating people, especially if you can trick them into thinking that the rewards are likely to come rolling in!

Incentive theory, which is closely related to expectancy theory, simply states that we are motivated to seek rewards and avoid negative experiences such as pain. My experience with phone companies has led me to expect pain from changing long-distance plans every other day, which overpowers the expected reward of saving a few bucks. What I expect, whether it's really the case or not, ultimately has a powerful effect on my behavior. When I have a message on my machine from a long-distance company, I just erase it.

Facing your opponent-process theory

Sometimes we're motivated to do things that aren't much fun, like going to the gym. Well, at least I don't think they're much fun. A lot of us engage in behaviors that seem more painful than pleasurable on the surface. This doesn't mean that we have a masochistic need or instinct. Motivations that may appear outwardly painful and not so pleasurable can be explained with the opponent-process theory of motivation.

A lot of people like to eat hot and spicy foods. Personally, I like to taste my food, not feel it for 20 minutes after I take a bite, but hey, to each his own. *Opponent-process theory* states that we are motivated not by the initial response or incentive that we receive, like the pain of hot foods, but by the reaction that occurs after the initial response.

For every response that occurs, there's an opposite reaction called the *opponent process.* After being exposed to a particular stimulus for a while, the initial response diminishes, and the opposite response grows stronger. What's the opposite response, the opponent process, of hot foods? Endorphins — those natural painkillers released by the body to combat pain. Spicy foods actually chemically burn our tongues, and our bodies combat those burns with these natural painkillers. It feels good when the endorphin painkillers kick in to soothe the burning. People who enjoy hot foods think that they eat spicy foods for the spice, but according to opponent-process theory, they're just a bunch of endorphin junkies, they're burning their tongues in order to benefit from the opposite or *opponent* reaction of endorphin release.

Launching Countless Bad Poems: Emotions

So far, none of the theories on motivation have addressed the power of emotion to spur us on or initiate action. Emotion and motivation are intimately related. When we need something or when a need isn't being met, we're motivated to satisfy that need. When our stomachs growl, we know we're hungry.

Feelings help us function

In addition to serving as signals of whether we've achieved our goals or not, Frijda identifies a couple of other functions of emotions. Emotions can prepare us for and alert us to potentially dangerous situations. Gavin De Becker sings high praises for this function of emotions in his book, *The Gift of Fear* (Dell Publishing). In a sentence, fear saves our lives. Have you ever been in a situation where you got that feeling that something just wasn't right? That "feeling" was your emotions alerting you to the possible presence of danger that you may have not consciously observed or been aware of. De Becker advocates listening to that voice more often and being more attuned to it — it's a powerful survival tool.

Positive emotions can provide us with relief from the trials and tribulations we all face. Happiness feels good. What would life be like if we never felt happy? Pretty miserable obviously! It's easier to have a good relationship with someone who is happy. Happiness leads to socializing, which may lead to romance, which may lead to children, which may lead to passing on whatever genes worked to produce that happy procreator in the first place. Emotions make us more attractive companions and allow for us to socially connect.

Another theory of emotions that has gained more support over the last few years comes from *evolutionary psychology*. Psychologists subscribing to this perspective view specific behaviors and mental processes as adaptive responses developed through natural selection. Emotions are assumed to be part of this adaptation process.

Cosmides and Tooby propose that we possess an extensive set of behavioral and mental programs (think computer programs) that help us address the challenges of survival. Each program functions independently, which creates a logistical nightmare. If you think getting ready for a camping trip is logistically difficult, try coordinating all the behaviors and mental processes that we possess. This is where our emotions come into play. Cosmides and Tooby view our emotions as "master programs" of sorts, working to organize and integrate all those behaviors and thoughts. From this perspective, our emotions serve a regulatory function. They help us figure out what we need to do in a particular situation and whether or not we've accomplished a desired goal.

But how do we know when other, more psychological needs aren't being met, like the need for self-esteem? When needs such as these aren't being met, our emotions let us know. Our emotions tell us that we're not meeting our motivational goals (in the form of disappointment, for example) or that we're meeting our motivational goals (maybe in the form of happiness).

An *emotion* is a complex phenomenon with three interrelated components:

✔ **Subjective experience:** When I have a particular emotion, I call this a *feeling*. My experience of sadness may consist of wanting to cry and lacking energy or motivation. This is my experience of sadness; it's subjective.

✔ **Physiological response:** All emotions are comprised of responses that involve brain and nervous system activity. When we're angry, our hearts beat fast, and our breathing rates increase. When we're sad we may feel tired.

✔ **Expressive component:** Each emotion is expressed and communicated in a unique way. Facial expressions, body language, posture, words, phrases, gestures, and numerous other means of expression accompany and communicate the experience of an emotion.

Which comes first, the body or the mind?

If emotions consist of three components, subjective experience, physiological reactions, and the expressive component, which comes first? Do I think and feel angry before my muscles tense up? Do I say I'm angry before I know I'm angry? Figuring this process out can get pretty confusing — it's kind of like the chicken or the egg argument for emotions. But don't worry; Farmer Cash is here to put all the eggs in the right basket. There are three main theories that address which of the components of emotion comes first.

✔ The *James-Lange theory* attempts to make sense of this mess. When we encounter a situation or stimulus that leads to an emotional reaction, our bodies react first. We all possess a set of automatic physical reactions to emotional stimuli. Our sensory systems respond by sending signals to the emotional centers of our brains, creating a state of arousal. After our physiological reaction, our brains analyze what is occurring. Finally, after arousal and appraisal, the subjective experience of the emotion occurs. Our brains then recognize fear, for example, after interpreting this long chain of physiological reactions. After we've recognized our experience of the emotion we are able to express this experience.

First we see the bear. Then our hearts start pounding, and other fear-related physiological reactions occur. The analysis may be, "My heart is pounding, and I'm running away from the bear. I must be scared." Only after the analysis, are you able to communicate, "I'm scared."

✔ The *Cannon-Bard theory* of emotion is a variation on the James-Lange theory. This theory also proposes that we physiologically react to stimuli before we subjectively experience an emotion, but there's a little twist. Cannon-Bard doesn't subscribe to the idea that the complex activities of muscle activation and the subsequent actions (like running from a bear) are the first physiological processes to get involved.

Specific parts of the brain that are considered less sophisticated are activated first. These "lower" parts of the brain then simultaneously send signals to three "higher-level" brain areas: the appraisal area, the arousal area, and the experience area. The main difference from James-Lange is that arousal, analysis, experience, and expression all occur at the same time, but only after more basic areas of the brain are cued or activated. So, I encounter the bear, my lower brain areas activate, and then I run, analyze my running, realize I'm scared, and yell out, "Help, I'm going to die" all at the same time. You can read more about the brain in Chapter 3.

✔ As if things aren't confusing enough, Schacter and Singer came up with a third variation on the emotional process. Their *two-factor theory* takes elements from James-Lange and Cannon-Bard but changes things around just a tiny bit. Instead of having an initial reaction from the body or lower brain areas followed by the evaluation process, the two-factor theory states that physiological reactions and cognitive appraisal occur together, creating a feedback loop and co-producing the subjective experience of an emotion. Information from the situation and the environment are used in the appraisal process. Emotional arousal is seen as *generic* (not specific to a particular emotion) until an evaluation is conducted.

Expressing yourself

When someone is smiling, is she happy? What about someone who glares at you, puffs out his chest, and turns red in the face? Can you guess what emotion he's experiencing? Of course you can. All emotions have an expressive and communicative component that consists of verbal signals, facial expressions, eye contact, and other body movements and non-verbal expressions.

Some people believe that the expressive components of emotions are innate or inborn. The same goes for our ability to discern what someone is feeling by observing these expressions. Some emotional expressions seem to be universal, such as smiling when happy and frowning when sad.

The culture we live in also has a lot to do with how and when we express emotions, including what emotions are appropriate to feel and express. Certain situations place constraints on these aspects of emotions as well. We don't typically cheer and laugh at funerals, and we don't usually scream angrily at people when they give us a compliment or a gift.

Our speech gives expression to how we feel in several ways:

✔ **Rate of speech:** Our rate of our speech can increase or slow down depending on how we feel.

✔ **Tone of voice:** Our tone of voice says a lot about the emotions we're experiencing.

✔ **Volume:** The volume of our voice can tell us quite a bit. When we're angry or excited we talk more loudly, for example.

Injecting a little fun

Consider the following experiment presented in Wallace and Goldstein. Research subjects are given a shot of epinephrine that activates their sympathetic nervous system. It engages their fight or flight response! Some subjects were told what the injection would do, and others were either told something misleading or told nothing about the injection. Then the subjects were placed into one of two groups: an anger-situation group or a euphoria-situation group. The anger group had to fill out an insulting questionnaire designed to make them angry. The euphoria group was put in a room with a researcher who was laughing, smiling, and having a good ol' time!

Both groups received the same drug, so their bodies produced the same physiological reaction and the same type of arousal. But did they experience this arousal as the same emotion? What do you think? The subjects in the anger group said they felt angry, and subjects in the euphoria group said they were happy. Keep in mind that both groups had the same physiological arousal so their experienced emotion was all based on the information provided to them by environmental cures applied to the generic experience of autonomic nervous system arousal. Just as the two-factor theory would predict, subjects apparently labeled their physiological arousal by evaluating the situation, or the context.

If you want to appear calm when you're angry, make an effort to speak slowly, use soft tones, and keep the volume down. If you're looking to intimidate someone, speak fast, in harsh tones, and very loudly. This will send the signal that you're angry.

Human beings experience a lot of different emotions: fear, sadness, elation, and disgust to name just a few. Take a second and think about your life: What emotions do you experience most often? As a therapist, I've seen the whole range, but love and anger are two feelings that come up time and time again — maybe more than any others. People want to talk about wanting love, not getting love, giving love, and so on. They also want to express their anger in a safe place where they know they won't be retaliated against.

Up close and personal with two favorites: Love and anger

Love makes the world go 'round. Or is it money? Whether love makes the world go around or not doesn't diminish the power that it seems to hold over a lot of us. Most of us want love, even if we don't want to admit it at times. It feels good to be loved and to love someone else. I think most people would have a hard time arguing that there's too much darn love in the world.

For those of you who think love is magical, I hope I don't burst your bubble with a psychological analysis of it. Hatfield and Rapson identify two specific types of love:

- **Passionate love:** Intense love with a sexual or romantic quality. It's the kind of love Romeo and Juliet had for each other. It's the kind of love you don't have for your grandmother!

- **Companionate love:** The love we have for friends and family members. There isn't much passion here, but there are high levels of attachment, commitment, and intimacy.

Robert Sternberg created his theory of love that outlines six forms of love. Each form is distinguished by varying degrees of *passion,* a strong desire for another person and the expectation that sex with him or her will be rewarding; *commitment,* the conviction that a person will stick around, no matter what happens; and *intimacy,* the ability to share our deepest and most secret feelings and thoughts with another person.

Sternberg's six forms of love based on varying levels of passion, commitment, and intimacy are:

- **Linking:** There's intimacy but no passion or commitment here. A relationship with a therapist is a good example of this form of love. I can tell my therapist my thoughts and feelings, but I don't necessarily feel passion for or commitment to her.

- **Infatuation:** Here, there's passion but no intimacy or commitment. This form of love is like lust. It's the one-night-stand or seventh-grade version of love.

- **Empty love:** This form is when we're committed, but there's no passion or intimacy. Some married couples are committed to each other out of necessity or convenience and stay together despite the lack of passion or intimacy.

- **Fatuous love:** Here, we have a high level of commitment and passion but low levels of intimacy. Romeo and Juliet seemed to be under the spell of fatuous love. I don't see how they could have become intimate when they never really got a chance to talk.

- **Companionate love:** This form of love is when you're committed and intimate but lacking in passion. It epitomizes a really good friendship.

- **Consummate love:** I guess Sternberg used *consummate* to describe this form of love because it's the total package: high passion, strong commitment, and deep intimacy. This has got to be "consuming."

Are the foundations of love formed in childhood? Some psychologists feel that our love relationships as adults are extensions of our childhood attachments. Children who have healthy attachments have more mature adult relationships with higher levels of intimacy and trust, and they're comfortable with higher levels of interdependency. Children who experience anxious or ambivalent attachments to their primary caregivers may "fall in love" too easily, seeking extreme closeness right off the bat and reacting intensely to any suggestion of abandonment. Glenn Close's character in *Fatal Attraction* must have had a hard time with attachments when she was a child. Children who avoid social interaction tend to be uncomfortable with closeness and have a hard time with being dependent upon others in their adult relationships.

Hatfield and Rappon proposed that each of us possess love templates in the form of mental schemas or scripts. Templates are formed early in life and are revised and solidified over the years as we experience various relationships with people. These templates shape the ways we think about relationships and determine what our expectations are when we enter into relationships. It seems that a lot of people on those TV dating shows have some pretty interesting love schemas because some of their expectations are, let's just say, interesting.

There are six basic love schemas that apply to romantic relationships. Each schema is differentiated by a person's comfort level with closeness and independence and how eager he or she is to be in a romantic relationship.

- ✔ **Casual:** No strings attached. Interested in a problem-free relationship. Dream on!

- ✔ **Clingy:** Seeks closeness (a little too much) and fears independence. Anybody got a spatula?

- ✔ **Fickle:** Uneasy with both closeness and independence. Can't make up his or her mind. Flip a coin already!

- ✔ **Secure:** Comfortable with both closeness and independence and doesn't rush things.

- ✔ **Skittish:** Fearful of too much closeness and perfectly comfortable with independence. Don't run!

- ✔ **Uninterested:** Just not into the whole relationship thing.

Everyone has an opinion on each of these love schemas. It's hard to judge people who may use one type of schema over another. Different schemas seem to apply to different periods of life, but most of us strive toward the secure schema. If someone feels that her schema is causing problems in her life, therapy is a good place to work these issues out.

Speaking of issues, anger is an issue that deserves a lot of attention. On the one hand, we often don't express our anger in healthy ways enough. But on the other hand, anger is expressed in inappropriate and extreme ways every day. Either way, anger is a natural emotion and is as important in our relationships as love.

Have you ever seen that T-shirt that has "I'm not prejudiced; I hate everybody" printed on it? Isn't that a wonderful message? That ranks right up there with the bumper stickers with the cartoon character, Calvin, from *Calvin and Hobbes* peeing on everything from the symbols of different car manufacturers to the Internal Revenue Service. Sometimes it seems like we live in a pretty angry society.

Where does anger come from? Lots of theories exist. One is that anger is a consequence of experiencing negative or painful feelings. All kinds of things can lead to negative feelings: unpleasant physical conditions, physical pain, limits on our movement, and even loud noises. I like to refer to this theory as the "grouch factor." Doctors theorize that we get angry when we

- ✔ Feel depressed. People who are depressed are more at risk for feeling angry. Even sadness and grief can generate angry feelings. It is not uncommon for people to become extremely angry when someone they are close to dies.

- ✔ Are prevented from engaging in something we want to do. Sroufe proposed the existence of an *anger* system. The system kind of works like a pressure cooker. We get more frustrated as we're blocked time and time again, which eventually leads to the experience of anger with one more blockade. There are no guidelines in this theory about where each of our breaking points is.

- ✔ Are separated from our attachment figure(s). An *attachment figure* is someone we have attached to or formed a strong emotional bond with. The theory is based on observing young children's reactions to being separated from their mothers. This theory seems to make sense even for adults though. Have you ever seen someone fly into a rage when their romantic partner wants to break things off?

Although it can be quite destructive, anger is a valid and important emotion, and there are some positives to it. Anger can be pretty adaptive. It can aid in self-defense and sometimes prevent someone from acting aggressively toward us. If someone is going to hurt us, sometimes a display of anger on our part might make him or her think twice. Keep in mind that some people react to anger with more anger so be careful. Anger can mobilize a lot of physical energy in a short period of time. It can also fuel our ambitions.

Anger need not be destructive, as long as it is expressed appropriately and constructively. Research shows that children who appropriately express their anger have less emotional and social problems growing up. Infants and toddlers sometimes use anger as a signal that they're frustrated and may need help with something, like eating.

Part IV
Barking Up the Right Learning Tree

The 5th Wave   By Rich Tennant

"They say your setting your bed on fire was a cry for help; pushing my car into the lake was a cry for help, and your failing grades are a cry for help. The next time you feel like crying for help, would you mind just crying for help?"

In this part . . .

In Part IV, I introduce you to the extremely important contributions that Ivan Pavlov, the "father" of classical conditioning, has made to the field of psychology. I briefly discuss his classic experiments and provide some good examples (at least I think they're good) designed to illustrate the basic principles of how humans learn. After talking about Pavlov and his dogs for a while, I introduce the second coming of learning theory, operant conditioning. I provide some basic definitions that cover the concept and some more edge-of-your-seat examples. Well, maybe they're not that exciting, but they're still pretty good.

Chapter 8

Pavlov's Dogs

● ●

In This Chapter

▶ Conditioning made easy

▶ Teaching an old dog new tricks

▶ Making connections

● ●

*H*ave you ever wondered why you get hungry for pizza when the door-bell rings? Maybe you don't. If not, a pizza company has spent a lot of money on an ad campaign that doesn't seem to be working. Why would you get hungry for pizza when the doorbell rings? The commercial presents the viewer with images of a pizza, melted cheese, and glistening pepperoni. This should whet your appetite at least a little bit. Then, a doorbell rings, and the pizza delivery person is at your door. The pizza people want you to think pizza when you hear the doorbell ring! How are they trying to do that?

Shifting focus from pizza to philosophy for a second can uncover the genius of the pizza makers in question. Well over a hundred years ago, a group of British philosophers tried to figure out the nature of thought. They considered thought to be a succession of integrated ideas that come together through experience. Any two sensory experiences that occur together will become associated with one another. When one experience or event happens, the other one happens automatically. These British philosophers called this process *associative learning* because events are associated with each other simply by occurring with each other. Every time I get on the freeway I run into traffic. Freeway → traffic. They go together. They're associated!

In order for associations to form, they must follow two very important rules:

- ✔ **Contiguity:** Associations are only formed when events occur together. For example, I feel depressed when I wake up every Monday morning and think about going back to work. Therefore, for me, work and waking up have become associated.

- ✔ **Frequency:** The more often two (or more) events occur together, the stronger the association will be.

The genius behind the pizza commercials must have studied the British associationists. Or, he or she could have learned about associative learning in psychology class. The commercials try to use the law of contiguity to get you to associate the sound of a doorbell with being hungry for pizza. That way, every time the doorbell rings, you'll think "Let's order a pizza" because you'll be hungry for it.

Doggy Drool

Kind of a gross title, huh? How would you feel if you conducted research on the salivation patterns of dogs? Personally, I would rather go to the dentist. That's just me. But one brave man, Russian physiologist Ivan Pavlov, was up for the job. Pavlov was actually studying digestion with dogs when he became interested in how the presentation of food automatically activated the salivation response in the dogs that he was studying. He found that the formation of saliva was automatic.

Try it. Think about something really tasty and see if your mouth waters automatically. Did it work? It should have because salivation is a reflexive response to food. It's the body's way of preparing to receive food. Saliva helps break the food down into digestible bits.

Pavlov constructed a device to collect the saliva directly from the dogs' salivary glands as the glands went to work. He could then measure how much saliva the dogs reflexively produced. Picture a dog strapped into a cage with a tube attached to its salivary glands and this wacky scientist counting each drop. Not even Hollywood could have come up with a more eccentric scene.

At this point, Pavlov was probably happy with his research, but one day, he noticed something strange — the dogs salivated sometimes even when the food wasn't presented. What was going on? Was something else causing the salivation? Pavlov came up with an associationist explanation. The dogs had learned to associate other stimuli with the food. But what? Pavlov conducted a whole series of experiments to figure out how the dogs had learned to automatically associate non-food stimuli with food in a way that produced salivation. A typical experiment went something like this:

1. Pavlov placed his dogs in their cages with the saliva tubes attached to the dogs' salivary glands.

2. He rang a bell and observed whether the dogs salivated or not. He found that they didn't.

3. Then, he rang the bell, waited a few seconds, and then presented the food to the dogs. The dogs salivated.

4. He repeated the bell plus food presentation several times. These pairings are called *trials*.

5. After Pavlov was satisfied with the number of trials, he presented the bell alone, without the food.

6. He found that the bell by itself then produced salivation.

Conditioning responses and stimuli

Pavlov's discovery became known as *classical conditioning*. After conducting his experiments, he outlined four necessary components in classical conditioning:

- ✔ **Unconditioned responses (UR):** Pavlov's dogs automatically, or reflexively, salivated when presented with food. They didn't have to learn or be conditioned to salivate in the presence of food. Pavlov called this response the unconditioned, or not-learned response. It happened without learning. Pizza companies count on the image of their tasty pizzas automatically making you feel hungry for pizza. It's probably a pretty safe bet, unless you've just eaten a huge dinner. That's why pizza companies don't usually show commercials just after dinnertime — they usually show the commercials before or during dinner.

- ✔ **Unconditioned stimuli (US):** The food that Pavlov presented to his dog is called the unconditioned stimulus. The US is the thing that causes or produces the unconditioned response. Food → Salivation. It's that easy!

- ✔ **Conditioned stimuli (CS):** The bell that Pavlov rang in a typical experiment is called the conditioned stimulus. It was *conditioned* or associated with the food through the process of pairing trials. The idea is that after enough trials, the conditioned stimulus will produce the desired response on its own.

- ✔ **Conditioned responses (CR):** Once the CS produces the UR on its own, the desired response is called the conditioned response. In symbolic form, it looks something like Table 8-1.

Table 8-1		Classical Conditioning
Trial Number		*Stimuli*
	US → UR	(food automatically produces salivation)
1	CS + US → UR	(bell + food produces salivation)
2		(bell + food)

(continued)

Table 8-1 *(continued)*

Trial Number		Stimuli
3		(bell + food)
...		(bell + food a few more times)
10	CS → CR	(bell alone produces salivation)

Becoming extinct

The power of classical conditioning is pretty impressive. Just think — if you appropriately pair two stimuli together, the CS will eventually get the job done alone. But when the pairing stops and the CS is producing the response by itself, the power of the CS eventually fades. If a CS is presented enough times without the US, the CS eventually will cease to elicit the CR. This phenomenon is called *extinction,* and it is a way to reverse the process of classical conditioning. For example, Pavlov's dogs learned to salivate at the sound of a bell. But if the bell kept getting presented without any delivery of food, the dogs would eventually stop slobbering to the bell.

But wait, there's more! Something even more interesting happens if the US is reintroduced sometime after extinction — *spontaneous recovery.* At this point, the CS's ability to elicit the response comes bouncing back, and once again the CS is capable of eliciting the CR. So, you can use classical conditioning to teach an old dog new tricks, and you can reverse the process through extinction. With this skill, you'll never be the boring guy at the party sitting in the corner. You can dazzle your newfound friends with classical conditioning tricks.

Here's a little something to try, just in case you're thinking about testing out classical conditioning for yourself.

1. Gather a few people together — family, friends, coworker, whoever. Get some packets of powdered, lemonade drink mix. This stuff is really sour without sugar. Give one pack to each participant.

2. Ask the crowd that you've gathered to dip their fingers in the lemonade and take a lick. (This is the US.) Ask them to observe if their mouths watered. They should have. If not, get yourself some better droolers.

3. Then choose a CS (a bell, a light, a whistle, whatever). Go through the process of pairing the bell (or any other CS that you choose) with tasting the lemonade (CS → US → UR over and over again). After 10 to 20 trials, go through a couple of trials where you present just the CS and ask the participants to observe if their mouths watered. They should have! That's classical conditioning. You can also play around with extinction and spontaneous recovery if you want.

One more way to reverse the effects of classical conditioning is worth mentioning. You've conducted the lemonade test, and you've successfully taught your Pavlovian subjects to drool at the sound of a bell ringing. If you want to reverse the effect, choose another US that produces some other response (UR) and classically condition the bell (CS) with the new US. This process is called *counterconditioning*.

Counterconditioning works especially well if the new US produces a response that is incompatible with the old CR. If the old CR was a watering mouth, maybe you could pick a new US that produces a dry mouth. I don't know what — maybe eating sand. I guarantee that, if you classically condition the bell with the eating of sand, the bell will have a very hard time producing the old CR, watering of the mouth, from that point on. Unless, of course, you reverse the process all over again. Remember though, you've got to give your subjects a break from time to time, and I wouldn't recommend the sand-eating demonstration as a parlor game.

Generalizing and discriminating

You may be thinking, "Big deal. We can teach dogs to salivate to a bell, so what?" Classical conditioning is actually a very important phenomenon in terms of human survival. It helps us learn things simply by association, without effort, and this can be very beneficial. After we've associated a CS with a US to the point where the CS produces the CR, we can expand automatically on that learning through a process known as *generalization*.

Generalization happens when we respond to something similar to the CS, I'll call it CS-2, and a CR is produced, even if we've never learned to associate CS-2 with the original US. For instance, if you learn to associate certain facial gestures, like a snarl or a sneer, with eventual violence, then the snarl or sneer (CS) produces fear (CR) whereas only a flying fist or a verbal threat (US) elicited fear (UR) in the past. You might then generalize from the CS-snarl and experience fear in connection with direct and non-adverted eye contact (CS-2). This generalization could save your tail. Generalization helps us adapt, because we apply what we've learned to new situations.

Generalization can backfire though. If, for example, I was attacked by a black-colored pit bull, I might then get scared every time I see a black-colored dog of any type, even a Chihuahua. Another example comes from the traumatic experiences of war veterans who suffer from post-traumatic stress. If they've experienced loud explosions and heavy gunfire and developed a strong fear reaction to these events, these individuals may react the same way when they hear a car backfire or some other loud noise. This can make life pretty difficult, considering that a lot of people live in urban areas with a lot of loud noises.

When we begin to overgeneralize what we've learned, we are not engaging in a process known as *discrimination.* We need to know how to *discriminate,* or tell the difference, between stimuli — between a gunshot and a car backfire, for example. Discrimination is learned when a CS-2 (or 3, or 4, and so on) is presented enough times without eliciting a response. We then learn that only the CS, and not the CS-2, is necessarily going to produce the CR.

Conditioning Rules!

All of this seems easy, doesn't it? You pair a couple of things together, and one eventually starts doing the job of the other. So far, the process is pretty straightforward, but some specific rules must be abided by in order to prevent this relatively simple procedure of conditioning from turning into an impossible task.

Contiguity is absolutely required in order for classical conditioning to occur. What if Pavlov had presented the bell (CS) after he presented the food (US)? What if he had presented the bell 15 minutes before the food? The CS must come before the US in order for the association to form.

Each of these questions represents a type of conditioning that isn't actually a very good conditioning technique at all. If Pavlov presented the US before the CS, a process known as *backward conditioning,* the dogs would have either made no association at all or an extremely weak one. If he presented the bell well in advance of the food, a process known as *trace conditioning,* the dogs again would have formed a weak association, if any.

The best way to ensure that a strong association is formed is to

- ✔ Present the CS just before the US and keep the CS "on" or "around" until the US appears. This way, the CS is seen as contiguous with the US.

- ✔ Conduct a lot of trials with the CS and US paired frequently. The strength of the association is a direct product of the frequency of the pairing.

- ✔ Select a strong or intense CS. A bright light conditions easier than a dim one. A loud bell conditions easier than a faint one. If you want your CS to produce the CR, give it some oomph.

Continuing with Contiguity

Again, I don't want to mislead you into thinking that all you have to do is frequently present an intense CS before a US and you get hassle-free classical conditioning.

The rule of contiguity states that if two stimuli are contiguous, an association will form. It actually might have been that simple, if it wasn't for a pesky graduate student named Robert Rescorla.

Rescorla questioned whether contiguity was enough. Maybe he thought that it all seemed too simple. He proposed that another rule be added to the list, the rule of *contingency*. Rescorla's idea was that a CS not only has to be contiguous with a US, it also has to be an accurate predictor of the US. If the CS is presented at random times (at 1 minute, 7 minutes, 2 minutes, 12 minutes, and so on for example) with the US, the CS wouldn't be a very good predictor of the US. The learner (animal or human) would gain no predictive power from experiencing the CS. The CS has to be presented with the US in a way that the learner can anticipate, with a fair degree of certainty, that the US is soon to come.

Adding another rule to the necessities of classical conditioning is quite the accomplishment for a graduate student. But Rescorla wasn't finished. Later, he and another psychologist, Allan Wagner, made another huge contribution to learning theory. The Rescorla-Wagner model (1972) simply states that in order for a CS to be maximally effective, it must be unexpected. The learning process is dependent on the element of surprise. If we expect the US every time we see the CS, we'll learn to associate it properly, but eventually, the strength of the association will reach a maximum. The strength will increase dramatically at first and then level off as the novelty of the CS wears off, and it becomes more "expectable." Therefore, the power or strength of an association is a function of the amount of surprise. The more novel the CS, the stronger the association will be.

Throwing You a Bone: Why Does This Work?

At this point, you know how to perform classical conditioning, and you know the rules that have to be followed in order to do it. (If not, check out the previous sections in this chapter.) Certainly, classical conditioning is useful. We can learn about our environment in ways that make us much more adaptable and capable. But why does it work at all? Why are we able to associate previously unrelated stimuli with each other?

Pavlov believed that the simultaneous activation of two distinct areas in the brain form associations between a CS and a US. This activation results in the formation of a new "pathway" between the new centers, kind of like a telephone wire being strung up between two previously unconnected homes. When the CS is activated, the US "gets a call" that is made possible by this new connection.

Clark Hull presented an alternative account. He felt that the association formed is actually between the CS and the UR, which then becomes the CR. Scientists are at their most creative when they figure out how to make two different theories compete with each other in predicting the outcome of an experiment. Their creativity is needed to dream up a critical experimental test. Holland and Staub set out to test this theory. They conditioned rats using noise and food pellets.

According to Pavlov, the rats learned to associate the noise with the food. But Holland and Staub pitted Pavlov's idea against Hull's — they tried to make the food an unattractive US. They put the rats on a record turntable, spinning them around to make them nauseous. After doing this for a while, they presented the noise again, and the rats didn't respond to it.

Pavlov thought that the original connection was between the noise and the food. But Hull predicted that devaluing the US would not make a difference in the rats' response, since he felt the critical association forms between the noise (CS) and eating (UR). It did make a difference, though. Hull's theory stated that the association was between the noise and the response, eating. Spinning the rats around on the turntable and making the food less attractive as a result should not have made a difference, according to Hull. Hull was wrong. There has to be a connection somewhere between the CS and the US. It can't be left out of the loop.

So, Pavlov rules the day! This isn't just rigid tradition. It actually has predictive value. Learning doesn't stop here however. Check out Chapter 9 for new adventures in learning about learning.

Chapter 9

Thorndike's Cats and Skinner's Rats

*A*thletes are some of the most superstitious people around, and only gamblers can outdo them in this category. When I played college baseball, I had one teammate, a pitcher, who wore the same undershirt without washing it for as long as he kept winning. Some of us kind of hoped that we'd lose so he'd wash his shirt. Other athletes carry lucky charms, perform rituals, or engage in elaborate routines to keep a streak alive or keep winning.

I had a couple of superstitions. I couldn't knock the dirt off of just one of my cleats with my bat. I had to do both, even if the other one was clean. And when running in off the field, I never stepped on the chalk line. The other players never questioned me about my superstitions; they had their own weird habits. When I started studying psychology, I began to wonder where this stuff comes from. Where did I learn that if I stepped on the chalk line I'd have a bad game? At some point in time, I must have stepped on the line and then had a bad game. I saw a connection between what I did (stepped on the line) and what happened to me (had a bad game). I drew a connection between my behavior and a consequence, in this case, a negative consequence. Psychologists call this *superstitious learning*.

When an actual connection exists between what we do and a particular consequence that follows, be it positive or negative, a specific type of learning takes place. We have learned that when we do A, the action is followed by B. Behavioral or learning psychologists consider all learning as a process of *conditioning*, a type of learning in which an association between events is made.

In Chapter 8, I introduce *classical conditioning*, a type of learning in which in which two events become associated with each other. In this chapter, I discuss *operant conditioning*, learning in which an important event necessarily follows a specific response. I know, I know, — that sounds kind of jargony. Try thinking of it this way:

Every month I get paid at my job. Am I paid just to sit around and take up space? No, I'm paid for performing the duties of my job, for working. I do something, and something happens. I work, and I get paid. Would I work if I didn't get paid? Probably not, for two reasons. First, I have better things to do with my time than to work for free. (My credit card debtors wouldn't be too happy with me either.) Second, according to operant conditioning theory, I work *because* I get paid. The "something" that follows my working behavior is a reward, a positive consequence. David Lieberman in 1993 stated that operant conditioning carries that name because responses *operate* on the environment in a way that produces a consequence.

Operant conditioning takes place all around us, in our homes, as well as in the workplace. Parents use rewards, or operant conditioning to get their children to do their homework. The following sections take a closer look at how operant conditioning works.

Cuddling Thorndike's Thrilling Kitties

From the introduction, you can see that when I do something, something happens. Then what happens? I keep going to work every month, so that paycheck I get must be having an effect on me. Way back in 1911, Edward Thorndike created a theory, known as the *law of effect,* that addressed this idea of a consequence having an effect on behavior.

Thorndike decided to look into this phenomenon by doing research with cats. He constructed the *puzzle box made out of* a wooden crate with spaced slats and a door that could be opened by a special mechanism. He placed a hungry cat inside the box and shut the door. He then placed some food on a dish outside of the box that the cat could see through the slats in the crate. Sounds kind of cruel, doesn't it? The cat would reach for the food through the slats, but the food was out of reach. The only way for the cat to get the food was for Thorndike or the cat to open the door.

We know that Thorndike wasn't going to open the door; he was conducting an experiment. The cat had to figure out how to open the door himself. I don't know about you, but I don't see a lot of cats going around opening doors. What did he do? It's suspenseful isn't it? What will our little cat hero do? Will he open the door and feed voraciously on the prized food just beyond his reach? Or will he meet his demise at the hands of a fiendish psychologist? Tune in next time. . . .

Anyway, the cat had to figure it out on his own, and Thorndike was a patient man. He waited and watched, waited and watched. The cat wandered around the box, stuck his little paw out, meowed, bounced off the walls, and acted in any number of random ways inside of the box. But then, something remarkable happened. The cat accidentally hit the latch that was holding the door shut, and the door miraculously opened! Hurray! The cat got to eat, and everyone lived happily ever after.

What did Thorndike learn from his little experiment? Nothing, he wasn't done yet. He put that poor cat back into the box to go at it again. No problem, right? The cat knew what to do, — just hit the latch. But when it got back into the box, the cat acted like it didn't know that it had to hit the latch to open the door. It started acting in the same random ways all over again.

Never fear, our faithful cat eventually triggered the latch by accident again and was rewarded once again by gaining access to the food. Thorndike kept performing this experiment over and over again and made a remarkable observation. The time that it took for the cat to figure out that the latch was the key got shorter and shorter with each subsequent trial. Why was the cat getting faster? Thorndike proposed that the food helped the cat learn the association between the triggering the latch and the escape.

His law of effect states, "Of several responses made to the same situation, those which are accompanied or closely followed by satisfaction to the animal will, other things being equal, be more firmly connected with the situation, so that when it (satisfaction) recurs, they (the responses) will be more likely to recur . . . The greater the satisfaction . . . the greater the strengthening . . . of the bond." Basically, the consequence of getting the food served as a reward for learning how to open the box. The opening-the-box behavior was like my job, and the food was like my paycheck.

Getting back to my original question of whether my paycheck has an effect on me or not — I keep working, just like Thorndike's cats kept opening the box to get the food. Therefore, the consequence of my action actually leads me to perform that action again.

Running Rats with Reinforcers

When a consequence of an action or event increases the probability that the event or action will happen again, we call that consequence a *reinforcer*. It's like a reward, and we know that when we're rewarded, we often do what we were rewarded for again. Operant conditioning is all about the effects that reinforcers have on behavior.

B. F. Skinner, one of the most famous behavioral psychologists, followed in Thorndike's footsteps in using animals to investigate operant conditioning. He constructed a box with a lever inside called a *Skinner box.* When an animal pressed the lever, a food pellet fell out of a feeder into the box. Skinner wanted to see if rats placed in the box could learn to press the lever in order to receive the food.

This task was a lot harder than one might think. Rats aren't used to pressing levers to get food. Skinner had to facilitate the process a little bit with a procedure known as *shaping,* rewarding successful approximations to the goal. Skinner rewarded the rats with food for performing a behavior that was close to, but not exactly, the required response. Shaping was done gradually so that the rats eventually got to the point where they pressed the bar and received their reinforcers of food. After the rats got the hang of it, they learned to press the bar for food the same way Thorndike's cats learned to open the door. The idea behind the actions was the same as well. The rats learned because the reward of the food "taught" them how to press the bar.

Thorndike's cats and Skinner's rats learned because they were rewarded with food. Food is a powerful reward for animals, but is just one type of reinforcer. Anything that increases the likelihood that a behavior will occur again can be used as a reward or reinforcer. It could be food, money, recess, or vacations.

Types of reinforcers

There are two basic types of reinforcement:

- **Positive reinforcement** is the use of any reinforcer that increases the likelihood that a behavior will occur again.
- **Negative reinforcement** occurs when the removal of noxious stimuli leads to an increased likelihood that a behavior will occur again.

Again, the basic idea of operant conditioning is that behaviors that are reinforced (either positively or negatively) are more likely to occur again. But is this true for all reinforcers? Are all reinforcers created equal? If Skinner gave the rats five dollars each time they pressed the lever, would they still have learned the response? Probably not. Differences between reinforcers exist and determine the impact that the reinforcers have on responses. Not all consequences are rewarding or reinforcing.

Two types of positive reinforcers are effective:

- ✔ **Primary reinforcers** are rewards that don't require shaping or prior training to be effective. Examples may be food or pleasurable physical sensations. David Premack in 1971 came up with the interesting idea that primary reinforcers can be identified by looking at what people spend most of their time doing. If they spend a lot of time watching television, riding bikes, or sleeping, these activities may be considered primary reinforcers. His *Premack principle* states that high probability responses can be used to reinforce lower probability responses. This is like using ice cream to get your child to eat his or her vegetables. If they want the ice cream (high probability response), they'll eat their vegetables (low probability response).

- ✔ **Secondary reinforcers** are things that become reinforcing through experience and learning. This result happens by associating the secondary reinforcer with a primary reinforcer by using the same principles as classical conditioning (see Chapter 8). Dolphin trainers blow a whistle as they reward the dolphins with fish. Eventually, the dolphins associate the whistle with food, and the whistle is reinforcing in and of itself. According to David Lieberman, some have argued, however, that the whistle is just a signal and not a substitute for the food. Research is still inconclusive on this issue.

After we figure out what someone or something considers reinforcing, we can set out to influence its behavior by rewarding it for performing the appropriate responses. For example, consider an office manager who is having a difficult time getting her employees to come back from lunch on time. What can she do? First, she has to figure out what is reinforcing for this group or for each individual. Then, she has to start rewarding anyone who performs the desired behavior, coming back from lunch on time. She could give them little gifts, money, or smiley-face stickers.

Back to negative reinforcement for a second. This one confuses a lot of people. How can taking something away or removing a noxious stimulus increase the probability of a behavior? Have you ever had a new puppy in your home or apartment that wouldn't stop whining while you were trying to sleep? If you kept it in another room or in the garage, you probably got up and went out to see what the problem was. What happened when you went to the puppy? It stopped crying. If you then went back to bed, I bet the crying woke you ten minutes later.

The problem is that *your* behavior is under the control of negative reinforcement. The puppy's whining is a noxious (and annoying) stimulus. When you go to the garage, the whining stops, increasing the likelihood that you'll keep going to the garage every time the puppy whines. You're being negatively reinforced for going to the garage — not to mention that your puppy got positively reinforced for whining! Who's in control of the situation, the puppy or you?

In the office manager example, if the boss yells at the employees every time they return late from lunch, they may start to come back on time just to get the manager off of their cases. This is another example of negative reinforcement.

Timing of reinforcement

What if the office manager waits until the end of the year at the office Christmas party to reinforce the timely workers? Chances are they would have forgotten all about the incidents and accepted the gift, while not experiencing any its reinforcing effects.

Research by G. R. Grice and K. W. Spence has shown that reinforcement must occur immediately, or as quickly as possible, following the desired response. If you wait too long, the connection between the response and the reinforcing consequence is lost. Thorndike's cats would have never gotten out of those crates if they were given a food voucher to be redeemed on their next visit to Cat Food Deluxe.

Bad rat! Very bad!

Both positive and negative reinforcements are consequences that are more likely to increase behavior. But what about that other consequence, *punishment?* Punishment is any consequence that decreases the likelihood of a response. One type of punishment is straightforward — the introduction of something noxious or aversive. Another type of punishment, *negative punishment,* involves removing something reinforcing, like taking a child's bicycle away.

We use punishment to influence people's behavior all the time. The office manager from the reinforcement example could have just punished her employees for being late. Parents punish children. Courts punish convicted criminals. Credit card companies punish people for late payments. Punishment is all around us.

I know that many of us use punishment. I also know that people criticize a lot of new parents for never punishing their children as an explanation for poor behavior. "What that kid needs is a good whipping." Modern parents sometimes rebut with a statement that punishment doesn't work. Does it?

Punishment in fact can be a very potent and effective means for suppressing behavior, but keep a few things in mind.

✔ Punishment should be the least intense form necessary to produce the desired response. Punishment shouldn't be too mild, though, because if you try to increase it gradually, the recipient may get used to each subsequent increase. Intense punishment is problematic as well. In order for punishment to be effective over a long period of time, you have to increase its intensity.

✔ To be effective, punishment has to occur as close in time as possible to the response being punished. If I wait three weeks to punish my children for breaking the lamp, they're going to be completely clueless as to why I am punishing them, and it will have absolutely no effect whatsoever.

✔ Punishment should also be firm, consistent, and accompanied with clear explanations of why the punishment is being administered.

Of course, a lot of people are uncomfortable with the idea of inflicting pain or suffering on another person in order to alter their behavior. The use of punishment can have some negative consequences:

✔ Fear may result. When people are effectively punished, they may learn to anticipate future punishment, and they may develop severe anxiety while waiting for the next shoe to drop. This can have a disruptive effect on their lives, sometimes leading to avoidance and apathy.

✔ Aggression can be another unfortunate consequence of punishment. I've worked in both jails and prisons, and I've seen men become angrier, more aggressive, and even fearful as a result of the harsh conditions that they face while incarcerated. When the time comes for them to be released and face the world in a reformed manner, they have become dysfunctional and institutionalized, often unable to make the transition to the outside world.

Disappearing from the face of behavior

What would happen if I suddenly stopped providing the reinforcement after successfully increasing a behavior's occurrence? The behavior would eventually cease, depending on how often it was reinforced. I guarantee that if I stopped getting paid at work, my working behavior would cease, and it probably wouldn't take very long either. This phenomenon is called *extinction,* the cessation of a behavior after the removal of a reinforcer. Just like punishment, extinction is used as a method to stop a behavior from occurring again. Chapter 8 has more information about extinction.

Scheduling reinforcement

Have you ever wondered why people keep going back to places like Las Vegas and Atlantic City time and time again to donate their money to the casino expansion fund? The bottom line with gambling is that the big winner is the house, the casino. But people can't stay away. The last time I was in Vegas I really enjoyed the multimillion-dollar casinos and resorts. I guess I have the gamblers to thank for that.

People keep going back because of something called a *schedule of reinforcement,* a schedule or determination as to what responses to reinforce and when to reinforce them. There are four different schedules of reinforcement, each with different effects on the response in question.

- ✔ Fixed ratio
- ✔ Variable ratio
- ✔ Fixed interval
- ✔ Variable interval

Perhaps the most common form of reinforcement is called *continuous reinforcement.* This involves reinforcing a behavior every time it occurs. Every time I pull the slot machine handle, I win! Yeah right, I wish. Continuous reinforcement is good for the shaping phase of learning or for what is called the *acquisition phase.* Anytime I am learning a new behavior, it is going to take time to learn it. Continuous reinforcement helps me learn faster. The problem with continuous reinforcement, however, is that it extinguishes quickly. If I'm reinforced every time I return to work on time from lunch, the minute my boss stops reinforcing me, I'll stop coming back on time.

Most reinforcement in our world, however, is more intermittent and sporadic. Of course we don't win every time we pull the lever on the slot machine. B. F. Skinner didn't design slots; B. A. Loser, the casino behavioral psychologist, did. Reinforcement on a less frequent basis is called *partial reinforcement.* There are two types of partial reinforcement schedules, each further divided by how predictably or randomly the reinforcers come.

- ✔ The first type of partial reinforcement is called a *ratio schedule.* With a ratio schedule, reinforcement is only given after a specific number of responses have been given. If a parent was using this schedule with his children, he might only give a reward for some number of A's his child gets or after a certain number of times his child cleans his/her room.

  - Ratio schedules can then vary based on whether a fixed number of responses or a variable number of responses are required. A *fixed ratio* reinforcement schedule (see Figure 9-1) involves always reinforcing for the same number of given responses. If I'm going to reward my child for every two A's s/he earns, that never changes, reinforcement follows every two A's.

- A *variable ratio* reinforcement schedule (see Figure 9-2) involves giving reinforcement for a varied number of responses provided. I might reinforce my child for two A's now, but then I might reinforce her for one A, three A's, or 10 A's. The key is to keep the recipient guessing. This approach has a powerful effect on the persistence of a response because people will keep doing the requisite behavior because they don't know when the reinforcement will come. It's much more resistant to extinction than continuous reinforcement.

Figure 9-1:
A fixed ratio rein-forcement schedule is methodical.

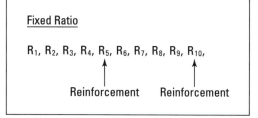

Fixed Ratio

$R_1, R_2, R_3, R_4, R_5, R_6, R_7, R_8, R_9, R_{10},$

Reinforcement   Reinforcement

Figure 9-2:
A variable ratio rein-forcement schedule is random.

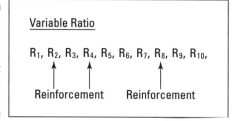

Variable Ratio

$R_1, R_2, R_3, R_4, R_5, R_6, R_7, R_8, R_9, R_{10},$

Reinforcement   Reinforcement

✔ The other type of partial reinforcement schedule, an *interval schedule,* is based on the amount of time that has passed between reinforcements.

- I get paid once a month. Time determines when I get paid. My pay schedule is an example of a *fixed interval* reinforcement schedule (see Figure 9-3). The time frame never varies.

- The other type of interval schedule is a *variable interval* reinforcement schedule (see Figure 9-4). Here, responses are reinforced per a varied amount of time passed since the last reinforcement. It would be like getting paid at the end of the month, and then getting paid two days later, and then getting paid three weeks later, and so on. Variable interval schedules are also very resistant to extinction for the same reason as variable ratio schedules. The responder never knows when he is going to get reinforced, so he has to keep responding to find out.

Figure 9-3:
Calling it a fixed interval reinforcement schedule doesn't mean it's neutered.

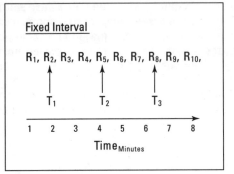

Figure 9-4:
A variable interval reinforcement schedule changes.

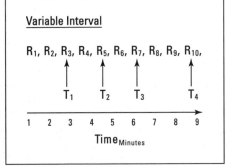

Variable interval reinforcement is what gambling is based on. Casinos program the machines to pay out on a variable interval schedule so that we'll just keep pumping the money in, waiting for that big payoff. You can't win if you don't play. So the next time you think you're "due" or bound to win because you've been sitting at the same machine for three days (without a shower, sleep, or anything to eat), remember that it's all variable. You never know when the machine is going to hit. And don't get ticked off if you finally give up and the next person who sits down wins it all! That's why they call it gambling.

Avoiding Tickets with Generalization

Have you ever noticed how people slow down on the freeway when they see a state trooper? That's probably because they've all gotten tickets from them at one time or another. What happens when a good old city cop is on the road? Nobody slows down. They just ignore him. Is this an example of a blatant disrespect for the law? No. It's an example of *stimulus control*, the idea that a response can vary as a function of the stimulus present at the time of reinforcement or punishment. Although both law enforcement authorities can give tickets for speeding, most of us know that city cops don't typically give tickets on the highway. The stimuli have different effects on our behavior because they have led to different consequences. Punishment only comes from the trooper.

Sometimes, when we learn a response due to reinforcement, we may automatically *generalize* that response to other similar stimuli. If I generalized my state trooper ticket experience to city cops, I would slow down for city cops, too. Or, if I'm reinforced for coming back from lunch on time, I might also generalize that behavior to coming to work in the morning on time. Generalization helps speed up the learning process because we don't have time to receive reinforcement for every single response we elicit. (For more information on generalization, check out Chapter 8).

Discriminating

Sometimes people can over-learn a response or behavior. They then engage in the response when they shouldn't because they've generalized a little too much. I think this happens to psychotherapists sometimes. We may be in a social situation, not working, when someone starts talking about how hard his or her day was. "Tell me how that makes you feel," may slip out. Everyone looks at the psychotherapist in question like a quack. Maybe it's time for a vacation.

I've also seen this phenomenon in movies. An ex-cop overreacts to seeing his grandson point a water pistol at him, and he takes the kid down to "remove the threat." These are problems of *discrimination,* responding to only one of two or more particular stimuli. The problem is remedied by presenting someone with both stimuli and only reinforcing the response to the correct one. Put grandpa in the middle of a hold-up and throw his grandson with a water pistol into the mix. Only reinforce the Detective Grandpa when he successfully neutralizes the threat of the robber (stimulus 1) and not for taking grandson out (stimulus 2). He's learned to discriminate between a real threat and a benign one.

Part V

Getting Personal with Social Psychology

The 5th Wave® By Rich Tennant

"How can you not feel confident? You're wearing Versace sunglasses, a Tommy Hilfiger sweater, Calvin Klein jeans, and Michael Jordan gym shoes. Now go on out there and just be yourself."

In this part . . .

Part V introduces psychoanalysis and the work of Sigmund Freud. I begin with the basic structure of the psyche and follow that up with Freud's theory of psycho-sexual development, along with a discussion on the famous defense mechanisms, such as denial and repression. I also introduce you to the second generation of psychoanalysts, Anna Freud, Erik Erikson, and others.

Next, I introduce you to personality theory and the most common personality types. This part goes on to cover topics such as knowing yourself, developing identities, forming relationships, and communicating — social stuff, as the title of Part V implies. I also discuss the influence that others have on our behavior and the different ways that individuals behave in groups. Finally, I take a look at developmental psychology and briefly trace development from conception to adolescence.

Chapter 10

Getting into the Mood with Freud

· ·

In This Chapter

▶ Building the structure of the personality

▶ Moving around inside the psyche

▶ Growing toward sexual maturity

▶ Defending oneself

· ·

Fewer names are more famous in psychology than that of Sigmund Freud. Was it because he had a sexy, Sean Connery-like personality? Well, not exactly. But his ideas are all around us. They show up in films, art, and even our everyday conversations. "You made a Freudian slip!" is a phrase you might hear at the office, on the elevator, or in your favorite television program. All of us make Freudian slips from time to time, some minor, some serious. Have you ever called someone by the wrong name because you were thinking of that other person? (I don't recommend it if you're seriously dating or married.) Although I wouldn't put him up there with Coke or Nike, Freud can be considered a household name, at least when it comes to psychology. You've probably seen Woody Allen anxiously rambling, perfectly demonstrating Freud's ideas of psychological defense mechanisms and psychic anxiety. And I bet you've had at least one "anal" boss at work who pushes your stress levels to new heights as he fixates on the smallest details and the most insignificant mistakes in your work. Freud's impact is unmistakable. But what exactly was he talking about?

Showing Some Personality

Freud formulated one of the most comprehensive theories of human personality ever created. The depths of his analysis and range of ideas are yet to be rivaled. But what exactly is a personality? We talk about personalities all the time. You've probably heard people justify dating an unattractive person. "He's got a great personality!" they say. Basically, *personality* is the organized psychological and physical components inside a person that create and determine that individual's unique characteristics and behaviors.

There are several key points here:

- ✔ Personalities are both psychological and physical. They exist as parts of our minds and brains.

  - We all know that psychological or mental abuse can hurt as much as physical abuse, and such abuse can shape our personalities. As our minds or mental life are affected, so too are our personalities.

  - As for the physical aspects of personality, if someone was to suffer brain damage from a car accident, his personality could be altered. He may be grouchier than usual, or more spontaneous and carefree. Either way, if his brain is altered, his personality could be affected.

- ✔ Our personalities create and determine what we do. What goes on inside your mind and brain shapes how you act, what you say, how you feel, and how you perceive the world.

- ✔ Perhaps most importantly, our personalities are what make us unique. Tens or hundreds of people around the world may have the same name as you or may look like you, but nobody has your identical personality. If you go to a party after work, are you the same person as you are at work? Of course you may act a little different, but most likely you're still the same basic person. This is because of your personality, your unique set of psychological and physical components that determine who you are.

This chapter explores Freud's thoughts on memory, instincts, and the famous defense mechanisms (actually the work of his daughter, Anna Freud) and how they contribute to make us who we are, possessors of a one-of-a-kind personality. Of course, no discussion of Freud would ever be complete without mentioning his theory of psychosexual development and the ideas about Oedipus and sex!

Your Unique Memories

What kind of personality would you have if someone erased all of your memories? Your first birthday? Your first day at school? Your wedding? Would you just be a blank blob of eating, sleeping, and wandering flesh? Freud felt that our memories and how they are arranged in our minds are vital parts of our personalities. He proposed that there are three basic divisions of memory that are differentiated by how aware or conscious each of us is of the material in those divisions: the conscious, the preconscious, and the unconscious. The unconscious is the most famous of the three.

The conscious and preconscious

My "active" awareness constitutes my conscious level of awareness. Here, I'm aware of those things that are current and in the moment, like the book on my lap, its yellow cover, the typeface in horizontal rows, and my stomach growling because I haven't eaten in six hours. My *conscious* awareness is dominated by the things I am hearing, seeing, and feeling, and if I've got a headache, trying to ignore.

The *preconscious* is made up of ordinary memories, such as birthdays, anniversaries, and how to ride a bike. We're rarely actively aware of our memories in the preconscious, unless deliberately conjured up or activated. But, they still play a powerful role in shaping who we are.

The unconscious

The *unconscious* contains the memories and experiences that we're not aware of. They're deep inside our minds and difficult to access. So the next time you can't answer a tough question, just simply tell the inquirer that the answer is locked away deep inside your unconscious. Thousands or even millions of things go on inside your mind that you're not aware of, you're unconscious or unaware of them.

Actually, Freud thought that your unconscious is filled with all your memories, thoughts, and ideas that are too troubling, disturbing, and horrible to keep in your conscious awareness. This is where you harbor your truest feelings, unfiltered and unedited by the niceties of everyday life. Your unconscious does not lie! So the next time someone asks you if you like her new hairstyle, tell her what your unconscious really thinks! Your unconscious is where your deepest and most basic desires and conflicts reside, it's the realm of secrets so dark that you're not even aware of them yourself.

The point is, depending on your memories and how aware you are of them, you may have a completely different personality than you do now. You may be the guy sitting next to you in the coffee shop, who knows? So relax, you're not a faceless robot in a sea of anonymity. Your conscious, preconscious, and unconscious memories help make you unique, giving you that special little personality that everyone, well, your mother at least loves.

Id, Ego, and Superego

Freud would have been a great Hollywood screenwriter. His "story" of personality is one of desire, power, control, and freedom. The plot is complex and the characters compete. Our personalities represent a drama of sorts, acted out in our minds. "You" are a product of how competing mental forces and structures interact. The ancient Greeks thought that all people were actors in the drama of the gods above. For Freud, you and I are simply actors in the drama of our minds, pushed by desire, pulled by conscience. Underneath the surface, our personalities represent the power struggles going on deep within us. Three main players carry all of this drama out:

- **Id:** The seat of our impulses
- **Ego:** Negotiates with the id, pleases the superego
- **Superego:** Keeps us on the straight and narrow

Each of these characters has its own idea of what the outcome of the story should be. Their struggles are fueled by powerful motives, and each one is out for itself.

I want, therefore I am

The initial structural component and first character in Freud's drama of personality is the id. Has an urge, impulse, or desire so strong that it just had to be satisfied ever overpowered you? A new car, sexual desire, a dream job? The answer is probably a resounding "yes!" Where does such desire come from? According to Freud, desire comes from the part of your personality called the *id,* located in the expanses of our mind. So look around, and look deep within. Look at your coworkers, look at your boss. It's in all of us, even the quiet old lady at the bus stop. Underneath that quiet, grandmotherly demeanor lurks a seething cauldron of desire.

The id contains all of our most basic animal and primitive impulses that demand satisfaction. It's the Mr. Hyde emerging from the restrained Dr. Jekyl. It's that little devil that sits on your shoulder, whispering temptations and spurring you on. Whenever I see a selfish, spoiled child in the grocery store demanding a toy and throwing a tantrum if he doesn't get his way, I know that's the id in action!

The id is a type of "container" that holds our desires. Relentlessly driven by a force Freud called the *libido,* the collective energy of life's instincts and will to survive, the id must be satisfied! We're all born with the id in full force. It's unregulated and untouched by the constraints of the world outside of our minds. When a baby gets hungry, I mean really hungry, does she sit quietly and wait until someone remembers to feed her? Anyone who's ever gotten out of bed in the middle of the night to feed a baby knows the answer to that.

But I don't want to give the id a bad rap. Where would I be without desire? My desire pushes me through life; it leads me to seek the things I need to survive. Your id does the same thing for you. Without it we'd die, or at the very least, we'd be really boring! So keep in mind that a large part of your personality consists of your desires and your attempts to satisfy them.

Enter the ego

Wouldn't it be nice if you could get everything you wanted, whenever and however you wanted it? Unfortunately most of us know otherwise. We all know how frustrating it can be when a desire goes unmet or gets stifled. Well, you can blame your ego for that. The *ego* is the second mental apparatus of personality. The ego's main function is to mediate between the id's demands and the external world around us — reality in other words. Does the Rolling Stones' song "You Can't Always Get What You Want" come to mind?

So far, it seems that, if it wasn't for reality, you and I would be a lot more satisfied. Even though the ego finds itself in conflict with the id, satisfaction is not abandoned. The ego is like a sports agent for a really talented athlete. Even though the athlete may demand a multimillion-dollar contract, the agent reminds him that he could price himself out of a job. So the ego negotiates with the id in order to get it what it wants without costing it too much in the long run. The ego accomplishes this important task by converting, diverting, and transforming the powerful forces of the id into more useful and realistic modes of satisfaction. It attempts to harness the id's power, regulating it in order to achieve satisfaction despite the limits of reality.

The final judgment

As if the ego's job wasn't hard enough, playing referee between the id and reality, its performance is under constant scrutiny by a relentless judge, the superego. While the ego negotiates with the id, trying to prevent another tantrum, the superego judges the performance. *Superego* is another name for your conscience. It expects your ego to be strong and effective in its struggles against the libido's force.

Usually, our conscience comes from our parents or a parental figure. As we grow, we internalize their standards, those same standards that make us feel so guilty when we tell a lie or cheat on our taxes. But does everyone have a conscience? There are certain people throughout history who have committed such horrible acts of violence that we sometimes wonder if they are void of conscience. How can serial killers such as Ted Bundy or Wayne Williams commit such horrible crimes? A strong bet is that they lack the basic capacity to feel guilt, so nothing really prevents them from acting out their violent fantasies. A famous psychiatrist once said that evil men do what good men only dream of.

It's All About Sex!

It could read like a newspaper headline: "Sexual Satisfaction Fuels Personality Development!" Well not really, but Freud's psychosexual theory of personality development was definitely about pleasure. What makes your personality so different from others? Freud's search for the answer to this question led him to the discovery that the clues to understanding the uniqueness of an individual's personality are found in infancy and childhood. Eureka, childhood is destiny! The personality that you live with today, the one that charms in order to get dates, makes lists and never gets anything done, ensures that the bathroom is always sparkling clean, was forged and molded in the fires of infancy and struggles of childhood. In fact, according to Freud, you were a unique final product by the time you hit puberty.

But what makes you so unique? Have you ever noticed how generic the ads in the "Personals" section of the newspaper are? "Single White Female looking for healthy nonsmoker for walks on the beach and good conversation." I don't know about you, but I'm always wondering what the real story is. What's that SWF really like? After the first few dates, when all the romancing wears off, will she still be tolerable? What are her quirks? Does she snort when she laughs? Does she spend too much time talking about herself? Is her apartment neater than an army barracks? This is where the personality rubber hits the road. Behind the generic masks that we all present lie those things that make us stand out, our quirks.

According to Freud, your unique character and quirks are the products of how your personality develops during childhood. As a child, and even as a teenager, you go through a series of stages in which you grow and mature:

- ✔ **Oral:** Birth to 18 months
- ✔ **Anal:** 18 months to 3 years
- ✔ **Phallic:** 3 years to 7–8 years
- ✔ **Latency:** 7–8 years to puberty
- ✔ **Genital:** Puberty to adulthood

It's like having five miniature personalities, each lasting a couple of years until you reach maturity. This reminds me of a typical high school freshman who begins school with one personality only to have an entirely new persona by the end of the year, complete with wardrobe and a secret language. It's Geek Von Bookworm one minute and Joe Slick the next. Each personality stage presents you with a unique challenge, and if you successfully overcome that challenge, you acquire a fully mature personality. (That's Mr. Joe Slick to you!) But, if you somehow fail to overcome the challenge of a stage, you'll be stuck or fixated there. This is where a lot of your personal uniqueness comes from, your "stuckness" or fixation at a particular stage of personality development.

Within each stage, you also find yourself focused on a particular part of the body known as an *erogenous zone*. It's kind of like focusing on your wash-board stomach when you're 18 years old and your love handles when you're 28; each stands out at a different time in your life. The pleasure sought by your inborn instincts is focused on sexual desire and gratification, through proper stimulation of each erogenous zone. If properly stimulated, you progress to the top of Freud's psychosexual peak, sexual and psychic maturity. If not, you're fixated on that particular zone and stuck in that particular stage of personality development.

Opening your big mouth

The *oral stage* is Freud's first stage of personality development. From the time of birth until about 18 months of age, an infant's life centers on his mouth. I used to look on with disgust, as my teenage friend would give his little brother things to put in his mouth. Cola can: in the mouth. Car keys: in the mouth. It seemed disgusting, even dirty, but he couldn't help himself. He put every-thing in his mouth. The main task of this stage is to satisfy oral desire by stimulating the erogenous zone of the mouth. Notice the infant's reflexive sucking and the way her head and mouth turn toward her cheek as it's gently brushed. Infants are born with a very well developed sense of taste, and their mouths are the most sophisticated tools they have to explore their world. Their mouths far outperform their hands and fingers in "grasping" the world around them.

One of the first objects "out there" in the world that provides an infant with oral satisfaction is his mother's breast. The mother's breast is a main source of connection and satisfaction. But could this ever be a problem? When was the last time you saw a 10-year-old breast-feeding? Eventually, all infants have to be weaned from their mother's breast. Weaning presents the infant with the first conflict between his desire and reality. If the infant fails to wean or is weaned harshly or incompletely, he will become fixated at the oral stage. He will develop an *oral character* in which he will be dominated by feelings of dependency and helplessness. Infants are not able to provide themselves with autonomous satisfaction; as long as they are in the oral stage, they depend entirely on (m)others.

Ultimately, as we successfully overcome the challenge of weaning and gaining control over our ability to satisfy our oral desires, we move on to the next stage of personality development. But for those of you that remain stuck there, you may find yourself preoccupied with oral things, like talking, eating, smoking, and drinking. You'll never grow out of the need for constant oral stimulation. So that guy with the big mouth at the office Christmas party, he's just an overgrown baby who never got over the fact that he couldn't breast-feed forever. But I wouldn't tell him to his face.

(M)other

For a lot of people, the first human they ever meet is their mother. With the exception of the nurses and obstetrician in the delivery room, mom's face is the first face you see. You're dependent on her for everything. You're not ready to be self-sufficient for a pretty long time.

She's the center of your world. Moms are held in pretty high regard in most (if not all) of the world. I once heard that the most common tattoo in the United States is "Mom" inside a heart. She's the (m)other because there's no other.

Take a minute to reflect on your childhood. It may be difficult to remember infancy, but most of us can conjure something up from the ages of 2 to 3 years. Did you have a pacifier? How long? Did you suck your thumb? Just how "oral" were you? Do you chew your pens now? Are you bitingly sarcastic? Freud may be tempted to say, "You are fixated!"

To poop or not to poop?

All babies have to grow up some time, and when they do, they graduate to the erogenous focus of the *anal stage,* Freud's second stage of personality development. Think pleasure, your relentless libido striving for satisfaction. Think defecation. Say what? That's right, Freud emphasized the control over defecating as the pleasure center from 18 months to 3 years old. The central conflict for toddlers is control! Kids in this stage want the ability to poop whenever they want and wherever they want. Like in their pants! But the reality that they have to hold it creeps in, conjuring images of long trips in the family car, "Are we there yet? I have to go!"

Who and what withholds such pleasure seeking, the desire to poop at will. Our parents and the constraints of reality do. (See "Id, Ego, and Superego" earlier in this chapter for more information about reality constraints.) In fact, some of your adult characteristics may be the consequence of how your parents handled your toilet training. Your creativity and productivity are indicators of how well you've successfully navigated the anal stage.

If you're stuck in the anal stage, you're dominated by anal satisfaction. This satisfaction can come in one of two ways:

✔ If you're messy, sloppy, or careless, it speaks of an expulsive rebellion against parental control.

✔ If you're withholding, obstinate, and obsessed with neatness, you've learned control in reaction to your toilet training experience.

Either way, you're in control. Maturity and success in the anal stage result in your ability to control yourself. So let go, but make sure you do it in the right place and at the right time.

Marrying your mom

Just when you thought that all of your personality traits had been described, Freud comes up with his third stage: *the phallic stage.* I've explained your orally fixated gum-smacking officemate. The pile of clothes on the floor of your room will never look the same after learning about the anal stage. But I've promised you sex, and it's time to deliver, well sort of. The 3- to 5-year-old child is focused on the erogenous stimulation of the genital area, the penis and vagina specifically. In the phallic stage, gratification begins with autoeroticism. That means masturbation to the rest of us. But our need for satisfaction soon turns toward our parents, typically the parent of the opposite sex. As our sexual satisfaction expands, we find ourselves within the realm of one of Freud's most controversial and strange contributions to the study of personality, the Oedipus complex.

As adults, most of us cringe at the idea of marrying someone like our mothers or fathers, least of all having sex with them, but we've all known a little boy or girl who wants to grow up one day and marry his or her parent. There's just one problem: Nearly every culture on the planet has a taboo against sex between parents and their children. Freud observed that children in the phallic stage of personality development shifted from self-gratification to seeking gratification from their opposite-sex parent. But the taboo is not the only thing that stands in the child's way; the other parent seems precariously in the way, an obstacle. How would your father feel if you tried to make a move on your mom, or vice versa? But the libido knows no bounds and must have satisfaction. It feels that the opposite-sex parent is its rightful object of desire. Why?

King Oedipus

Freud found ancient support for his ideas about a child's sexual desire for his or her parents in the famous (or maybe not) Greek play, *Oedipus Rex.* The basic story is about a king who has a male child who prophets predict one day will kill the king and marry the queen. To prevent this, the king takes the child to the woods and leaves him to die. The child is discovered by some peasants in the woods, however, and is raised to be a healthy adult. One day, he returns to the city to make his fortune, but on the road to the city, he encounters the king, neither of them aware of their relation to each other. There is a scuffle, and the king is killed. As the son arrives in the city, he soon makes his fortune, rising to the top of civic society. He soon attracts the eye of the mourning queen and eventually marries her, thus fulfilling the prophecy.

This is where Freud gets a little complex. Basically, all children are initially attracted to their mothers because she's often their primary caregiver. She's their primary source of pleasure and satisfaction. She's the end all and be all of satisfaction. From there, kids split by sex (or gender, as most people refer to it).

Boys

For the male child, this attraction to the mother continues to develop into what Freud called the *Oedipus complex.* The male child's father blocks him from his mother. This gets to be really frustrating for the male child. It's so bad that the frustration eventually blossoms into full-blown hatred for his father. You might say, as the prophets in *Rex* did, that his hatred for his father becomes murderous.

This complex is riddled with conflict as boys find themselves afraid of their fathers because they want their mothers all to themselves. Freud called this fear *castration anxiety.* The male child is afraid that his father will cut off his genitals. Because of this fear, the male child takes an alternative route: If you can't beat 'em, join 'em. Junior learns to identify with his father, adopting his masculinity and seeking his own "mother" of sorts. He can't have sex with his mother, but he can live vicariously through his father. This supplies him with symbolic access to his mother and satisfies his libidinal desire.

Girls

Freud was thoroughly criticized for his neglect of female sexuality. So, he consulted the Greeks again, finding a similar Oedipal tale about a woman named Electra. Electra gets someone to kill her mother to avenge the death of her father.

For girls, their attraction shifts to their fathers because they come to resent their mothers for a very strange reason, *penis envy.* According to Freud, little girls stop desiring their mothers because they realize that they lack a penis like their fathers. How can they have sex with their mothers without a penis? So what about that "can't beat 'em, join 'em" philosophy? Like little boys, little girls also can't identify with their fathers because they lack a penis. So what are they supposed to do? They spend the rest of their lives looking for a penis. Essentially, they spend the rest of their lives looking for a man to make them complete.

Many of Freud's ideas have been met with harsh criticism. You may be sitting there right now saying to yourself, "Come on, this is too much!" In order to benefit from Freud's ideas and get past the preposterous nature of such a thing as wishing to have sex with your mother and murder your father, think metaphor; think analogy. Freud's ideas are best understood when processed more symbolically. For example, try to picture Oedipus as a frustrated little kid that has to share his mother's attention with his father. Daddy stands in the way, he must be eliminated. Remember, don't get caught up in the theatrics!

That's a lot to take in, I know, and it all seems a little weird. Did I say a little? Okay, it seems really weird! How does it relate to personality? If a boy or man successfully aligns himself with his father, he turns his conflict into a deep striving for success and superiority in society, conquering women, conquering the business world, and becoming the captain of the football team. This is a successful response to the male castration anxiety of the phallic stage. Unfortunately, not all men get to this point. If he finds himself fixated because he fails to join forces with Dad, he's been successfully emasculated. He becomes a failure at life, unable to strive for achievement because of the disabling guilt generated from competing with his father for his mother's attention.

With successful resolution of the Electra complex, a girl finds herself equipped to deal with her adult sexual and intimate relationships. She turns her penis envy into a healthy search for a good "fatherly" husband. But if she fails, she becomes fixated and may be overly seductive and flirtatious. I know, I know. . . but women's liberation happened a long time after Freud!

Taking a time out

With successful resolution of the conflicts of each previous stage, children enter into a more quiet time of psychosexual development called latency. The libido loosens its grip on the personality, and the impulses cease to dominate. Kids find more freedom to explore and expand on the skills they've gained from each subsequent stage. Latency lasts from about 6 years old until puberty. Things cool down, so to speak. There's no rivalry with the opposite-sex parent. There's no battle for control over satisfaction. It's a time for basic social exploration like making friends and forming little social cliques. I think this time period matches everyone's basic notion of childhood a little better than Freud's previous stages. It's less perverse and conflict ridden for sure.

Peaking sexually

With the onset of puberty, the smooth ride of latency begins to speed up again. The flames of earlier conflicts are rekindled. Desire begins to dominate the picture again, but this time it's different. The self-centered pleasure-seeking child of earlier stages gives way to a more mature form of satisfaction. A concern for the pleasure of others begins to shape the direction of psychosexual development, and the child is now open to learning how to engage in mutually satisfying love relationships. Keep in mind that Freud never stated that all people reach this point of full maturity. This point is more like an ideal, something to strive for, a lifelong project. But if somebody doesn't make it (at least some of the way), he could easily drift back into selfish phallicism. This seems to conjure images of the selfish lover who doesn't care about the pleasure of the other partner: As long as he gets what he wants, he's just fine. But if you make it, eat your heart out, Don Juan! You'll be attentive and actually care if the other person in the interaction is enjoying his or herself.

Defensive? I'm Not Defensive!

So you're walking along your favorite hiking trail in the mountains and a bear jumps out, rises up on its hind legs, and looks really hungry. What do you do? Stand and fight or take off running? If this situation poses a threat, you may have to defend yourself. But is defending your body from physical harm the only time you go on the defensive? I've had to defend my reputation one or two times . . . or more. Either way, sometimes we have to defend or protect ourselves psychologically. This is an important aspect of our personalities.

Anna Freud (Sigmund's daughter) brought us the concept of defense mechanisms. We can be afraid of anything: bears, bullies, or gossip. Our impulsive behavior can get us into trouble or force us into disfavor with someone we love. Have you ever scared yourself? We can fear the wrath of our own conscience, or its tool, guilt. "Stop being so defensive!" is something you've probably heard, but don't worry; we all are "defensive." Freud believed that your characteristic ways of defending yourself against your anxieties are strong determinants of your overall personality. How do you cope? How do you psychologically defend yourself? How do you protect yourself from painful thoughts, impulses, or urges?

The Freuds proposed several important defense mechanisms:

✔ **Repression:** Keeping a thought, feeling, or memory of an experience out of consciousness. "Forget about it!" Many things may be the objects of repression, forbidden impulses or desires or a painful, emotionally difficult situation. Are you sitting there doubting? "I'm certainly not repressed in any such way!" Well, try to picture your parents having sex. Not easy is it? What do you do when you're at a party or family gathering and someone brings up an embarrassing situation from your past? "Remember when. . . ?"

Freud's little girl

Anna Freud was Sigmund Freud's daughter. She followed in her father's footsteps and made some substantial contributions to his theory of personality. For some reason, the Freuds emphasized anxiety and protection in their work on personality. Kind of makes you wonder what kind of home Anna grew up in. I can see it now. She brings home a C- on her psychology final. How could she have missed that question on the id, ego, and superego? Maybe she was too busy thinking about defense mechanisms! Anna took much of what her father created and applied it to children's problems and helping them in therapy. Her additions to Sigmund's theories both supported and expanded his earlier work. Most people have never heard of her, but make no mistake about it, Anna seemed to inherit her father's gift for understanding the human personality.

✔ **Denial:** Refusing to accept that something exists or happened. It can also involve altering the meaning of an event so that its impact is diverted. If something important to you goes wrong, you may just say to yourself, "That's not so important after all." This is the common "sour grapes" response. Images of my freshman year in college come to mind as I pitifully and unsuccessfully asked seniors on dates. "I didn't like her anyway," I'd cry, instead of facing the dejection. Repression would have been nice, but when in doubt, deny it! Denial is one defense mechanism that most people can relate to and commonly use. Don't try to deny it!

✔ **Projection:** Attributing a threatening urge, impulse, or aspect of oneself to someone else. The guilty conscience turned jealous lover defense! Any unacceptable impulse may be projected. This is kind of like the best offense is a good defense. Instead of acknowledging that you're mad at someone, you might accuse him or her of being mad at you. When someone feels aggressive impulses, he or she often uses projection. The individual attributes his aggression to someone else, and the once aggressive person becomes fearful of the potential attacks of others. So the next time someone tells you that you are being paranoid, think about whom you may be angry with.

✔ **Rationalization:** Creating an acceptable but incorrect explanation of a situation. I once knew a habitual thief who only stole from big businesses. He would never think of robbing the Smiths, but super-megastores look out! He explained that big business makes money from "ripping people off," so he's just trying to even the score. Kind of like a modern day Robin Hood I guess. Unfortunately for him, the judge he faced for his crimes was not a believer in fairy tales.

✔ **Intellectualization:** Thinking about something "logically" or coldly and without emotion.

Therapist: "Mr. Jones, your wife has left you, and you've recently lost your job. How does that make you feel?"

Patient: "I've found that the organization in my home has been much improved, less clutter now; her things took up so much room. As for the job, the economy had been slowing down for some time, I could sense that it was coming."

✔ **Reaction formation:** Doing the opposite of what you would really like to do. Ever gone out of your way to be nice to someone you really disliked? I know, I know, love thy enemy. But if being neighborly is just a reaction formation, maybe I could find another defense mechanism that leaves me with a little bit less egg on my face. I think I'd rather project than suck up to someone I really don't like.

✔ **Regression:** Returning to an earlier or more childlike form of defense. Physical and psychological stress may sometimes lead us to abandon our more mature defense mechanisms. If you've resorted to whining when asking your boss for a raise, consider regression.

Our interactions with the world around us can be wrought with conflict and anxiety. Sharing office space, having a roommate, and dealing with a persistent bill collector are just a few examples of everyday conflicts we face. The Freuds made unparalleled contributions to our understanding of how our characteristic ways of coping comprise our basic personality. It would be a mistake to assume that psychologically defending ourselves is a negative behavior; it is basic to our survival. Our defenses protect us and keep us from becoming overwhelmed. Without them, we might all end up having a nervous breakdown.

Chapter 11

Developing an Award-Winning Personality

A personality is a stable system of tendencies to act, think, and feel a particular way. Describing someone's personality is in essence developing a picture out of the various bits of information available about that person. Describing someone's personality almost always means taking a bunch of behavioral characteristics and reducing them to a more restricted set of qualities and attributes.

Personality theories assume that a few general characteristics can serve as a summary for what a person is like. The qualities that first come to mind when I think about a person are usually the qualities that are most central to him or her. The more central that quality is, the more useful that aspect is in predicting his or her behavior and distinguishing him or her from other people.

The theories and ideas that I cover in this chapter all have at least one thing in common: They all emphasize adaptation as a major component of personality. In fact, the function of personality is adaptation and maximum adjustment within the world. From this perspective, personality is viewed as a survival tool of sorts. Animals evolved fur to keep them warm and sharp claws to defend themselves against the threats in their environment. We humans developed personalities!

An important thing to keep in mind as you read about these personality theories is that nobody fits perfectly into the categories presented. An important concept in psychology is the principle of *individual differences*. No one *is* a personality theory: The theories are *tools* for understanding the complexity of human behavior, thought, and emotion.

Knowing Who's a Nerd

Whether we realize it or not, each of us has a theory of personality that we use as our own little way of classifying people so we can tell them apart. When I was in high school, people were classified as nerds, jocks, or partygoers. Such a simple-minded scheme, but it came in handy from time to time.

So, each of us is a little personality theorist, but many specific groups of personality theorists are also out there. Astrologers, psychics, theologians, poets, and many others have been trying to classify people for centuries, each using their own insights into personality to develop theories.

Take the following personality description:

> You have a great deal of unused capacity that you have not turned to your advantage.
>
> Sometimes you have doubts as to whether you have made the right decision or done the right thing.
>
> At times you are sociable; at other times you keep to yourself.
>
> Security is one of your goals in life.

Do these characteristics describe you? If so, is a secret personality-analyzing computer chip imbedded in the binding of this book? Or are the above descriptions so vague and general that they would apply to anyone reading them? I vote for the latter. The *Barnum effect* is when personality theories are so general that they could apply to most everyone and tell very little specific information about a particular individual. It was named after P.T. Barnum, the famous circus owner who allegedly perfected this technique in his sideshow fortune-telling acts. After learning about the Barnum effect, I hope you never again see another fortune cookie or horoscope in the same way.

Stroking Freud's Ego

Remember the ego? You know, that symbol of American freedom and the U.S. Postal Service? No, that's an "eagle." The ego is Freud's master negotiator between desire and morality. (See Chapter 10 for more on Freud.) Remember now? Even though a lot of people were and remain pretty impressed with Sigmund's ideas, many of Freud's colleagues and contemporaries decided to go their own way and develop their own personality theories. Many of these individuals felt that Freud did not give the ego enough credit in shaping our personalities. Most of them felt that it was more than just a mediator. For some, the ego became synonymous with personality itself.

H. Hartmann

H. Hartmann was a follower of Freud who lead the dissent and march toward emphasizing the Ego in personality. For Hartmann, the Ego played two key roles in shaping personality:

- Reducing conflict
- Promoting adaptation

Sigmund Freud talked a lot about conflict among the id, the ego, and the superego. Basically, a lot of tension exists between a person's desire and the reality of satisfying that desire in a socially acceptable and appropriate manner. Hartmann's Ego was similar to Freud's in that it helped to satisfy the Id's desire and appease the Superego's rules. But his Ego was out for itself in a way that Freud never mentioned.

Hartmann's Ego is a central part of the personality that has its own desire or need for satisfaction, while Freud's Ego was more like a referee with no real agenda of its own. What satisfies the Ego according to Hartmann? Thinking, planning, imagining, and integrating are all the sexy stuff of Hartmann's Ego. Built-in satisfaction occurs when humans engage in these processes, and this accomplishment pushes all of us toward greater independence and autonomy. Being independent and self-sufficient is a satisfying feeling. Children get pretty happy at the prospect of being seen as a "big boy" instead of a baby. Little do they know what's waiting for them when they are actually grown up . . . poor things.

Feeling phrenological?

In the eighteenth and nineteenth centuries, a scientist named Franz Joseph Gall tried to classify people's personalities based on the shapes of their skulls and the unique patterns of lumps on their heads. Don't worry though, no one is using that technique anymore — apparently lumps tell us very little. Many thinkers who made legitimate contributions in other areas came up with relatively useless theories for personality. A good personality theory allows us to accurately describe individuals and distinguish them from one another. Bad personality theories are often guilty of something called the *Barnum effect* (see the section "Knowing Who's a Nerd" earlier in this chapter).

Balance is the key

My ability to control my impulses and to adapt to the demands of the situation is called *ego control*. It's important though, not to get carried away with too much ego control, so that it turns into over-control. All work and no play make Johnny a very dull boy. (I always wondered where that saying came from. I don't think it came from psychologists.) Balance between complete lack of control and being too rigid is important. Flexibility is the key!

Robert White

Robert White, another psychoanalyst, added to Hartmann's ideas about the Ego. This strive for self-sufficiency and the satisfaction that comes with it stem from a drive White called *effectance motivation* — the motive or need to feel like we can make an impact or have an effect on our surroundings. It's kind of like having a little community activist inside all of us, pushing us to "make a difference" but in a more personal and individual way.

White added another need to this idea, the *competence motive* — the need to make an effective impact on the world around us. So, having an impact is not good enough, it's more satisfying to have an effective impact. This is more than the effectance motivation; we have to have a competent effect. Sometimes I wonder if teenagers who paint graffiti aren't just out to satisfy their effectance motive without much regard for the competence motive. Call me crazy, but scrawling your name on a wall is not very artistic. Don't get me wrong though, I've seen some pretty impressive graffiti art; I'm just wondering about those "taggers."

Our needs for effectance and competence push us toward mastery, a desire to be an effective person. Children's games such as King of the Hill and Follow the Leader seem to reflect our need to be in charge. Be aware though that Hartmann and White weren't saying that we all have a need to be leaders of others, just a need to be leaders of ourselves — to have self-control. We actively seek information and stimulation in order to master our world and ourselves. It's kind of like the Manifest Destiny of personality. Domination is not the issue either. Healthy satisfaction of these motives is adaptation acquired through proper impulse control and flexibility when faced with necessary adjustments and challenges. I could feel like a master if I subject other people to my will, but this would not be a healthy satisfaction of mastery need.

Alfred Adler

Alfred Adler, yet another psychoanalyst, tried to address the idea of where this need for mastery actually comes from. The need for mastery and our drive to achieve is the result of a complex process of self-evaluation.

Essentially, Adler felt that all of us have certain ideal images of ourselves and that we all possess aspirations that we strive toward. These needs are specific manifestations of a general need to carve out a niche for ourselves in a big, ambiguous, and anonymous world. When a discrepancy exists between our ideal self-image and what we're actually doing, *inferiority feelings* arise, and we form an *inferiority complex*. This complex pushes us toward realizing our ideal selves and a need for mastery. So what we're actually mastering is not actually the world, but our ability to live up to our own expectations. I guess I'm alright by Adler, then. I've got some pretty low aspirations — easily achieved mastery, I guess.

Erikson's Psychosocial Theory

Erik Erikson had close ties to the psychoanalytic/Freudian theory of personality. But like the others who jumped ship, he had some very powerful ideas of his own. Erikson didn't spend much time talking about the lustful Id or the judgmental Superego. He was focused on the Ego, but in a very different way from Freud.

Erikson viewed personality as a product of social interactions and the choices we make in life. He presented the Ego "in development" as personal identity, shaped and molded by our experiences. As we relate to other people, we go through a series of stages in which the goal is to develop a coherent sense of self, of who we are. Each stage presents us with a challenge or a crisis in which we go in either one or another direction. When a personality "fork-in-the-road" is present, our choices have a strong effect on who we are. The following are Erikson's stages of psychosocial development.

Basic trust versus mistrust

How do you know that the sun is going to rise tomorrow morning? Experience tells you so. How do you know whether you can trust that your needs will be tended to? Experience tells you so. The basic experience of interacting with an attentive and trustworthy caregiver early in life turns into a basic trust of the world. (The basic trust versus mistrust stage of development encompasses a baby's first year of life.) A sense of predictability and continuity in those who care for us develops, as they take care of both our basic and complex needs. This basic trust also includes trusting yourself, knowing that, when caregivers are not available, you can take care of yourself.

But what if mom and dad drop the ball? If there is a consistent lack of responsive care giving and a child's needs are not adequately met, he may never learn to trust his environment. Inconsistent or intermittent care can also lead to a lack of trust. Either way, when a child's sense of basic trust is undermined, it can lead to withdrawal and sometimes even to a complete walling-off from relationships.

Autonomy versus shame and doubt

As babies turn into toddlers, their abilities (language, social, physical, and cognitive) rapidly expand. They become walking, talking, and question-asking machines. They're into everything! It's hard to keep them corralled. This rowdiness and persistence is an expression of a toddler's independence. As their bodies and minds grow, they gain confidence and explore their worlds.

But what if mom and dad are too overbearing? Kids between the ages of 1 and 3 need to go it alone. If parents tell them not to touch things, not to talk, and not to try on their newfound confidence, children may develop a sense of shame and doubt in themselves. Shame is not the same thing as guilt. *Shame* is more a feeling of self-disgust or extreme dislike for oneself. *Guilt* usually involves letting other people down, but shame is more of a condemnation of oneself. Caregivers need to balance safety and guidance with a healthy promotion of exploration and experimentation with independence.

Initiative versus guilt

Building on successes in the first two stages, a preschooler continues to expand her sense of independence but now in a more refined way. Raw independence is channeled into more purposeful and responsible behavior. Actions contain less of a sense of rebellion and more of a sense of self-initiative. The word initiative implies starting or originating. During this period, the unique desires of a child emerge and really start to give definition to their little personalities. They may want to help around the house or dress in their favorite clothes, even if their favorite clothes are a Halloween costume.

I've got to admit, I have issues. I hate being called "irresponsible." Maybe I'm still stuck in this stage, but either way, I feel really guilty when I fail to act responsibly. This is what can happen when a preschooler fails to develop a sense of initiative. Guilt can arise from feeling too anxious or misguided in your actions. It's kind of like letting yourself down. You're not cutting it! You're lazy! You're irresponsible! Help, I need therapy!

Industry versus inferiority

"Time to shape up!" — that's what you hear between the age of 6 and adolescence. Playing around and experimenting with the environment will no longer be tolerated. A child is expected to be achieving something when they engage in something. Pointless and messy play is viewed as a lack of industry. You are expected to be the "captain of industry" of the elementary school — accomplishing, not farting around. Playing football in the front yard with the neighbor kids is not kid's play, it's a demonstration of your leadership and organization skills and your ability to accomplish a goal. Well, I know these examples are a little extreme, but the point is that the goal of this stage is to focus one's childhood abilities toward specific goals and tasks. It's no longer alright to scribble . . . parents don't applaud that anymore. They want results. Now they want you to color between the lines. And that's just for starters.

What if a child views playtime as a time to unwind and relax from the pressures of the school day? Could he be heading toward inferiority? No, using playtime to relax is purposeful. But if there is an apparent lack of goal-directedness in a child's behavior, a sense of being a "slacker" or being without purpose can lead to feeling inferior.

Identity versus identity confusion

When I was a teenager, I went through quite a few identities before I settled on "surfer." I'd dye my hair purple one month and dress like a gangster the next. I know, I know, I was a wannabe. But according to Erikson, this behavior was a normal part of development. During adolescence, teenagers experiment with new identities and views of themselves. There's a push to find out who one really is and what he or she is all about. Erikson called this an *identity crisis*. If a teen successfully navigates the abysmal waters of teenage identity confusion, he emerges with a more solid sense of self and a clearer identity. If not. . . .

Identify confusion is the state of unresolved identity crisis. I used to think that my 30-year-old buddy who still wears Duran Duran T-shirts, spikes his bangs, and rolls up his pant legs was in a state of identity confusion. But in fact, he's successfully resolved the issue of who he is — he's the same guy I knew in eighth grade: no confusion there. Sometimes though, teenagers get lost in the confusing search for a genuine identity, sometimes withdrawing and never really feeling a true sense of "me."

Intimacy versus isolation

When does being a bachelor, living the partying and dating lifestyle, get old? For many people it's during their young-adult years, between 18 and 35 or so. When I was in my early twenties, I remember seeing this guy in his forties at the local nightclub standing against the bar trying to lure the twenty-some-things over for a drink. I don't know, but that looked pretty pitiful to me. This is a value judgment of course, but according to Erikson, there is a time when one's ability to find and develop intimacy is a primary task of personality development. After somebody knows who he is, he turns to developing close relationships with other people who know who they are. The goal is intimacy. Perhaps this is why so many people get married during these years?

I have no idea whether that guy in the nightclub was intimate or isolated from intimacy based on a casual observation and a poor attempt at playing armchair (or dance-floor) psychologist. Erikson did state, however, that people who fail to develop intimate relationships during these years are likely to experience social isolation. Considering my nightclub example, I realize that intimacy may appear to be romantic in nature. This is not the case though: Intimacy is about developing close relationships, whether the relationships are with friends, lovers, or otherwise. Either way, individuals with difficulty developing friendships or making romantic connections may find themselves isolated.

Generativity versus stagnation

Something surprising often happens with older convicts in prisons. A prison is an environment full of tough, sometimes mean guys who typically don't care about who they hurt when they commit their crimes. But a lot of the older inmates take on the "big brother" role for the younger guys coming in. Now, you're probably sitting there saying, "Sure, they're big brothers alright, teaching them better crime skills." But that's not it at all. The older convicts actually try to warn the younger guys, attempting to guide them away from the lifestyle that they've lived for so long. This is a good demonstration of what Erikson called *generativity* — the need to be needed and to feel like one is guiding the "next generation." A sense of wanting to leave a legacy and to have an impact on younger people develops during middle adulthood.

When people feel that they've done nothing or can do nothing for the next generation, they develop a sense of *stagnation* instead of generativity. It's as if they're stuck in isolation with no one to pass their wisdom on to. This process is a strange thing to watch, kind of like an internal alarm that goes off. People want children and grandchildren, or they want to coach little league. If individuals don't have an ability or opportunity to satisfy this desire, they develop a feeling of being stagnant.

Integrity versus despair

As life winds down and old age is upon us, we often sit back and reflect on things we've accomplished and whether our lives were well spent or wasted. If a man feels a sense of satisfaction with the way he lived his life, he will feel *integrity,* a basic sense of wholeness or of being complete. If not, *despair* is likely to follow. Ever wonder why elder adults like to tell stories from their lives? It may have something to do with this process of looking back and reflecting. So, if you don't want older folks to fall into despair, act interested and laugh even if you don't think the stories are funny.

Relating to Objects

In keeping with the social focus on the personality theories covered in the previous sections, yet another expansion of Freud's theory has become one of the most dominant forces in personality theory over the last 50 years. It is called *object relations theory.* The basic premise is that interpersonal relationships are the basic foundations of personality. Essentially, our personalities are the product of our mental representation of other people, ourselves, and the relationships between the two. That is, it's not actual people and our relationships with them that are important but our thoughts and ideas about these people. The "objects" in the theory are other people. "Relations" are the relationships. Simple enough right?

Object relations theory is not really one theory at all but a collection of theories from a variety of thinkers. The three most popular contributors to this body of thought are Melanie Klein, Ronald Fairbairn, and D.W. Winnicott. Another prominent figure was Margaret Mahler. Mahler developed a nice synthesis of much of the others' works, and she is the main focus for this discussion.

All of the object relations contributors basically share two broad emphases:

- ✔ The idea that a person's pattern of relating to others is established during the interactions of early childhood

- ✔ The assumption that whatever pattern is formed, it tends to recur over and over again throughout a person's life

Mahler stated that newborns are born without the ability to distinguish themselves from things that are "not self." Infants are in a virtual state of psychological fusion with the objects in their environment.

For those of you who are mothers and have carried a baby, you may know a little about this. In all reality, a mother and her fetus are biologically intertwined. They're not joined at the hip, just seemingly everywhere else. They are physically connected, and when one thing happens to the mother, it also happens to the fetus and vice versa.

Mahler extended that idea in a more psychological sense. When an infant is born, she is in state of personality fusion with her mother or primary caregiver. Is this because of the beautiful, harmonious love that they share for each other? Not exactly. This fusion is more a function of the dependency of the infant and her undeveloped survival skills. So as we grow and our personalities develop, this fusion breaks down, and an infant gradually develops a more differentiated personality that is separate and distinct from her mother's personality, and others' as well. That's good — I was going to say, "Get a life!"

With the goal of a completely differentiated personality in mind, here are the stages of personality development presented by Mahler:

- ✔ **Autistic stage (birth to 2 months):** The infant is in a sleeplike state of psychological isolation similar to being in the womb. This is a time of total union where the baby can't tell the difference between himself and his mother. In the infant's mind, the mother in fact is just an extension of the infant. The autistic stage is a closed system, and all emotional energy remains referenced to the baby's own body, not directed outward to external objects.

- ✔ **Symbiosis (2 to 6 months):** Now, a dim awareness of an "other" begins to emerge. This other is experienced as some "thing" that satisfies hunger, thirst, and other discomforts. The relationship is as if the other exists only to serve the baby's needs. (Sometimes I think old-fashioned husbands think this about their wives!) There is still no distinction made between "I" and "you." We are one in the same.

- ✔ **Hatching (6 to 10 months):** At this point, the infant's world begins to open up a little bit and expand. What is "hatching" is a sense of difference between the infant and the objects in the world around him or her. However, this can be a scary thing, and the comfort of symbiosis is not long forgotten.

As infants begin to psychologically open up to the big, bad world, they often require something to take with them on their journey. This comforting "thing" is called a *transitional object*. Remember Linus from *Peanuts?* He took his blanket, his transitional object, everywhere. It comforted him. Now, Linus seemed a little older than 10 months, so did he have some issues or what? Infants also develop stranger anxiety during hatching. *Stranger anxiety* is where infants become weary and sometimes even fearful of people they've never seen or met before.

✔ **Practicing (10 to 16 months):** This stage is where little Johnny gets carried away with his independence. Children are fully aware of their separateness, and they try out their independence. Some psychologists think that kids go through this stage again when they hit their teens. Ever hear a child at this age use the word *no?* I bet you have! Repeated use of *no* is a great example of "practicing" independence. So the next time some bratty 15-month-old kid yells, "No!" at you, just be patient. They'll soon realize that they're in this big scary world all by themselves. Sounds a little cruel, huh?

✔ **Rapprochement (16 to 24 months):** Just when Junior thinks he's running the show, something starts to happen to his confidence — he realizes he's all alone. That can pretty scary for anyone, let alone for a 1½-year-old child. The solution? Reengage with mommy! This is like running back home after not being able to make rent in your first apartment, although I'm not sure how embarrassed the 20-month-old is.

✔ **Object constancy (24 to 36 months):** After a child has returned home so to speak, he is eventually able to develop a strong enough sense of self and security to go out on his psychological own again. This stable sense of self is developed in part by the child realizing that some consistency exists between his fluctuating moods and his mental states. It may sound kind of strange to think that just because there's a change in mood, a pre-object constancy child would experience a less stable sense of himself, but he does. Before this stage, with each passing mood and thought, children experience uncertainty about their identity. But as this stage begins, they develop a more sure sense of themselves.

Collecting Your Unconscious with Jung

Ever wondered where someone's dark impulses come from? Do you sometimes feel like you're not yourself, that you're living out someone else's life? If so, then call Shirley Maclain. She'll have you convinced that you're feeling that way because you're really King Henry the XIII reincarnated. However, before you get too carried away, I'd like to bother your highness with an alternative explanation.

A psychologist named Carl Jung (*young*) brings us one of the most metaphysical and esoteric theories of personality around. It's popular though, because it's almost as if it speaks to things that we've known are there personally but couldn't quite put our fingers on. Jung was conventional in one way, he too talked about the *Ego* and the *unconscious*. But he challenged a lot of people's thinking with his other major component of personality theory, the *collective unconscious*.

Jung's Ego was seen as the center of conscious awareness. There's been a lot of talk by other theorists about the Ego's role in adaptation. Jung was no different. His Ego is the center of all conscious and willful attempts at adaptation, and the Ego can only work with things that a person is currently aware of. It only deals with the known. So what else is out there other?

The *personal unconscious* and the *collective unconscious* represent the unknown parts of a person's personality for Jung.

- ✔ **The personal unconscious:** Consists of forgotten information and other memories that are not currently conscious to the Ego. The personal unconscious is comprised of everyday information and our own mundane personal histories. Remember that day you skipped school and decided to go the beach instead? No? Well, don't worry. All of your forgotten memories are being kept safe in your personal unconscious. Lucky you!

- ✔ **The collective unconscious:** If the personal unconscious contains information from your personal history, what does the collective unconscious contain? It contains the history of humankind inherited in the structure of our minds. All the common themes and struggles since the days when we chased woolly mammoths and grunted instead of spoke are kept there, influencing our behavior in ways that we often don't realize. The collective unconscious is unavailable to normal consciousness. In fact, only artists and visionaries have much access to it. Jung felt that they were tapping into something much deeper and more important than the personal trials and tribulations of an individual.

Within the collective unconscious exist primeval images and symbols that give rise to the fairytales, myths, and other stories passed on from generation to generation. Jung called these images and symbols *archetypes*. Jung spent a lot of time emphasizing three in particular: the shadow, anima, and animus.

- ✔ The *shadow* represents the darker side of humanity. It challenges a person's typical moral conception of himself. The shadow may or may not represent the "devil inside," but it definitely challenges anyone's view of himself as basically good. Jungian psychotherapists will often work to get their patients in touch with this part of themselves. So, if you're not up to the task, avoid seeing a Jungian therapist!

✔ The *anima* represents the essential feminine energy and aspects of an individual. It's like the yin of the yin and yang. (Or is it the other way around? I always get confused.) Either way, the anima produces mood and guides our actions based on emotion. The anima within us allows for us to be more social and conscious of our relations to things and people. Both men and women have anima. So for you tough guys out there, don't fight getting in touch with your feminine side.

✔ So if the anima represents the feminine side of our unconscious, the *animus* must represent the masculine side. The animus is the rational force or guide in our lives. A man or woman who is pure animus is exacting, judgmental, and is a "know-it-all." Remember, all of us have both the anima and animus in our collective unconscious, complementing each other and working together to guide us in a balanced approach to life.

That brings us to a final point on Jung's contribution to the realm of personality psychology, his theory of *introversion* and *extraversion*. Are you cautious, contemplative, and hesitant? Do you get excited when faced with the unknown and just dive right into things without much thought, shooting first and asking questions later?

Introverts are thoughtful and deliberate. They don't like taking chances and sometimes have a hard time adapting to our fast-paced world because they're stuck overly analyzing things. Extraverts on the other hand are spontaneous and sometimes thoughtless, which can sometimes get them into trouble at times. They're generally good in new situations, but they sometimes make unnecessary mistakes.

The good news is that Jung thought that each of us has some relative mixture of both. It's not an either/or thing. It's like something my students say when I ask them if they agree with some of the psychological theories I'm going over, "It depends." Or when I ask them if they would rather have an in-class or a take-home final, "It depends." Here's a tip: "It depends" is a pretty safe answer because take-home finals can be deceptively hard. They're "sneaky hard."

Learning from Others

The subject of television and violence has caused a lot of controversy over the last few years. Many people feel that the constant barrage of violent images is creating a more violent character for our society. There's little argument that violence in our schools is higher today than ever before, but why? This is a complex issue, and many causes and explanations have been put out there. Some explanations have even suggested that there are simply more violent personalities in the world. After all of the personality theories discussed so far, what do you think about the concept of a "violent" personality?

In 1977, Albert Bandura conducted a now-famous study looking into this concept of a "violent" personality and turned his theory into a broader theory of personality in general. The experiment is now called the Bobo Doll study. Bobo dolls are those plastic blow-up figures with a weighted bottom that bounce back when you hit or kick them. The experiment consisted of an adult punching and kicking a Bobo doll while a young child watches. Then, the child is put into the room with the Bobo doll by himself. Can you guess what happens? Little Johnny turns into Little Rocky. He punches and kicks that Bobo doll just like he saw the adult do it.

Bandura's *social-learning theory* explains this phenomenon. Basically, people can learn something just by watching or observing it. This is one of those "no duh!" theories in psychology. But hey, no one else put the theory out there the way Bandura did. Social-learning theory has become a powerful theory of personality and its development. Our personalities are a product of our observational learning experiences from those around us. We're all just a bunch of copycats. If you saw your parents being obnoxious, you'd be obnoxious too.

Bandura continued to add to his copycat theory of personality by addressing the question of why we do what we do. In other words, what motivates us to act in the ways that we do? He introduced two very important concepts to address this:

- *Self-efficacy* is a personal belief in one's ability to successfully perform a behavior. This belief is based on what Bandura called the *self-appraisal process.* This process is simply an analysis of one's actions and evaluation of successes and failures. A sense of one's capabilities arises from this: How does a particular behavior develop and a belief formed? We're motivated by these beliefs and inhibited by our expected failures. We do what we think we can do and vice versa.

- *Self-reinforcement* is as simple as giving yourself rewards for doing things. Some parents give their children rewards or reinforcement for doing their homework or cleaning their room. Bandura believed that we all do this for ourselves as well. So the next time you do something, give yourself a little reward. It will help your self-efficacy.

Representing Ourselves

Some psychologists emphasize the way people represent themselves and their experiences of the world as core aspects of their personalities and the way they act. Most of us have been to an office party or holiday party at school where some genius tries to be helpful by giving everyone a nametag.

I'm always tempted to put something goofy on mine or to use someone else's name. The tag is a crude form of representation, or presentation, of our self to other people. Sometimes I'll put a nickname on mine — I've had a few. Nicknames are good examples of a "tag" that tells us a little more about a person than her everyday name. When you meet someone nicknamed "Stinky" or "Psycho," you get a different impression than you would from "Lefty" or "Slim."

Nametags, nicknames, and common names are all examples of representations of who we are. They are convenient and shortened ways to organize a whole lot of information about someone. Ever have a conversation about a movie and forget the name of the main actor? "You know, that guy who was in that one movie with that one woman?" Just saying "Brad Pitt" is so much easier than explaining the person's characteristics every time you want to talk about him. This way of organizing information about people and the world is the product of the human mind's tendency to impose order and structure on our experiences.

Schemas

The structured representation of experience is based on recurrences of similar qualities of a person or experience across repeated events. This order takes the form of *schemas* or mental constructs for "Joe," "Brad Pitt," or "me." Joe is my neighbor who plays his music too loud. Brad Pitt is a famous actor that every man envies. Me? I'm that guy who envies Brad Pitt. After these structured representations of people, including myself, are developed, they are used to recognize and understand newly encountered information.

Cognitive personality psychologists emphasize the schema-based representation of experience as the central organizing construct in human personality. Two basic types of schemas play a role in establishing regularities and patterns of personality: self-schemas and socially relevant schemas.

Self-schemas are the organized units of information about yourself; sometimes these are called *self-concepts*. What is the concept of "you," or "Me?" An in-depth discussion of how a person's identity is developed is beyond the scope of this section, but no matter what the exact details are, our identities are represented in the form of schemas. These self-schemas are integrated conceptual networks that incorporate our own and others' opinions of us. They provide detailed information about us, from demographics (like how old we are) to our values and can be updated automatically through experience or revised through conscious attention and effort.

Scripts

The other key component in establishing personality, *socially relevant schemas,* involves the representation of categories of other people, environments, social behavior, and stereotyped expectations. These are sometimes called *scripts.* Is an actor in a movie presenting his off-screen personality or simply acting out a script that tells him how to act, when to speak, when to cry, and so on? It's a script of course. Imagine, now, that we're all just acting out a "personality" script of our own, written by the author of experience and development. These scripts determine the ways we act.

It may seem that our personalities are pretty simple. But we all have some sense that we're more complex than that. Walter Mischel (1980) attempted to add some flavor to this rather dry version of personality. He introduced five specific classes of scripts to give shape to this robotic-like conceptualization: *competencies, encoding strategies, expectancies, subjective values,* and *self-regulatory mechanisms.*

There is so much more to personality than meets the eye, and one important aspect of your personality is your personal collection of skills and abilities for solving problems and analyzing the world. Mischel called these *competencies.* How we engage and overcome the challenges in our lives in part defines our personality. Are you a "go-getter" or an "analyzer?" Have you ever built something like an extra room, a playhouse, or maybe a doghouse? How did you go about doing it? Some people sit down and figure everything out in advance, drawing out a blueprint with precise measurements and specifications. Others just get what supplies they think they might need and figure it out as they go along. A good way to test yourself is something I call the "Directions Test." When you buy something that needs to be assembled, do you look at the instructions, or do you toss them to the side?

Because cognitive personality theory puts so much emphasis on information and how it is stored and interpreted, an important aspect of personality involves the strategies and constructs we use to organize information. This is the process of building those complex schemas and scripts that will eventually guide our behavior. *Encoding strategies* are a person's unique way of attending to and interpreting the world. It is pretty easy for two people to witness the exact same event and come up with two entirely different interpretations of it. Anyone who's ever had an argument with a wife, husband, or significant other can vouch for that.

You're only as special as your expectations of a situation. Are you an eternal optimist or a pessimist? *Expectancies* consist of expectations or predictions that one event will necessarily follow another. These expectations set up the rules for what to do and how to manage specific situations. If the rules match the reality of a situation, then the behavior will be effective, and a feeling of mastery will develop. If not, I guess the only option is to keep on trying.

Do you work for free? Not many of us do. Most of us work for the incentive of getting paid. Incentives act as motivators toward a certain behavior. We're not all tempted by the same things though. Our *subjective values* represent what things are important to us as individuals and determine what we are willing to do to earn them. Hey, if you like getting little golden stars on your paycheck instead of a raise for a job well done, knock yourself out. That's what makes you so unique.

What are your goals in life? Do you have a master plan or a blueprint? You may not realize it, but according to Mischel, all of us have what he called *self-regulatory systems and plans.* You set a goal, you go for it, you analyze whether you meet that goal or not, and you make the necessary adjustments. Each of us has a unique way of doing this that characterizes our personal style.

Ultimately, according to this representational view of personality, how we see ourselves and view the world, and the ways that these views get planned out in the form of behavioral blueprints represent personality.

Regulating Ourselves

Does is ever seem like you're being guided by some higher power or force? What if I was really just a complex robot sent here from another planet to research Earth and report back to my alien superiors? Seem a little far-fetched? Some cognitive personality psychologists seem to think that this view is not so far off after all. No, they're not proposing that I'm a robot or that any of us are (well, maybe not most of us), but they do suggest that we are guided by a complex system of self-regulatory mental processes that form our personalities.

Think of it like a personality thermostat. The neat thing about a thermostat is that it is internally regulated. When you set your home thermostat to a certain temperature and select "Auto," the heating and cooling systems are engaged when necessary to maintain the desired setting. If the temperature drops below the setting, the heater kicks in. If it gets above it, the air conditioner kicks in. Psychologists Ajzen and Fishbein (1988) proposed that the human personality works in the exact same way.

The "acts" of personality consist of forming behavioral intentions that are then employed to reach a particular setting. Here, a form of mental algebra is performed in which several types of information are integrated, resulting in a likelihood or probability of a particular behavior being performed. If the probability is high enough, an intention is formed, and the behavior is carried out. A behavior becomes important enough to perform through cognitive analysis and intention formation.

Intentions are formed based on the analysis of two specific types of information: likelihood of an outcome and desirability of that outcome. In this view, our personalities are kind of inherently lazy, often forming intentions based on those behaviors most likely to succeed. We go by the path of least resistance. The desirability of the behavior is based on its personal meaning and on whether people that are important to you want you to do the behavior. I am much less likely to form an intention for a behavior that someone I couldn't care less about desires me to do.

Chapter 12

Catching the First Boat off Isolation Island

*O*ne of the things that distinguishes psychology from other social sciences is the focus of its investigations and applications. Although psychologists do focus on groups at times, they focus a majority of their work on individuals. Therapy, for example, is typically an individual affair, even if it's group therapy.

Americans love the classic individual. John Wayne walked tall and independently for years. Rambo single-handedly took on entire divisions of enemy soldiers. These guys stood on their own. They were individuals who resisted the pressure to go along with the crowd. They seemed to know who they were, and they were never willing to compromise on that issue. Sometimes that's called integrity. One of the meanings of the word integrity is wholeness or completeness, and these guys were complete individuals. They had strong character and dominant personas. They knew who they were, and no one could tell them otherwise.

In case you haven't noticed, however, psychologists take nothing for granted. If I had John Wayne in therapy and he came in with his macho, "I know who I am, and I'm not going to change" attitude, I'd take the bait. I'd say, "Okay, who are you?" It's easy to take knowing who you are for granted. Until someone asks, most of us go around assuming we know who we are. This is the age-old question of *self*. What is a self, and how do I know if I have one? What is my identity? Who am I?

Feeling Self-Conscious

Have you ever seen a dog stand in front of a mirror? Sometimes they bark at themselves or stand there with a puzzled look. Believe it or not, the ability to recognize oneself in the mirror is pretty advanced, and dogs have yet to demonstrate that they can do it. Some psychologists argue that it is a uniquely human ability, although at least one study has shown that teenage chimpanzees can recognize themselves in a mirror.

When we've developed a sense of self-awareness, we've achieved a state of self-consciousness. Why do I say "developed?" Aren't we aware of ourselves at birth? Actually, it may take up to five or six months for an infant to develop anything even remotely resembling self-consciousness.

The mirror technique is one of the tools that psychologists have used to test infants' and toddlers' levels of self-consciousness. The simplest form of this test involves just setting an infant down in front of a mirror and watching her response. Some researchers have shown that 5- to 6-month-olds will reach out and touch the mirror image, suggesting they think it's another baby, or at least different from them.

In 1979, Michael Lewis and Jeanne Brooks-Gunn conducted a sophisticated version of the mirror test. They applied some blush to the noses of two sets of children — 15- to 17-month-olds and 18- to 24-month-olds. The idea: If the kids look in the mirror and see the blush on their nose, they'll touch it or try to remove it in some way. But this requires the child to realize that the person in the mirror is himself. So what happened? Just a few of the 15- to 17-month-olds actually reached up and touched their noses, but the vast majority of the 18- to 24-month-old children did it. So, these children must have recognized themselves in the mirror.

Showing up in the buff

I used to have this recurring dream where I would find myself naked in some public place. In one of the dreams, I was back in elementary school, and the only thing that I had on was a fur coat, with nothing underneath. I was pretty worried about what these dreams meant. Did I have a fur-coat fetish, or was I just an exhibitionist? I was glad to find out that these dreams were probably about self-consciousness. Each of us has different situations that exemplify feeling extremely self-conscious and exposed. For some people, the situation is public speaking, and for others, it's dancing in a nightclub.

Self-consciousness and self awareness are the same thing. Being self-conscious just means being aware of oneself. But, too much of anything can be bad. Usually when someone says she is "self-conscious" she means that she is aware of some flaw. This is not the type of self-consciousness I am talking about in this section.

- ✔ Body awareness
- ✔ Private self-consciousness
- ✔ Public self-consciousness

Becoming aware of your bod

Body-awareness begins with a simple question: Where do I physically begin, and where do physically I stop? Remember the movie *Malice* with Bill Pullman, Nicole Kidman, and Alec Baldwin? In one scene, Bill and Alec are sitting in bar, and Alec asks Bill to name the part of his body that is most expendable. In other words, Alec wants Bill to choose the part of his body that he could lose without taking a severe blow to his sense of self. If you've seen the movie, you know why he asks this creepy question — it's foreshadowing.

What part of your body is most important to your sense of self? It may sound strange, but being able to tell the difference between your body and someone else's body is crucial to self-consciousness. Think about newborns. The physical connection between a child and a breast-feeding mother is undeniable, and a child's realization of a sense of difference, or separateness, from the mother only develops in time.

Keeping it private

How well do you know yourself? Are you always trying to figure yourself out? The internal focus on your thoughts, feelings, motivations, and overall sense of self is called your *private self-consciousness*. When you "look within," you're privately self-conscious. But if you "look within" a little too much, you're "privately spaced-out."

Showing it off

One day I was leaving for work in the morning, and when I got outside to my car, I realized that I'd forgotten something. So, I did the "big finger snap" and the "one-eye squint," made an about-face, and went back inside. What are these things? They sound like something from a *Seinfeld* episode, but we all know what they are — those behaviors that you do when you forget something. Why did I make these gestures? If I didn't, I'd look like an idiot for walking to my car and then walking back again for no apparent reason. Why did I need a reason? Someone was watching me!

This is the *invisible audience* phenomenon — a sense that we're "on stage" when we're in public and that people are watching us. Teenagers always seem to be "on stage." If they trip over a crack in the sidewalk, they turn bright red and run off giggling. This is an example of our *public self-consciousness* — our sense of ourselves in the presence of others, our public image.

The most noticeable aspect of our public self-consciousness is our awareness and focus on appearances. We don't spend billions of dollars a year on nice clothes, gym memberships, and diets for nothing. Our public self-consciousness is a big part of who we are and how we see ourselves.

Identifying Yourself

One easy way to find out who we are is to ask other people. Our identity is often deeply tied to the way other people see us. When you look into the mirror, what do you see? Have you ever wondered how you look to other people? Do they see the same person who you see in the mirror? When your understanding of your self-concept consists of other people's reactions to and views of you, it's called your *looking-glass self,* one of the most basic concepts of self. We are, after all, social creatures, and it would be hard to argue against the idea that at least part of our self-concept depends on the views of others.

Daniel Stern's theory of self-concept gives us a good look into how we first begin to identify ourselves as a unique "self." From his studies on infants, he proposed that we all are born with an innate ability to become aware of ourselves through a series of experiences.

You are what you do

The most interesting aspect about identity is that, as we grow older, we change the way we define ourselves. Elementary school children often define who they are by the things that they do. Very young children may identify themselves by saying, "I run. I play. I ride my bike." When these children become teenagers there's another shift in how they define themselves.

They use more psychological concepts such as beliefs, motivations, desires, and feelings. "I want to go to the dance," or "I feel very sad today." How do adults define them-selves? Probably by combining both types of self-definition: activity and psychological concepts. "I'm a sad psychologist who can't golf."

Our *emergent self* is with us from birth and basically consists of our subjective experiences of joy, distress, anger, and surprise. Feelings! Our *core self* begins to arise between the ages of 2 and 4 months, when our memories start to form and we develop a sense of our physical capabilities. Next comes the *subjective self*, which emerges when an infant realizes that she can share her experiences with other people. A good example of this is when a baby tries to give you a drink off her bottle before she drinks it. And last but not least, our *verbal self* develops as we use our language ability to organize our sense of who we are.

Arnold Buss again gives us a good look at what *identity* is. Two aspects comprise our identity:

- Personal identity
- Social identity

Forging a personal identity

My *personal identity* consists of those things that make me stand out in a crowd — like my massive biceps and Adonis-like physique. Actually, I'm thinking of something a little more psychological, even though our physical appearances make up part of our identity. According to Buss, our personal identities are comprised of a *public self* and a *private self*, each with their own components. Three important aspects make up our *public self:*

- **Appearance:** As I mention earlier in this chapter in the "Showing it off" section, being aware of our appearance is very much a part of our identity. This is not a uniquely western perspective — cultures all over the world engage in elaborate and sophisticated attempts to improve appearances and enhance personal beauty, as defined by each particular culture. Some philosophers state that a sense of aesthetics is essential for the good life — central to our self-concepts.

- **Style:** James Dean had style! The way he talked, his body language, and his facial expressions were undeniably "Dean." All of us have a peculiar way of speaking and moving. Our handwriting is unique. These things give us a style. Don't get confused by the James Dean example though, style isn't about being "cool." My style is unique to me, whether it's cool or not. It's the "Dr. Cash" style, and no matter what others may say, I think it's pretty cool.

- **Personality:** Personality theories attempt to account for our individuality based on the differences between our personalities. If someone put my personality inside another person's body, would people recognize me? Maybe not at first, but they may eventually start to notice something. People may notice that something is up because our personalities make us unique; they make us identifiable as "me." Our personalities are enduring, and they don't change easily. Because of their consistency and stability, our personalities are good representations of who we are, even if we act different from time to time. Chapters 11 and 12 are all about personality.

Our *private selves* consist of those things that are most difficult for others to see and observe. When a patient comes in for psychotherapy, a psychologist has a difficult time helping him if he refuses to talk about his private self — his thoughts, feelings, and daydreams and fantasies.

- ✔ **Thoughts:** Knowing what someone is thinking is hard, unless he tells you. Some people are better than others at figuring out what people are thinking, but that's really nothing more than a sophisticated guessing process. My thoughts are unique to me.

- ✔ **Feelings:** Mental health professionals often evaluate new patients at psychiatric hospitals with something called the *mental status examination*. The professional observes the patient, partly to figure out how the patient feels. This observable aspect of how someone feels is the *affect*. But what about what the person says? I've often not seen someone's depression even when she tells me that she is extremely sad. This is called *mood,* a person's own private experience of feeling. When patients tell me how they feel, I have to take their word for it. It's pretty hard to tell someone that he's not sad when he tells you he is.

- ✔ **Daydreams/Fantasies:** Who would you be without your daydreams and fantasies? Again, our fantasies are typically private, especially the sexual ones. They are unique to us; they define us.

Carving out a social identity

What's your name? Where are you from? What's your religion? Each of these questions is a component of one aspect of your *social identity* — those things that identify you with a particular societal category. *Group affiliation,* consisting of a person's vocation, things he does for recreation, and cliques. Our social identities are comprised of the following factors that when taken all together equal the social "you."

Kinship

Most of us are aware of how central *kinship* is to our social identity. Our relatives are our "kin," and they often give us our last names. In the United States, last names are legal names and a fairly reliable way to identify people. Although many people have the same name, many more do not. In Arabic culture, a last name is not the primary way to identify someone's kin. Legally, last names are often used for identification, but a person is socially identified by who his father is, and a father is identified by who his oldest son is. Instead of being "Mr. Josef Khoury," an individual would be "Father of Josef"

or "Abu Josef." The son, "Josef Khoury," would be "Son of Josef (the father),"
or "Bin Josef," or "Josef Josef." For more on family, see "Cavorting with Family
and Friends" later in the chapter.

Ethnicity and nationality

Ethnicity is another important aspect of our social identity. Are you White,
African American, Native American, Latino, Other? Often, you can find these
common categories on job and school applications. The categories are rather
arbitrary in name, but they do include a lot of information. Some people are
more comfortable not identifying ethnic differences between people because
they fear discrimination. But, ethnicity is very much a part of who people are
and the culture that they use to structure their lives.

Nationality is not the same as ethnicity. I could be a born-and-raised Canadian
citizen with Japanese ethnicity. Both ethnicity and nationality are important
pieces of information because a Peruvian citizen of Japanese descent may be
a very different person than a Canadian citizen of Japanese descent.

Religious and group affiliations

Religious affiliation is a very important aspect of someone's identity. In Israel,
for example, most of the inhabitants of the city of Nazareth are of Arabic eth-
nicity, but there are two distinct religious groups: Muslims and Christians.
Their religious identity is a core aspect in determining who they are.
Americans also often identify themselves by religious denomination: Roman
Catholic, Presbyterian, Lutheran, Muslim, Jewish, Hindu, and so on.

Group affiliation refers to things such as our vocations and social clubs. Many
people identify themselves by the type of occupation that they hold. "I'm a
fireman!" "I'm a cop!" I'm a psychologist. Still another important dimension of
our identity are the kinds of social clubs and cliques we affiliate with. One
would be pretty hard pressed to deny the strong identification many college
men have with their fraternities. Other people see themselves as "cowboys"
because they strap on boots, jeans, and a cowboy hat and go line dancing at
the local cowboy disco. No matter what you're into, it often gives you a sense
of uniqueness that goes beyond the other aspects of personal identity.

Mustering up some self-esteem

Unfortunately, sometimes having a *looking-glass self* can be a bad thing. (See
"Identifying Yourself" earlier in this chapter.) As long as other people see us
in a good light, all is well. But this is often not the case. Children are sometimes belittled, put down, or verbally abused by their parents. Others don't
hold them in the highest esteem, so, in turn, they often don't hold themselves
very high either.

Sorry for the depressing introduction, but most of us have come to understand the concept of *self-esteem,* an individual's evaluation of her self-worth, through its absence. A lot of us are pretty quick to point out if someone we know has low self-esteem. Have you ever seen the "Self Improvement" section in the local bookstore? It's usually pretty big, and I've yet to find the "You're Already a Great Person!" section at my local bookstore.

Buss provides a good review of six main sources of self-esteem:

- ✔ **Appearance:** We usually feel better about ourselves when we feel attractive. A lot of social psychology research has demonstrated that people judged to be attractive are granted more favors and preferred for social interaction than those who are not. Looking good and feeling good!

- ✔ **Ability and performance:** We feel better about ourselves when we get good grades, perform well at work, and generally are able to do things successfully. The more a person is able to accomplish for his or her self, the more likely he or she is going to feel good about his or her self.

- ✔ **Power:** When we feel like we're in control of our lives, we're more likely to feel good about ourselves. There are at least three sub-sources of the sense of power — dominance, status, and money. Domination can be achieved by coercion, competition, or leadership. Status and money pretty much speak for themselves. I'm not saying that unknown, poor people feel bad about themselves, but they might feel better if they had some status and a bigger bank account.

- ✔ **Social rewards:** Three types of social rewards make us feel good about who we are.

  - • Affection: When people like us

  - • Praise: When someone tells us we're doing a good job

  - • Respect: when others value our opinions, thoughts, and actions

- ✔ **Vicarious sources:** This source of self-esteem is like feeling good about yourself because of things "outside" rather than "inside." *Reflected glory* makes us feel good when we get a boost from being around or being associated with successful, powerful, or popular people. It's the I-know-famous-people form of self-esteem. Having nice material possessions can also make us feel better.

- ✔ **Morality:** Morality involves being a good person and living according to the standards and rules of social conduct. Being a good person never hurts self-esteem. For the most part, morality is a relative term. But, when someone feels that he's taken the moral high ground (however he defines it) in a situation, he is likely to have a more positive self-esteem.

In addition to these sources of self-esteem, some research also suggests that some aspects of personality can make an impact on self-esteem. Shyness and social loneliness both have been found to be associated with a sense of lower self-worth. On the flip side, people who are more optimistic and sociable typically report feeling better about themselves. It seems, then, that being social and having good relationships are important to feeling good about oneself. That brings me to the topic of relationships, as I leave the realm of the isolated self behind.

Getting Attached

Humans are unarguably social creatures. Some of us are very social, while others are less so, but most people have a desire to socialize at least a little bit. In fact, if a person has an extreme disinterest in social interactions, he or she may have a form of mental illness called *schizoid personality disorder*. Personality disorders are tackled in depth in Chapter 16.

The most basic relationship is between two people — husband and wife, brother and sister, friend and friend. How do we cross the divide between our isolated selves and the people in the world around us? Psychologists have approached this problem by looking at what is typically our first relationship, mother and child. I realize that this is not the first relationship for everyone. Some people are raised by their grandparents or by foster parents. So, in actuality, the earliest relationships that we all have are between our primary caregivers and ourselves, and these people may or may not be our mothers.

Even monkeys get the blues

Researchers often analyze the primary relationship between a caregiver and a child by using a concept called *attachment*. John Bowlby is considered the dominant figure in attachment research. (Does that mean he has high self-esteem?) Bowlby's view is that infants are essentially dependent on their caregivers for providing the necessities of life (food, shelter, stimulation, love, and so on). For the most part, infants are helpless, except for their ability to "attach" to and form a relationship with their primary caregiver(s). This connection or attachment ensures that the infant's needs are met. When an infant finds himself in a threatening situation, he attempts to reconnect to his primary caregiver. This is called *attachment behavior* — anything an infant does to attain or maintain closeness to someone seen as better able to cope with the world. A primary caregiver is viewed as an *attachment figure*. If we know that our attachment figures are available when we need them, we feel more secure.

Bowlby viewed attachment as an essential aspect of leading a productive and psychologically healthy life. In fact, when attachment is lacking, infants often suffer from depression, anxiety, and a generally poor psychological well-being. In the 1950s for example, mental health professionals began to investigate the effects of long-term hospitalization and institutionalization on infants, and they documented severe problems. The adverse effects of inadequate or absent care during infancy and early-childhood were undeniable. Children need access to caregivers who they know and whom they are connected to.

In 1959, H. Harlow conducted an interesting experiment with monkeys. He put baby monkeys in a cage with two different dummy versions of mother monkeys. One of the dummies was made of soft-cloth and had no food; the other one was made of wire but had food for the babies to eat. The babies preferred contact with the soft dummy over the wire dummy in spite of the presence of food. Harlow conducted another experiment in which he deprived baby rhesus monkeys of social contact with other monkeys for as long as six months. When these monkeys were released to be with others, their behavior resembled that of a depressed and anxious human with severe levels of withdrawal, self-harming behavior (such as biting themselves), and nervousness.

Attaching with style

It should be undeniable that attachment represents an essential relationship for all of us, but we all know that the ideal and the reality are often two different things, and the area of attachment is no exception. Some of us are in therapy today because of the relationships we had with our primary caregivers. If Bowlby presented us with the ideal, what else is there?

Various *attachment styles* theories address the variations on Bowlby's ideal relationship. They used the *strange situation* technique to determine the nature and extent of children's attachment. In the strange situation, a child and her primary caregiver are put in a room with some toys to play with. Then, the primary caregiver gets up and leaves the room. Researchers observe the child's reaction and record it. After a while, a stranger comes into the room, and the child's reaction is recorded again. Finally, the primary caregiver comes back into the room, and the child's behavior is recorded one last time.

Researchers designed the strange situation to answer the following questions:

- ✔ Does the child use the caregiver as a secure base from which to explore the environment? A *secure base* is a safe place where a child can launch his world explorations.
- ✔ When the caregiver leaves, does the child fuss or react with protest?
- ✔ If there is a protest, is it because the child prefers to be with the caregiver, or is it because the child fears that the caregiver won't return?
- ✔ When the caregiver returns, does the child welcome him or her back, or does the child react in some other, more resentful or distant manner?

The answers to these questions lead to three basic attachment styles:

✔ **Secure:** Securely attached children exhibit the following behavior:

- They use their primary caregiver as a secure base from which to explore their environments.

- They protest a little when their caregiver leaves but eventually calm down, seeming to trust that he or she will return.

- While with strangers or other adults, they're friendly but not overly so.

- Upon reunion, they go to the primary caregiver and seek connection.

✔ **Anxious/ambivalent:** Anxious/ambivalently attached children act in the following ways:

- They do not use their caregivers as secure bases to explore from.

- They sometimes resist initial contact with the caregiver but staunchly resist any attempt to break it off after it has been established.

- They are avoidant or sometimes aggressive in the presence of strangers.

- They cry excessively upon separation and are difficult to console.

✔ **Avoidant:** Avoidant attached children act as follows:

- They seem to need less contact from the caregiver.

- They are indifferent when left alone or cry only because they are alone and not because they seem to miss the caregiver.

- Upon the return of the caregiver, they either avoid or ignore him or her.

Before anybody designs his own little "strange situation" at home to see how much his children love him or not, let me tell you about *goodness-of-fit*. Goodness-of-fit refers to how well the primary caregiver and the child are matched in terms of temperament and personality. This fit can have an effect on attachment style and should be considered before anyone writes himself or herself off as a horrible parent or the "unlovable child."

Caregivers and infants sometimes can look like they're engaged in a harmonious dance, perfectly synchronized with each other. Other times, they may look like they've both got two left feet. If a mother is high strung and energetic, she may not do well with a mellow baby, or vice versa. Remember that the style of interaction and how smooth it goes over is a powerful factor in establishing a secure attachment. So, if you're having trouble and you think that your child is poorly attached, take a look at the style of interaction and see if anything can be done to smooth it out.

Cavorting with Family and Friends

Ever wonder why so many people get depressed during the holidays? Maybe they're not looking forward to going into debt to finance all those gifts. The holidays may remind other people about how lonely they are. I've got an alternative explanation though: The holidays are when a lot of us get together with family. Families are pretty good at embarrassing us in front of our dates by pointing out our weight and receding hairlines or belittling our pitiful salaries. That can pretty depressing! Fortunately, families are good for some things.

A *family* consists of at least two people related by blood, marriage, or adoption. Doesn't it seem like American families have changed over the last 20 years? A lot of American marriages end in divorce. Children are learning to have two sets of parents, half-siblings, and split holidays. Even though the modern face of the family has changed, many of the basic functions of a family have not.

The *McMaster model of family functioning* breaks down six major components of, you guessed it, family functioning:

- **Problem solving:** The family's ability to resolve issues and maintain family functioning.

- **Communication:** The clarity and directness of information exchange in a family. You knew that this one was coming.

- **Roles:** Involves the different behaviors of and responsibilities between each family member, including meeting basic needs, performing household tasks, and providing emotional support and nurturance.

- **Affective responsiveness:** Each of the individual family member's ability to express and experience a wide range, intensity, and quality of emotions.

- **Behavior control:** The rules and standards of conduct. We could never belch at the dinner table in my family.

- **Overall family functioning:** Addresses whether a family can accomplish its daily tasks across the other five areas. If you had to give your family a grade, what would it be?

Parenting with panache

A good friend of mine recently had a baby. Just when I was about to offer him some psychological advice on parenting, he started talking about all the advice people had been giving him and how it bothered him. I kept my opinion to myself. "Crying opens up their lungs." "Don't give them a pacifier." There are almost as many opinions on how to raise your children as there are people on the planet. Fortunately, psychologists have been trying to simplify things.

Children of divorce

There's been a lot of controversy over the effects of divorce on children. Many parents stay together "for the sake of the kids." Most research tends to show that children are not necessarily adversely affected by the divorce of their parents. Boys, though, have been found to do a little worse than girls in the long run. However, the most important predictor of how children will cope with a divorce is the nature of the marriage. If the parents always fight and have a tumultuous relationship while married, the divorce is also likely to go poorly. Researchers often advise couples to not argue or discuss divorce-related issues in front of children and to keep overall conflict to an absolute minimum.

Baumrind took on the task of trying to boil down parenting into something a little more manageable She came up with three main parenting styles: *authoritarian, authoritative,* and *permissive.*

✔ **Authoritarian:** These parents are rigid and dictatorial. Some kids feel like prisoners in their own families — their parents are overly strict, rigid, and don't listen to anything that the children have to say. They're like the drill sergeants of parenting. What they say goes, and there's no discussion about it. Unfortunately, all that toughness tends to backfire. Authoritarian parents tend to have children that are either overly passive or excessively rebellious and sometimes hostile. They could learn a lot from the next style of parenting.

✔ **Authoritative:** These folks tend to approach parenting with a more democratic style. Parents from previous generations often criticize how "today's" parents try to reason with their children too much. "What that kid needs is a good spanking!" Authoritative parents listen to their children and allow them to have input, while maintaining parental authority and control. Children seem to thrive in this environment, and they tend to act more sociable, feel more capable, and be more well-adjusted in general as they grow up.

✔ **Permissive:** There are two types of permissive parents:

• **Indulgent:** Ever been to one of those backyard, beer parties in high school? Well I haven't either, but from what I hear they can get pretty wild. I've always wondered where those kids' parents are. Oh, I get it; they've got the "cool parents." Indulgent parents are involved with their children but shy away from taking an authoritative role and instilling discipline. They sometimes even enable their children to engage in questionable behavior because they don't want to alienate their kids.

• **Indifferent:** These parents are more neglectful. This indifference can be due to many factors, including career, drugs, or self-centeredness. Either way, permissive parents tend to have children who often report feeling ill equipped for dealing with the demands of growing up.

Embracing your rival: Siblings

Ever wonder what siblings are good for? Those of you who are only children may even have fantasized about having a brother or a sister. Some of us think that siblings are only good for fighting or stealing your boyfriend, but psychologists have actually found that there's more to it than that.

Siblings have a powerful effect on our development as people. They create a family environment that would be very different without them. They're also good sources of friendship, companionship, and affection. Sometimes they can even be role models. Three other distinct functions that siblings provide for each other are

- ✔ **Mutual regulation:** Acting as sounding boards and testing grounds for new behavior, like practicing a break-up speech before delivering it to a boyfriend

- ✔ **Direct services:** Easing of household burdens and sometimes providing practical support, such as rides, help with homework, or fashion advice

- ✔ **Dealing with parents:** Siblings often help by forming alliances and coalition building; this involves sticking together in times of need

Many people are familiar with sibling rivalry and discord. Research has shown that the most common negative qualities associated with siblings are antagonism and quarrelling. Some people think that the fighting goes away as we grow older. Actually, the basic emotional character of sibling relationships remains pretty stable. Interactions can change, but the feelings remain much the same.

Getting chummy

How does that old saying go? "Friends are forever?" Or is it "Diamonds are forever?" I never can remember. I don't have many diamonds, so it doesn't really matter much anyway. Throughout this chapter, my intention has been to demonstrate how our social lives grow and expand. I've gone from self, to caregivers, to parents, to siblings, and now I've reached friends. Friendships are important. Why do we remember Tonto's name? Because he's the Lone Ranger's friend.

Psychologists Willard Hartup and Nan Stevens provide us with a nice review of research related to friendship. They basically define *friendship* as a relationship between mutually attracted people engaged in a reciprocal relationship of exchange. Friends are different than non-friends in that our relationships are typically mutual. There's a lot of giving, and taking, and giving again.

Good friends support us and help us cope with all of life's problems. Making friends isn't necessarily easy — it requires a fair amount of social skill. It doesn't hurt if you're socially well-adjusted either. (See Chapter 13 for more on social adjustment.) Being equal and fair helps. Knowing how to manage conflicts when they arise also helps maintain friendships.

Who are our friends? Our friends tend to be people much like ourselves. They are typically similar in age, gender, ethnicity, and ability. A lot of times they have a similar lifestyle. Especially as we get older, our friends tend to be people we work with, which means that they are typically of the same socio-economic class as us as well. Darn, no rich friends for me!

Why do we have friends? To borrow money from, why else? Actually, friendships have been found to have a positive effect on our psychological well-being. People who have good friendships tend to be more sociable, helpful, and confident. Friends are good for your health. So go out there and make a few!

Chapter 13

Knowing Thyself and Knowing Others

*O*ne thing is for sure — we live in a pretty complicated world. The environment is like a symphony made up of a bunch of different instruments, each playing their own little part to create a coherent tune. Our perception of a coherent song depends a lot on our perceptual capabilities. If our perceptual capabilities are not in working order, we may think that the symphony is playing out of tune. Some of the loudest instruments in the symphony that is our environment are other people. They seem to dominate the music, standing out as central aspects of our perceptions of the environment.

What's so special about perceiving the world in an organized manner? Ever been lost in a city without a map? It's not much fun. But fun is the least important reason that makes the ability to organize our perceptions so important. Perceiving the environment in a coherent fashion is necessary for our survival. It seems that human survival has always depended on understanding the complexity of our environment.

Other people make up an extremely powerful force within our environment that is seemingly more important than the weather. Humans are, after all, social beings. Our survival, then, would seem to depend on our ability to understand our human environment, to say nothing of the weather. Social understanding is vital. Alliances, enemies, allocations of resources, divisions of labor, relationships, communication, and self-understanding are important aspects of our social understanding. Each of us must possess a basic level of *social skill* to get along within our human environment. Phillips gives us a good working definition of social skill: the ability to communicate and interact with others in a way that allows for one's needs and goals to be met without interfering with other's goals.

The following sections contain a discussion of four very important social skills: understanding other people's behavior, understanding our own behavior, getting along with and helping other people, and communicating.

People Watching

The area of psychology devoted to understanding how we go about understanding people, including ourselves, is known as *social cognition.* The word cognition is used because the focus is on the specific thought processes involved when we observe people and make inferences about them based on those observations.

We are always people watching. Have you ever gone to a public place like a park or a busy shopping mall and just watched people? It can be pretty interesting. You may notice people's clothes, the bags that they're carrying, the conversations that they're having, and so on. You're noticing all kinds of things about them and using those observations to draw conclusions.

Don't think so? How many times have you called the young guy in the business suit driving a BMW a yuppie? Have you ever said to yourself that the teenager with purple hair and a pierced nose is just looking for attention? How do you know these things? Maybe, the yuppie is really a well-dressed car thief, or that the purpled-headed kid is conducting a psychology experiment. How do you know? Have you had a conversation with them? Probably not, but you don't have to talk to them in order to begin drawing conclusions about them based on what you see, hear, and experience.

The complex process of drawing conclusions about people's intentions and characteristics, based on our observations of them, is called *person perception.* We all use some assumptions in the person-perception process:

- ✔ We assume that people are *causal agents* — they play an active part in producing their own behavior. This statement seems like a no-brainer, but do we assume that a cloud floats across the sky because it caused itself to float? Do weeds grow in my flowerbed because they want to, just to irritate me? I hope not; they would be some pretty rude weeds if they did. The point is that when we see someone acting in a particular way, we often infer that they intended to do so. (See Chapter 1 for more on figuring out why people do what they do.)

- ✔ Another automatic assumption in the person-perception process is that we think that other people are like us, thinking and feeling in the same ways as we do. Thinking like this allows us to use ourselves in trying to understand other people. I know I cry when I'm sad, like when the Yankees lost the World Series in 2001. So, when I see someone else crying, I assume that they're crying because they're sad too, and maybe they saw the Yankees lose as well.

As a scientist of human behavior and mental processes, I know how difficult it can be to understand and organize my observations of other people. Psychologists have come up with specialized techniques and instruments to measure and organize their observations. Barker and Wright felt that behavior is like a river, with its continuous stream of actions connected without any apparent seam. It would be pretty hard to take one piece out of a river. So, how do we take a piece out of the stream of human behavior, the *behavioral stream?* Newston and Engquist stated that we all possess the natural ability to select "breakpoints," or freeze-frames, of behavior as natural informational units.

We pull out samples of people's behavior that appear to have separate intentions. This is kind of like looking at someone's hair and seeing the mass of it move in unison. We don't assume that each strand moves to the beat of its own drummer; they all move in response to the movement of the head as a whole. Maybe a better way of looking at it is to think about watching a football game. Is it easier to pay attention to the players on the front line who move like a big, mindless mass or the quarterback, running-back, or wide receiver who moves independently of the line? We notice the "independent movers."

We also have a natural tendency to notice abrupt shifts or changes in behavior. (See Chapter 16 for more on changes in behavior.) If someone walking toward us gradually moves in our direction, we're less likely to notice the movement than if the person jumps 3 feet to the side in our direction. Behaviors that stand out are more likely to be noticed.

Explaining others

Trying to explain other people's behavior is pretty hard to do. You can't look inside their minds and can only guess as to what's going on in there. This doesn't stop people from trying to explain others' actions.

Judging on the fly

Have you ever experienced love at first sight? I've always wondered how that works. How can you fall in love with somebody based on just looking at him or her? Maybe research in the area of *snap judgments* can help answer that question. Snap judgments of people are instantaneous, automatic, and unconscious evaluations.

We base our snap judgments on two types of cues:

- ✔ **Static cues:** Things that are relatively unchanging about a person like their appearance, gender, and body-type (not including clothing). We use this information to make *evaluative judgments* about the person. These judgments can be right or wrong. I might evaluate a person wearing a bow tie as fun-loving and easy going, or I might see him as nerdy and uptight. Either way, I'm using an aspect of someone's physical appearance to make a judgment about what kind of person he or she is.

✔ **Dynamic cues:** Things that tend to change depending on the situation, such as facial expressions and mannerisms. When I see a smile, I might evaluate that person as generally happy, or I might think that he or she just heard a funny joke. The point is that we use relatively basic information to make snappy evaluations of people's personalities or about their lives.

Making an impression

Snap judgments are really just the beginning of our attempts to figure other people out. We all make snap judgments, even though we're often unaware of doing so. In the process of *impression formation,* we go beyond snap judgments and make more in-depth inferences about the kind of person that someone is. Consider the following adjectives describing a person: hardworking, tense, skillful, cold, industrious. What kind of person is this? Regardless of your conclusion, you are attempting to pull these words together, based on your experience and knowledge, in a way that paints a summary picture.

Solomon Asch came up with a popular theory of impression formation that focused on the existence of *central traits* that color our interpretations and the meanings of other observed traits. It's like we have an internal sense that certain traits go together. For example, an attractive person may have an easier time getting someone to help him or her change a flat tire than an unattractive person. This is probably because we assume that the attribute of attractiveness is automatically connected to the attribute of gratefulness. I'm not going to help an unattractive, ungrateful person change his tire.

Implicit personality theory

Bruner and Tagiuri considered our internal sense of traits that belong together as part of an *implicit personality theory.* We learn that certain traits go together because we've either been told that they go together or we observe them going together. I was told a thousand times that polite people don't interrupt, so I guess I'm pretty rude because I interrupt all the time. Interrupting and rudeness "belong" together in my implicit personality theory.

Basically, implicit personality theories are stereotypes. Stereotypes are an inevitable consequence of our attempt to make sense of our social world. Stereotypes are like shortcuts for thinking. We couldn't possibly store independent evaluations of every single person that we've ever met. This would take up way too much space in our memories. Instead, we categorize people, and sometimes this categorization results in the formation of stereotypes. Unfortunately, in our attempt to simplify the world, we often over-generalize negative aspects of people, which too often leads to prejudice and racism.

Figuring out the causes of others' behavior

We not only make snappy judgments about people based on limited information, but we also attempt to determine why people did what they did or what caused a particular behavior. According to Heider, all of us have a tendency to perceive behavior as either being caused by the person herself (internal cause) or by the environment (external cause).

The last time I went to Las Vegas, I witnessed an elderly woman win a progressive jackpot of $50,000. As I stood back and watched people crowd around her, I heard her telling her new-found fan club all about her strategy. I couldn't help but laugh, thinking that her strategy had nothing to do with it. It was pure luck. In that situation, I attributed her success to an external, environmental cause, the programming of the particular slot machine she was using. She attributed it to her skill. Maybe she should write *Slot Machines For Dummies*.

When making an attribution, we tend to focus on three important pieces of information:

- ✔ **Consistency:** People generally behave in the same way across different situations. That same behavior gives us a sense of their consistency. When someone exhibits a consistent behavior, we attribute that behavior to his or her personality. Something internally belonging to that person causes the behavior. The more inconsistent someone is, the more we attribute the behavior to the circumstance. I don't lose in Las Vegas because I am a loser; I lose because of the circumstance. I hope.

- ✔ **Distinctiveness:** I used to think a buddy of mine had a real problem with women. Before I knew it, he always got slapped and shuffled back over to complain to me. It was only after I saw how he treated other people, including men, that I realized he was lousy with everyone. His behavior was distinct because he acted the same with all people. He responded to all people in the same way, not just specific people. Because his behavior did not vary by context or environment, it was probably an internal trait.

- ✔ **Consensus:** When Tom goes to the movies, he buys popcorn and a soda, gives his ticket to the usher, finds a seat, sits down, faces forward, doesn't talk, and watches the movie. What does this tell you about Tom? Absolutely nothing. Why? Probably because Tom is engaging in typical moviegoer behavior. There's a consensus that all people act in a particular way when going to the movies. This leads me to consider that Tom's behavior is due to the situation. If Tom stood up and started screaming when the movie came on, he would be acting outside of the consensus and thus possibly showing more of his true personality through this unique act.

Numerous possible combinations of these three pieces of information exist: high consistency, high distinctiveness, low consensus, and so on. Consistently we find that the combination of high consistency, low distinctiveness, and low consensus leads to a *personal attribution* (internal cause or explanation for their behavior). When I act consistently across situations, respond to the same stimuli the same way every time, and act differently than other people in that same situation, it's probably me. High consistency, high distinctiveness, and high consensus lead to an external attribution. When I act the same across situations, but I respond differently to the same stimuli, and everyone else is doing it, it's probably the situation or the external environment. So what would you attribute my passion for polka music to? Doesn't everyone love polka?

Making mistakes

With all of this judging going on, it begs the question of whether or not we're accurate in our attributions. A consistent mistake that all of us make is called the *fundamental attribution error*. Most of the time we underestimate the role of external causes as determinants of other people's behavior. We have a tendency to see what they do as inherent to them, as actor-caused. We may think that because we lack significant information about their behavior across situations, and so when in doubt, we attribute it to the actor. The more information we have, the better judges we become.

We also have a tendency to see our own behavior as due to external causes more than we see other people's behavior as due to external causes (Jones and Nisbett). Again, this tendency probably exists because we have access to more information when it comes to ourselves. We also tend to attribute our successes to internal causes and our failures to external causes, and vice versa for other people. If I had won the $50,000 jackpot in Vegas, I'd probably do the same thing as the elderly woman who won — attribute the win to my innate ability to pull a slot handle really well. And she'd probably sit back and laugh at me, thinking it was all luck.

Explaining yourself

Do the famous people who endorse products on television commercials actually use the products they promote? Does Michael Jordan really wear that brand of underwear? Does Tiger Woods really drive the car he endorses? Maybe they do, and maybe they don't. I don't know Michael or Tiger, so all I can do is guess. But let's just say for the sake of discussion that they do use the products they endorse. If I asked them why they endorse those products, what would they say, and what would these responses tell us about how well they know themselves?

Festinger and Carlsmith performed a classic experiment that gives us some insight into the "Tiger Woods question." They asked research subjects to perform a dull and boring task and then offered the subjects money to tell other people that the task was really interesting. There were two groups. One group was paid $1 each, and the other was paid $20 each. The subjects that received only $1 reported that the task was more interesting than the $20 subjects did when asked about their true feelings, as opposed to their "endorsement" feelings. The $20 created a larger gap between the subjects' actions and what they thought they felt. This experiment demonstrates *cognitive dissonance,* the process of changing one's beliefs to match one's actions. If I do something that contradicts my beliefs, I will alter my beliefs to match my behavior.

The subjects that were paid $1 must have figured that, if they were only getting bribed with one measly dollar, they must not have been so bored after all. The bigger the bribe, the more we perceive the task as being contrary to our true beliefs. In this case, the extra money represents an easy explanation for our behavior.

What does this tell us about our famous product endorsers? If they do use the products they endorse, they may do so because they don't want to admit that they only endorse the products for the money. Michael Jordan may not want to admit to himself that he really doesn't find his underwear comfortable because he loves the money that the manufacturer gives him to say that they are. So, he may change his attitude to match his behavior. In fact, I really don't know why MJ wears a particular brand of underwear, but it serves as a good illustration.

Cognitive dissonance tells us a lot about how we know things about ourselves and engage in the process of *self-attribution.* Daryl Bem developed a theory of self-perception that states that we know our own attitudes by drawing inferences based on observing our own behavior in the same way that we observe others. We know ourselves in the same way we know others — by observing behavior. When faced with dissonance between what we do and what we believe, we often change our belief because we use observations of our external behavior as a way to know what we believe.

When trying to figure ourselves out and judge our own behavior, a lot of us are guilty of some pretty interesting distortions. Three particularly interesting distortions are

- ✔ **False consensus effect:** This distortion is a tendency to overestimate how common our opinions and behaviors are, especially the undesirable ones. "Everyone's doing it!" We tend to see a consensus that is consistent with our opinion, whether or not one exists. I bought bright pink high-top sneakers in sixth grade because I thought that they would be the next big thing. They lasted one school day.

- ✔ **False uniqueness effect (FUE):** There's a saying in Alcoholics Anonymous, "You're terminally unique!" The phrase is used for people who think that their problems are so different from everyone else's that no one could possibly understand them. The FUE is the tendency to underestimate how common one's beliefs are, especially the desirable ones. After I tossed my bright pink shoes, I went out and bought a totally unique pair of $100 kicks. Can you imagine my shock when I saw every other kid at school wearing the same shoes?

✔ **Self-handicapping:** When I was in college and I knew I had a tough test coming up, one that I was pretty sure I was going to fail no matter how much I studied, I wouldn't study for it at all. That way, when I failed it, I could blame it on not studying instead of my lack of ability or intelligence. When people create excuses for failure in order to protect their self-esteem or self-image, they're engaging in self-handicapping. Sometimes I think professional athletes do this. If they drop the game-winning pass, they may fall on the ground and pretend that they're injured or cry to the referee that the defender interfered with them. Yeah, yeah, yeah — we know you blew it, plain and simple. But you're the one that's got to live with yourself.

Communicating Is Easier Said Than Done

One of Ronald Reagan's nicknames was "The Great Communicator." Supposedly, he could really get his point across, and people really responded to his speeches. I personally haven't taken the time to analyze Reagan's communication skills. But whether you're the president of the United States or just trying to order a hamburger at the local drive-thru, communication skills are vital to being a socially skilled person.

Hargie, Saunders, and Dickson developed a model of *interpersonal communication* that identified several important components of the communication process. Each person involved in a communication brings with them particular motives, knowledge, attitudes, personality characteristics, and emotions to the situation that influence the communication process. Different situations bring about different styles or aspects of communication. I may communicate differently if I'm in a formal setting, as opposed to an informal one. I usually refrain from profanity in a job interview for example but use it readily when watching a sporting event.

All episodes of communication are goal directed, and several goals may be pursued simultaneously. A conversation varies as a function of the intended goal. If my goal is to visit with an old friend, I may talk about different things than if I'm conducting a psychological evaluation.

There are also several *mediating processes* that shape the communication process. Any psychological process that affects the meeting of a communicative goal or the outcome of communication can be a mediating process. One important processes is called *focusing* (what one pays attention to), which can have a major impact. How you connect current conversational information with previous knowledge is also important, and *inference* — going beyond the surface information being communicated — is also important.

Another important aspect of the communication process is *feedback* — information provided to me by the other person about how effectively I am communicating — and how I use it. I use this feedback to change the way I communicate to better meet the conversation goals. Some people seem to just ramble on, oblivious to signals from the other person in the conversation that they're not making any sense. These people are not picking up on the feedback. Here's a hint: When someone falls asleep while you're talking to her, that's important feedback.

Being a great communicator involves being good at three specific communication skills: asking questions, explaining, and listening.

Asking questions

An important feature of all effective communication is the process of *questioning* (Hargie, Saunders, and Dickson). Questions are a good way to open a conversation, gather information, and express to the other person that I am interested in what he's talking about. There are several different types of questions. "Where were you on the night of November 12 at 10:00 p.m.?" Just a little advice if the police ask you this question — call a lawyer. This example is a *recall* question, asking you to remember basic information. Other questions ask the responder to analyze, evaluate, or problem solve. *Closed-ended* questions require just a yes or no or identification response. *Open-ended* questions require description and elaboration.

There's an art to being a good questioner. Giving the responder a context and structure to frame the question within often helps. You might start out by saying, "I have three main questions." Something like that often helps. The point is to clue the person in to what you are talking about, kind of like providing a conversational roadmap of sorts. Sometimes we need a cue to answer a question appropriately; this is called *prompting and reviewing*. Previous statements can also help the respondent.

Explaining

In addition to being good at questioning, the gift of gab often requires a certain level of skill at explaining oneself. Explanations provide information, clarify, and are often used to demonstrate a point.

When making a point in a conversation, an individual can often bolster his or her argument by providing a solid explanation for the position being taken. Good explanations are clear, focused, and linked to the listener's knowledge base. Being brief and avoiding a lot of "ums," "ers," and "ya'knows" also helps. These terms interrupt the fluency of the communication and can lead to people losing interest.

Sometimes it helps to pause and review so that the listener can organize and absorb what has already been explained. It's also very important to use language that is appropriate to the audience or listener. If you're too technical, too gross, or too basic, you may lose their interest.

Listening

A third very important aspect of effective communication is listening. One-way conversations are poor excuses for communication. If no one is listening, there's no "co" in communication. Hargie, Saunders, and Dickson give a few hints to being a good listener:

- ✔ Be physically prepared and prepare the environment. Turn off the radio; reduce extraneous noise. Sit so that you can hear the person speaking.

- ✔ Be aware of your biases and preconceived ideas and mentally prepare yourself to pay attention.

- ✔ Keep yourself focused by asking yourself questions in your mind about what the speaker is talking about.

- ✔ Don't interrupt if you can help it.

- ✔ Mentally identify the main point of the speaker's communication and organize what he or she is telling you into categories like who, what, when, why, and how.

- ✔ Don't use *blocking techniques,* such as denying someone's feelings or changing the topic.

- ✔ Maintain eye contact.

- ✔ Nod.

- ✔ Orient your body toward the speaker and maintain an open posture. Don't cross your arms or turn away.

- ✔ Don't fidget or fool with stuff around you. Doing your taxes while someone is talking is a dead giveaway that you're not really listening.

Asserting yourself

One of the most common problems I see in my clinical practice is that people don't know how to stand up for themselves and communicate their needs in a direct and confident manner. Complaints about pushy coworkers, jerky bosses, and grouchy spouses are commonly the result of a lack of assertiveness. For some people, assertiveness seems to come naturally; they're just good at telling people what they think in a way that doesn't put anybody off.

I'm not talking about being aggressive — that often involves a certain level of hostility and a denial of the other person's rights in the interaction. I am talking about something a little milder than aggression, *assertiveness.*

Assertiveness can be defined as standing up for one's rights and expressing one's thoughts, feelings, and beliefs, in a direct, honest, and appropriate manner that respects others. Ever have someone cut in line while you were at the grocery store? Did you tell them to go to the end of the line, or did you keep your thoughts to yourself only to get mad later on, wishing you had said something? What about ordering food at a restaurant and getting something you didn't order? Did you just eat it anyway or did you send it back? It sounds easy, but a lot of people won't say anything for fear of being seen as a jerk, being disliked, or hurting the other person's feelings.

Assertiveness is a social skill that you can learn. Typically, when people get better at being assertive, the overall quality of their relationships improves. They no longer feel that they can't say what they really think or that they have to keep quiet for the sake of friendships. When people learn how to communicate assertively, they awaken to a whole new realm of possibilities in communication.

Want to be more assertive? *Basic assertions* are expressions such as "No, I don't like that movie" or "Thank you but I've had enough fruitcake." *Empathic assertions* are statements used to convey that you understand the other person's position even if you're not going along with it. "I understand that you prefer fast food over Italian, but I'm really craving spaghetti." When someone begins with a basic assertion and then progresses into more straightforward statements with little ambiguity, she engages in *escalating assertiveness.* This is a good skill to use with pushy salespeople, as this example demonstrates:

> **Salesperson:** Can I help you find something?
>
> **Customer:** No thanks.
>
> **Salesperson:** Well, we've got these great deals in women's apparel today.
>
> **Customer:** Really, I'm not interested.
>
> **Salesperson:** How about. . . .
>
> **Customer:** For the third time, can you please leave me alone? I don't want your help!

A final useful tool in being assertive is to use "I language" — making statements from a personal position rather than pointing out the other person's behavior and using the "you" word. Instead of telling my boss that he's been hounding me and he's starting to tick me off, I may say, "I feel that you've put unfair pressure on me compared to the other employees. When I perceive that happening, I feel angry." Easier said than done I know, but it works pretty well. Try it!

Fry developed a quick list of verbal defense strategies that can be used against manipulative and rude people:

- **Broken record:** Simply repeating oneself over and over again. "I said no! What part of no don't you understand? I'll say it again. No! No!"

- **Fogging:** Agreeing with what someone is saying but not changing one's position. "You're right, I should watch what I eat. I have gained a few pounds." All the while thinking to yourself, "I'm going to eat whatever I darn well feel like eating."

- **Meta-level:** Taking a conversation to a more abstract level than encompassed in the original conversation. "I think this is a good example of how hard it can be to get one's point across. I've often wondered how we could get past this." I like to call this the old therapist switch-a-roo! "What is the ideal weight anyway? Being heavy used to be a sign of beauty and prosperity. I'm just beautiful and prosperous, not fat."

Chapter 14

Conforming Like a Contortionist: Social Psychology

I'll never forget the time that I saw news footage of two groups of Buddhist monks fist-fighting for control over a monastery. I was shocked to see people who I stereotypically thought of as peaceful acting so violently. The image was disturbing, but also a strong demonstration of how our individual behavior can be overpowered by a situation or by the force of a group. These typically peaceful individuals seemingly were overcome by the situation, some of them engaging in behavior that they themselves could not explain if asked.

Psychology would be incomplete without taking into account the social influences on why we do what we do. We're pushed and pulled by the dynamics of our personalities. We act instinctively based on our genetic makeup. Our behavior varies as a function of how we think about things, and we're subject to social influences as well.

Social psychology is the study of the social causes of and influences on our behavior. The power of these forces is not to be underestimated, as this chapter demonstrates. The study of these social influences completes the final aspect of the biopsychosocial model of human behavior. (See Chapter 1 for more on the biopsychosocial model.) Social psychologists have long suggested that many of the answers to the question of human behavior lie in understanding such things as our group norms, gender roles, conformity, and group pressure. This chapter explores some of the social influences on our behavior and how being around other people has a powerful effect on our individual behavior.

Playing Your Part

Unless you're a hermit, and you live in a shack in the middle of the desert, you exist within a *social matrix* — a multi-layered configuration of social relationships ranging from parent-child to coworker-coworker relationships. Picture yourself in the middle of a huge multi-ringed circle with each ring representing a level of social organization.

Each of these circles carries a set of expected behaviors, rules that dictate what each individual is supposed to do. Each social group's rules or behavioral expectations are called *norms.* Cultures have norms, families have norms, and even subcultures have norms. A subculture may consist of a small social group, often organized around a recreational activity. A gang may be considered a subgroup with its own subculture. Gangs have their own language, clothing styles, and rituals that delineate clear rules for the behavior of each individual member.

Americans prefer to see themselves as rugged individuals; we wince at the idea of following norms. But norms are not all that bad. They simplify complex social situations, allowing us to think of things other than how we should act and what we should say. Social situations operate more smoothly when norms are clear. Argote for example, found that groups that work together do so more efficiently and effectively when there are clear and agreed-upon norms.

I think you would be pretty hard pressed to find a culture in this world that has a norm of punching someone in the face upon greeting that individual. In fact, some norms seem to be universal, unlike punching someone in the face. Brown in 1965 found that people almost universally speak more respectfully to others of higher status and more casually to those of lower status. This manner of addressing others can even be seen in the structure of some languages, such as Spanish or French, in which the way a verb is conjugated depends on how well you know the person you're speaking to.

Certainly, universal norms exist, but some variations exist as well. If you're a Palestinian Christian, you'll firmly resist any food offered to you while visiting someone's home and only accept after much counter-insistence by the host. Americans on the other hand, may even ask for something to eat or drink without thinking twice. Another common variation in a cultural norms concerns waiting in line. Some cultures don't seem to appreciate the orderliness of waiting in a single-file line when ordering food at a fast-food establishment, but others do. The norm of *personal space* (the physical space or area around us) too can vary by culture. Some cultures seem to need less personal space than others.

A *role* is a specific type of norm that defines how a person should act in a specific situation. Each of us has certain roles we play (student, employee, brother, sister, parent, and so on) that dictate different behaviors for different situations. Typically, there are clear roles to be played. A classic example of these clear rules being bent is when a parent tries to be a "friend" to their teenage child. Being a parent is not the same thing as being a friend, and when the lines are blurred, the so-called parent is violating the parental norm. Of course this begs the question as to why an adult would want a wacky teenager for a friend in the first place.

A powerful role that determines our individual behavior is our *gender role* — the behavioral expectations outlined for males and females. Boys wear blue; girls wear pink. Boys are tough; girls are soft. Girls are caring; boys are selfish. The list goes on and on. Society is full of gender roles that determine appropriate behavior for girls and boys. I always get a kick out of watching old movies where the women had to sit sidesaddle when riding a horse. Apparently, it wasn't lady-like for a woman to spread her legs in order to straddle the horse. I guess they didn't have many female rodeo stars back then — it would be pretty hard to ride a bull sitting sidesaddle.

A lot of changes have occurred in the definitions of gender roles over the years. Men with earrings or men wearing makeup are good examples. Women wearing pants? The nerve! Today, women routinely work outside of the home, and I've even seen a man cry once or twice. He must have had something in his eye. Regardless of the specifics of each gender role, we are a long way off from androgynous roles for both men and women.

Getting carried away

Role definitions are a powerful determinant of our behavior, and the definitions sometimes overpower our individual personalities and preferences. In 1972, Phil Zimbardo conducted a famous experiment known as the *Stanford prison experiment* that illustrated the power of roles. College students were recruited to participate in a mock-prison situation in which they were randomly assigned to be either guards or inmates. The experiment took place in a makeshift prison in the basement of the psychology building at Stanford University.

Each of us seems to naturally know what the roles of both inmate and guard entail. Zimbardo had to discontinue the experiment within a week because of what he saw happening. The otherwise normal and healthy college students began to take their roles far too seriously. The guards treated the inmates inhumanely and with harsh disdain, and the inmates began to truly hate the guards and focus only on the circumvention of the "prison" system and survival. In other words, they really got caught up in their roles and forgot about the reality of the situation.

Ganging Up in a Group

In a classic episode of the *Twilight Zone,* everyone gets plastic surgery when they reach adolescence, and everyone picks the same transformation so that everyone looks the same, Ken for the men and Barbie for the women. One girl decides to keep her natural look and is subsequently tormented and ridiculed for wanting to do so. She was under enormous pressure to conform, to give into group pressure, and to go along. Groups exert all kinds of pressure on their individual members. Sometimes groups have explicit rules that keep people in line. Other times the rules or pressures are subtle.

Conforming

Conformity is defined as a change in behavior that results from real or perceived group pressure. Much to people's surprise, we conform a lot more than we think. How many purple houses are there on your block? Not many I bet.

In an old study from 1937, Sherif looked at how people would change their judgments based on the answers of other people. Subjects were asked to estimate how far a light moved across a dark room. Sherif found that, when other people were present and offered a different estimate, the subject would change his or her answer to be closer to the others. The other people's answers influenced the subject. Asch in 1955 found the same thing when he put people in a group and asked them to estimate the lengths of lines. Subjects changed their answers to go along with the group consensus. Both of these experiments are good examples of how an individual will conform under group pressure, even if the pressure is subtle.

Obedience is an extreme form of conformity, often involving going against one's better judgment or truest intentions. When I think of obedience, visions of dog-obedience school pop into my head — me standing there with a leash around my neck, jumping up to get my treat for performing the requested trick. Sounds extreme doesn't it.

Most of us would like to think that we would walk out of an experiment in which we had to torture someone with electric shocks. The majority of subjects in one famous study didn't stop applying the shock treatment in just such a case (see the "Shocking, no?" sidebar in this chapter). Why? Eight factors have been identified that seem to increase conformity and obedience:

> ✔ **Emotional distance from the victim:** The more personal contact someone has with an individual, the less likely he is to act without compassion. It's harder to be cruel when the victim has a face.

- ✔ **Proximity and legitimacy of the authority:** When an authority figure is close by, obedience is more likely. The authority also has to be seen as legitimate. We're more likely to be obedient to an individual that we see as possessing genuine authority, as opposed to a poseur.

- ✔ **Institutional authority:** When an authority figure is part of an accepted institution, obedience is more likely. I'm more likely to comply with the suggestions of a judge than some guy sitting next to me at the bus stop. Recognized institutional authority has a powerful effect on obedience.

- ✔ **Group size:** Groups of three to five people have a maximum effect on conformity pressure, any less or more than this, and the effect is less powerful.

- ✔ **Unanimity:** When groups are in complete agreement, it's more difficult for a single individual to resist conforming.

- ✔ **Cohesiveness:** The more a group feels that it is bound together and tightly organized, the more power the group has over its members. I used to play softball on a team without uniforms, and it just didn't feel right. We needed uniforms to be a "real" team. Uniforms are one way to increase cohesiveness because when we look the same we have a sense of unity.

- ✔ **Status:** People with higher status have more influence.

- ✔ **Public response:** People conform more when their behaviors are made public. It's easier to disagree privately or anonymously.

Shocking, no?

Stanley Milgram, in 1965, conducted an obedience experiment that borders on the extreme. Subjects were seated at a control panel with a switch for delivering electrical shocks to a "subject" on the other side of a partition. The "subjects" were actually experimenters pretending to be participating as real subjects. The premise: The "subject" is to be shocked each time that he or she gets a question wrong. With each subsequent wrong answer, the shock gets stronger and stronger. The shocks start at 75 volts and go up to 450 volts. At some point, the "subject" is yelling and pleading with the real subject to stop administering the shock. An experimenter stands next to the real subject with a clipboard and a white lab-coat insisting that the real subject continue with the experiment and continue to administer shocks, despite the "subject's" protests and obvious pain.

Actually, the "subjects" did not receive any shock at all; they only pretended to get shocked. Now ask yourself, "When would I have stopped giving the shocks?" Maybe you think that you would have stopped the second the "subject" started yelling and asking you to stop. I'm sure the subjects in Milgram's study thought the same thing. However, the shocking (sorry about that one) outcome was that 63 percent of the real subjects went all the way to 450 volts in compliance (or obedience) with the experimenter. Now that's pretty obedient!

Although conformity and obedience are not necessarily bad things, learning how to resist both may be important, just in case. Nazi Germany is perhaps one of the most horrific examples of the dangers of conformity. I contend that maintaining a degree of individual diversity is important in any social group. The best way to prevent conformity may be to maintain a sense of and respect for human uniqueness. Freedom of speech and religious tolerance are also good protections against conformity. As long as people feel comfortable being themselves and they can freely speak their minds, conformity is a little more difficult.

Doing better with help

"There's no I in TEAM!" A lot of coaches use this line in their pep talks, trying to convey the idea that the better a team plays together, the better their results will be. Social psychologists have found that this idea is true to a certain extent. When we're in the presence of others, we're more aroused and energized, and dominant behaviors are strengthened. This phenomenon is called *social facilitation.*

Robert Zajoncin found that when we do something relatively simple and routine, being in the presence of others improves our performance. But when a task is complex, having others around can hinder our performance. So, it may be a good idea to conduct that calculus contest somewhere other than Madison Square Garden. Although, tug of war is probably okay.

Kicking back

When I was in junior high school, teachers often asked me to participate in group projects. It usually went something like this: Four less-motivated students would pair up with the smart kid and let the smart kid do all of the work. These motivationally challenged pupils would then ascribe their names to the project in order to get the credit. This is an example of *social loafing —* the tendency for people to put out less energy and effort when engaged in a group task that ignores individual accountability.

Psychologists Latane, Kipling, Williams, and Harkins found, for example, that when people were put in groups of six and instructed to clap as loud as they possibly could, the amount of noise produced was less than that of one person clapping alone. People "loaf" when engaged in activities as groups. These loafers are *free riders* who rest on the efforts of other people in the group, kind of like those people who just mouth the words in the school choir. Hey, if I'm not being watched, then why should I exert myself? I won't get credit for my individual effort anyway.

Remaining anonymous

Ever wonder why groups of people who do really awful things often wear uniforms? Take the Ku Klux Klan for example. What's with the pointy hats? Researchers have found that diminishing individual identity and diffusing individual responsibility reduces people's inhibitions. This reduction of inhibitions can result in people doing things that they may not do if they were alone or more easily identifiable. When this happens, they become *deindividuated.*

A certain amount of freedom seems to accompany blending into a crowd or being anonymous. Maybe, we're less afraid of getting caught. Children have been found to steal more when they are deindividuated. It seems that anonymity and a lack of unique identification facilitate antisocial behavior — something to think about when you consider how anonymous American society really is. Some of us don't even know our next-door neighbors.

Thinking as one

Groups can have both positive and negative effects on individual behavior. We may perform some tasks better when working within a group and be lazier while performing others. In 1971 Janis introduced another potentially adverse effect of group participation, a phenomenon known as *groupthink.* When groups work to suppress disagreement and dissent in order to maintain group harmony, they are engaged in groupthink.

Dissent can sometimes threaten the cohesiveness of a group. When people start expressing ideas contrary to the group's views, the group sometimes reacts negatively. Galileo was one of the most famous victims of groupthink in history. He discovered evidence regarding the solar system that challenged the prevailing thought of the day. Did he receive high praise and honors? Not quite! He was locked away in prison for being a heretic, a dissenter.

Groups work hard, both consciously and unconsciously, to prevent dissent. Janis identified eight symptoms of groupthink that can be present in a group:

- ✔ **Illusion of invulnerability:** When groups think they are untouchable, they're more likely to squash dissent.

- ✔ **Belief in the group's moral superiority:** When a group thinks it is ultimately moral, it'll ignore its own immorality.

- ✔ **Rationalization:** A group becomes more close-minded as it collectively justifies its actions.

- ✔ **Stereotyping the opponent:** When an opponent is viewed in biased or prejudiced terms, statements that contradict the group's views are ignored.

- ✔ **Conformity pressure:** There is strong pressure on individuals to go along with the group's will and to not disagree; otherwise, they'll be cast out.

- ✔ **Self-censorship:** Group members keep their dissenting opinions to themselves rather than rock the boat.

- ✔ **Illusion of unanimity:** Internal dissent is kept out of sight and away from the group's view; therefore, dissent appears not to exist.

- ✔ **Mindguards:** Some group members take an active role in protecting the group from dissent or contrary information. They're like the "thought police" in George Orwell's book, *1984.*

Groupthink can cause a lot of problems. Alternatives to the status quo may go unexamined, thus preventing a complete survey of any problem at hand. Risks may be ignored. Overall, the decisions that a group makes can be compromised.

Some ways to avoid groupthink are to

- ✔ Encourage everyone to express their opinions and viewpoints

- ✔ Invite outside people in to give alternative viewpoints

- ✔ Assign individual group members to play the devil's advocate role

Persuading

The power of persuasion is something I think we all wish we had a little more of. The greatest example of this power comes from a movie series, *Star Wars.* Jedi warriors possessed the ability to influence the thoughts of others by using "the force." It was called the "Jedi mind trick." I think the car salesman who sold me my last car used the Jedi mind trick on me. He used the dark side of the force I think.

Persuasion is a powerful force in all social interactions and arrangements. People don't just use it to sell products. Persuasion is used in a wide variety of applications, from formal to informal. There are two paths to persuasion:

- ✔ **Central route:** The central route occurs when the "persuadee" actively processes the potentially persuasive information. Verplanken in 1991 found that when people think deeply about something, any associated change in attitude or opinion is more likely to stay changed.

- ✔ **Peripheral route:** This communication is less direct than the central route and involves associating the intended message with other images, sometimes positive and sometimes negative. Classic examples are using Fabio to sell a butter substitute or hard-bodied models to sell gym memberships. The peripheral route is not direct and requires substantially less thinking. The persuaders are counting on our minds' natural ability to associate things. Remember classical conditioning? (If not, check out Chapter 8.)

Psychologists Petty and Caccioppo warn that if you're going to try to persuade people, don't warn them that it's coming. Distracting them helps because they won't be able to mount a counter-argument to your claims. In addition, four key components make up any persuasive argument:

✔ **Communicator characteristics:** A message is more likely to be persuasive if someone perceived as credible delivers it.

- Expertise is often a powerful indicator of credibility. We listen to experts. One thing to keep in mind, though: Just because someone says that she's an expert doesn't mean she necessarily is. When in doubt, always check credentials, education, training, and experience.

- We're also more likely to be persuaded by someone we see as trustworthy. I buy my oatmeal from the company with the old, trustworthy, grandpa guy in the commercials. Would he lie?

- Most of us still find attractive people's messages more persuasive. Attractive people can be physically attractive or have an appealing personality.

- Similarity plays a role. The more they are like us the better.

✔ **Message characteristics:** Should a persuader appeal to someone's emotion or to her reason and critical thinking? Here's a breakdown of these and other message characteristics:

- **Reasoned approach:** In 1983, Caccioppo and others have found that when trying to persuade highly educated or analytical people, a reasoned approach is best. These individuals seem to like to think things over, analyzing the information before making a decision. They're not necessarily smarter, but they are typically more involved in and up on recent information.

- **Emotional approach:** Those of us who don't have the time or inclination to read every consumer review when we go to buy a new car trust other people and are more swayed by emotional appeals. "My sister said she loved her new car. I think I'll get one."

- **Fear factor:** A lot of persuasive messages use fear to scare people away from harmful or unhealthy behaviors (as you can see in Chapter 23 on stress and health). These messages work. Fear-evoking ads are all around us — anti-smoking, drug abuse prevention, and political campaigns, for example. There's only one catch. If you're going to scare people in order to persuade them, you have to provide concrete information on how to deal with or how to change their behavior; otherwise, they may resign themselves in the face of the fear.

- **Two-sided argument:** This is another helpful tactic to employ in your quest for persuasion. A two-sided argument is one that acknowledges the other position, giving the impression of fairness and objectivity. Advertisers have been using this technique for years, conducting "taste tests" and other comparative challenges with their rivals. We know what they're up to!

✔ **Mode of message communication:** How a message is presented is important. The best way to present persuasive information is to make the persuadee play an active part in processing the argument. Active arguments capture the perceiver's attention and carry an expectation that the perceiver will comprehend the message, remember it, and then take action. As we increase the energy that we invest in mentally processing a message, we increase the likelihood that it will stick. Passive reception of a message, like listening to a lecture, is less likely to have an impact. People have to get involved in the message.

✔ **Characteristics of the audience:** Sears in 1986 found that older people are less likely to change their attitudes and opinions than people who are younger. Our early twenties are years in which we are particularly vulnerable to persuasion. This is a time in many people's lives when choices abound and information is being exchanged at a rapid rate. People are in college, entering the work force, and expanding their social networks. They're exposed to a whole new world of information, and this can make resisting persuasion more difficult.

Finally, here's a little tip on how to resist persuasion. With each of us being bombarded by persuasive messages every day, it helps to know how to stay committed to our own beliefs and attitudes. In 1970, Kiesler found that a good way to resist persuasion is through the process of *attitude inoculation.* Attitude inoculation involves exposing people to weak, or weaker, arguments against their position in order to inoculate, or firm up, their resistance to counter-arguments. This process gives them practice and confidence in refutation. It's kind of like warming-up before the big game. If I want to bolster someone's position on increasing handgun regulation for example, I might present him with weak arguments against increased regulation.

Easy as pie

There's a great rock video out by a band named Cake that demonstrates the influence of persuadee participation perfectly. In the video, a man walks around a beach, asking real people to put headphones on and listen to the new song. They're encouraged to comment on the song. This is a much more powerful advertising technique than if the man just walked up with a sign that read, "Check out Cake's new song. In stores now!" The persuadees are participating in their own manipulation. It's beautiful. I don't know if the video makers were thinking this way, but if they were, they hit on a great persuasion technique!

Being Mean

Although most of us would like to think that we're civilized, it's hard to ignore all the violence and aggression around us. Some of the most horrific acts of aggression were committed in the twentieth century, not in some savage society in our remote past. Examples abound — Pol Pot's Cambodian genocide, the Holocaust, Mao Tse-tung's killing of 26 million people, and in recent years, the Rwandan civil war. These are mass atrocities, but every day, we're confronted with smaller-scale, but nevertheless as horrible, acts of violence and aggression. Domestic violence, child abuse, murder, rape, and assault are all around us. Unfortunately, most of us have had some experience with at least one of these forms of violence and aggression. Why do we act this way? Why are we violent toward one another? Psychologists have searched for answers to these questions by studying *aggression,* a form of violence. *Aggression* can be defined as any behavior that is directed at and intended to hurt another person or persons. Two subtypes exist:

✔ **Hostile aggression:** Driven by anger and is and end in itself

✔ **Instrumental aggression:** Used to serve some other purpose, such as intimidation or extortion

Most of the theories about aggression ask why we commit hostile aggression. What if I can't help it? Several theories exist.

Maybe I was born with a violent instinct and a genetic predisposition to act aggressively. It does seem that some children are born more aggressive than others. Freud felt that we are born with aggressive instincts, and genetic studies have shown that identical twins are more likely to be more equally aggressive than fraternal twins (Rushton et al, 1986).

Some research also shows higher levels of the hormone testosterone in both men and women convicted of violent crimes when compared to those convicted on non-violent crimes (Dabbs, 1988).

Blaming the boob tube

I've watched violent television all my life, and I don't consider myself a violent person. The research is clear though, the more violent a child's television viewing is, the more aggressive the child is (Eron, 1987). There's little denying it. Hearold in 1986, conducted a comprehensive review of over 230 studies and concluded that watching aggressive behavior leads to aggressive behavior. My question is, why is there so much violence on television? Do we get something out of it? Is it an emotionally arousing persuasion technique used by corporations to sell their goods? I don't know, but I think we should look at reasons behind the inclusion of so much violence on TV.

Our brains may actually have something to do with it as well. Specific centers in the brain seem to be implicated in producing and inhibiting aggressive behaviors. Individuals with severe damage to the frontal lobes of the brain have long been observed as having more difficulty controlling their aggressive impulses because this inhibition is seen as one of the functions of the frontal lobe. This difficulty with controlling aggression is a disinhibition process.

Maybe I'm just frustrated? I'm one of those drivers who gets angry when I'm stuck in traffic. Now, I don't curse out my window at people or get into fistfights, but I sure do get frustrated. In 1989, Berkowitz found that sometimes frustration leads to aggression, and sometimes it doesn't. When we get frustrated, we get angry, and when we feel angry, we're predisposed to act aggressively. It's like our bodies and minds are poised, or on alert, to act with aggression. The trigger comes when we make a cognitive evaluation of a situation and conclude that the person who is ticking us off did so on purpose. This scenario is likely to produce an aggressive response (Weiner, 1981). So if you step on my toes, you'd better hope that it was an accident.

Maybe I'm just a product of my environment? I may have learned how to act aggressively by watching other people do it. Albert Bandura would agree. *Social learning theory* holds that aggressive behavior is learned by observing others and by seeing them rewarded for such behavior. Little boys are often rewarded for being tough. We pay boxers tens of millions of dollars to beat people up. We reward aggressive acts on a regular basis in our society. What child wouldn't see the benefits of aggression in such an environment?

Television violence has come under fire in recent years because of the dramatic increase in youth violence. Americans watch a lot of television. Even as far back as 1972, Gallup polls reported that Americans watch an average of seven hours of TV a day. I'm sure that number is higher today. Regardless of our opinions on violence and television, the fact is that there's a lot of violence on the tube. In 1990, Gerbner found that seven out of ten programs contain violent scenes, with primetime programming containing five violent acts per hour. No doubt about it, we get a heavy dose of violent images from television.

Lending a Helping Hand

I've always marveled at people like Mother Teresa who devote their entire lives to helping others. Her sacrifice was unquestionable. What drives people to help in this way? It certainly wasn't money. I never saw Mother Teresa driving around in a Rolls Royce. *Altruism,* having concern for and helping other people without asking for anything in return, seems to have been a favorite topic among social psychologists. Maybe, they studied altruism with such zeal because it's an integral part of our everyday lives. Nearly every day, we're presented with a situation in which someone needs our help, even if it's those sad, late-night commercials showing starving children in developing nations.

I think that most of us like to see ourselves as helpful people. If we're not particularly helpful, then at least we're willing to help in certain situations or when the need is severe. Hundreds, if not thousands, of studies conducted by social psychologists have investigated why, when, and who we actually help. Some of the findings are surprising, even shocking.

In New York City, 1964, a woman named Kitty Genovese was brutally murdered outside of her apartment by a man with a knife. She struggled with the attacker and screamed for help for nearly 35 minutes. No one came to her aid. There were later reports by 38 of her neighbors stating that they had witnessed the crime and heard her screams, but they did nothing to help her.

What happened here? Why didn't anyone help her? I'm sure that as you're reading this you're saying to yourself that you would have helped. When I first heard this account I thought, "What was wrong with those people?" Think about it though. What are the chances that all 38 people were cold, callous individuals who didn't care about a woman being murdered within earshot? The chances aren't good. The Kitty Genovese story illustrates the main point of social psychology — the power of the situation was a major factor in determining each individual's behavior.

Why do we help?

Before I introduce you to some of the main theories of why we perform altruistic acts, I want to conduct a little mini-experiment.

The next time you're in a public place, try one of these out:

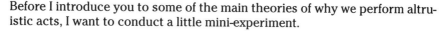

- ✔ **Experiment #1:** Drop five coins on the floor near a group of people and act like you don't notice. Time how long it takes for someone to help you. Try to remember as much about them as you can.

- ✔ **Experiment #2:** Pretend to trip and fall in the same public place. Make the same observations.

If you performed these experiments, what happened? Who helped you? How long did it take? Do you know why they helped you? I know — it was probably because of your stunning good looks. Believe it or not, as I cover later in this section, attractiveness does make a difference.

Theories about why we actually help cover a wide range:

- ✔ **Social exchange theory:** Helping as a type of trading process.

- ✔ **Selfishness theory:** We help to get something out of it.

- ✔ **Genetic theory:** Helping is part of our genetic makeup.

Foa and Foa introduced *social-exchange theory,* the idea that helping is part of a reciprocal process of giving and receiving social "goods" such as love, support, and services. Each of us tries to minimize our costs and maximize our benefits, just like any good businessperson would do. In helping situations, if the benefit of helping is higher than the cost of not helping, we are more likely to help. This kind of makes sense if you consider that sometimes helping people involves putting ourselves at physical risk or serious inconvenience.

In the 1950s, Ayn Rand wrote *Atlas Shrugged,* a famous philosophical novel that promoted the "virtue of selfishness." If each of us looks out for numero uno, all will be well. Rand was not alone in thinking that selfishness wasn't all that bad. Similar to social-exchange theory, other social psychologists, including Carlsmith and Gross, have argued that helping behavior is driven by our own selfish interests. We give in order to receive. Some rewards are external, like praise and notoriety, and others are internal, like reducing negative feelings such as guilt.

These theories sound pretty cynical don't they? I'm sure that the money I drop in the Salvation Army donation can on the street corner comes straight from my heart. But research does give some credence to these selfish theories. Krebsin found that men who showed the most physiological distress (increased heart rate, rapid breathing, and so on) were more likely to help someone than those who were less distressed. If we're not bothered, I guess we don't bother to help. Okay, I admit it. I only put money in the Salvation Army can so that nagging person ringing the bell will shut up! Or do I?

In 1991, Daniel Batson came to the rescue of our sense of goodness with his theory that we help people because each of us has a natural *empathy* for other people, especially those we're attached to.

Hoffman found that even infants seem to possess the naturally ability to "feel for" others. They cry when they hear another baby cry. Are they just crying because the other baby's crying is hurting their ears? No, it's because they are in touch with the other baby's pain. A lot of us can relate to feeling upset at the sight of another person's misfortune. This natural empathy may encourage us to help.

I empathize about your sympathy

Some people get confused between empathy and sympathy. Empathy involves a more personal understanding of someone's suffering, and sympathy is more distant and impersonal.

It's kind of like imagining being in someone else's shoes (empathy) versus feeling sorry for the person who's actually in those shoes (sympathy).

But if empathy doesn't take care of it, we always have our *social norms* for helping. Gouldner's *reciprocity norm* holds that we should return help to those who help us. You scratch my back, and I'll scratch yours. In turn, we don't hurt those who help us. Never bite the hand that feeds you! There's only one catch to this theory: Sometimes, people can get offended if you offer them help. If they can't return the favor, they may feel demeaned by the offer. Reciprocity works best when it's between equals.

How often do you help those people who stand on the side of the street holding the "Will work for food" signs? Do you feel a responsibility to help them? They're hoping you do. Another norm (see "Playing Your Part" section at the beginning of the chapter), the *norm of social responsibility* holds that people should help others who need it. Weiner in 1980, however, found that we typically apply this norm only in situations in which we perceive the person needing help as not having caused the situation due to her own negligence or fault. If we think that the person only needs help because she "did it to herself," we're not likely to use the norm of social responsibility. Do you think that the guy standing with the sign on the side of the street made some bad choices or somehow screwed up? Ask him; you never know until you ask. You may be eschewing your social responsibility.

Richard Dawkins wrote *The Selfish Gene* in 1976 and proposed that people are altruistic because their genes compel them to be. The idea of *kin protection* states that genes promote altruistic behavior toward kin or family in order to ensure the survival of the group's genetic makeup. Following this line of reasoning, I'm much less likely to help someone I don't know. Why would I? They don't share my genes. The more genetic material I share with someone, the more likely I am to help him or her. That's it. Nothing fancy.

When do we help?

One of the most remarkable findings in altruism research is the idea that people are less likely to help when they're in the presence of others than when they're alone. This sounds kind of strange doesn't it? I would have thought that the fear of looking cold or uncaring in front of others may encourage people to help more. The research shows otherwise. When we're in crowds, we're actually less likely to notice that other people need help. In New York City, for example, people are always surrounded by other people. It's a crowded place, and most people don't take the time to notice everything and everyone around them. It's easier to fade into a crowd.

Strangely enough, when others are around, we are also less likely to interpret someone's behavior as indicative of needing help. We look to others for a sign as to how we should respond in a situation, and if they don't act alarmed, we typically won't either. If the situation is ambiguous, not a clear-cut helping situation, our interpretation of the event in the presence of others is likely to be that intervention is not required. This is especially true if the other people are strangers.

A final problem with helping in the presence of others is called *diffusion of responsibility*. We always think someone else will do it. If no one else is around, we've got to help. But if others are around, we assume "they'll do it." What happens when everyone assumes that everyone else is going to offer assistance? Help doesn't get offered. That's exactly what two researchers, Latane and Darley, found in a 1968 study.

It's not all bad news when it comes to groups though. Test in 1967 actually found that when someone in a group takes action, others are more likely to jump in. These people serve as *prosocial models* and are a strong influence on altruistic behavior. The problem is getting someone to make the first move. Until someone does, the negative forces of the bystander effect are active. The *bystander effect* is when we don't get involved in a situation when there are too many people standing around; we just stand there. So go ahead and be a hero. Make the first move — someone has to.

What about feelings? I've always wondered about the origins of the tradition of buying cigars for friends when a baby boy is born. I still don't know where it comes from, but altruism research has shown that happy people tend to be more helpful people. Does that mean that sad people aren't helpful at all? It actually depends on how rewarding helping others is to the person experiencing sadness. If they're not self-absorbed and self-focused, altruistic acts can be very rewarding for those who are sad. Feeling good, doing good! Feeling bad, doing good! Sounds good, especially if I'm feeling bad.

The pious among us are often viewed as helpful. Many non-profit organizations are operated by religious organizations. But are religious people really more helpful? When people indicate that religion is very important in their lives, they have been found to give 2.5 times as much money to charity as those who indicate that religion is not very important. The verdict is in — religious individuals are definitely generous, and in at least one study, they're more generous than non-religious individuals.

Who gets helped?

Crowley in 1986 found that women get helped more often than men, and attractive women get helped more often than unattractive women. I guess the ugly men out there are out of luck. Luckily for them, similarity to the helper seems to be a factor. Emswiller in 1971 found that the more someone looks like or dresses like us, the more likely we are to help them out. So, if that ugly guy can find another ugly guy when he needs help, all is well!

Chapter 15

Growing Up with Psychology

*H*ave you ever wondered what it would be like to have a psychologist as a parent? What if both parents were psychologists? Would that be a good thing or a bad thing? Would the average dinner-table conversation sound something like the following dialogue?

Parent: How was your day today?

Child: Fine.

Parent: Fine, huh? That's funny; somebody doesn't look like he had an alright day. What about it honey? How was your day, really?

Child: I got into a fight with that big, stupid bully at school again. Well, I didn't really get into a fight. He just took my lunch pail and threw it into the trashcan.

Parent: How did that make you feel? Frustrated? Angry? What role did you play in the situation?

Child: You know, just once I'd like to hear you say that you'll do something about it or protect me somehow. Maybe you could teach me how to defend myself. I'm tired of being in therapy at the dinner table. I'm going to my room.

Parent: Well, I guess I messed that one up. How does that make me feel?

I don't know if having a psychologist as a parent is necessarily a good thing or a bad thing. Some people seem to think that everything the child does would be overanalyzed. In some respects, that's not completely fair. If a parent was a pediatrician, would people expect her to leave her medical knowledge at the door and not treat her own children if they became ill? Of course not. However, anything can be overdone.

One of the largest areas of psychological study is psychological development. Although most people only think of children when they hear the term, developmental psychology covers the entire span of human life. This approach is called *lifespan psychology* — the study of human psychological development from conception to death.

Some of the areas traditionally covered in lifespan psychology are covered in other chapters in this book. Personality development, for example, is covered in Chapters 11 and 12. Self development and the development of relationships are covered in Chapter 13. Therefore, this chapter focuses on physical and motor development, cognitive development, and social development. In addition, I only cover the periods of development from conception to adolescence because these seem to be the most emphasized areas in developmental research.

From Conception to Birth

The process of psychological development begins with conception. Genetic processes, which play a big part in the future development of behaviors and mental processes, originate with the union of a woman's egg and a man's sperm. Each coupling creates a new genetic combination called a *genotype* — the genetic makeup of each individual. Through a complex process that's best understood by geneticists and biologists, our genes express themselves in what is called our *phenotype* — the actual manifestation of genetic codes in observable biological and psychological processes as shaped and impacted by our environment. So, I may have the genotype for being tall and muscle-bound but if I suffer from malnutrition and never lift weights, I might be letting my genotype down.

$X + Y = $ It's a boy!

Both the sperm and the egg are specialized cells in the body that contain half of the genetic material necessary to make a whole person and are called *sex cells* because they are involved in sexual reproduction. Human beings contain 46 chromosomes. We get 23 chromosomes from our mothers and 23 from our fathers. Non-sex related cells contain a full set of genetic material with 46 chromosomes. Our chromosomes determine the unique aspects of our biological and psychological makeup. They are the genetic building blocks of our cellular construction.

The 23rd pair of chromosomes, the sex chromosomes, determines the sex of the child. Sex chromosomes can be either X chromosomes or Y chromosomes. Sperm cells can carry either an X or a Y chromosome, but an egg can only carry an X. When the sperm and the egg get together, their unique combination determines the sex of the child. Boys have a 23rd chromosome pair that contains one X and one Y (XY) chromosome. Girls have two Xs (XX). Because the mother can only give an X chromosome and the father can give either an X or a Y, the father's sex-chromosome contribution plays the deciding role.

The role of genetics in human behavior and mental processes has been part of the decades-long debate known as the *nature versus nurture* debate. Proponents of the nature argument believe that our behavior is genetically determined. Biology is destiny, so to speak. The nurture advocates believe that the environments we grow up in determine our psychological makeup. This debate has been basically squashed in the last 25 years by the position that both biological and environmental factors are involved, with different weight being given to one or the other depending on the psychological process in question.

Uniting and dividing all in one night

Our biological development begins with the process of sexual reproduction. So it goes that our psychological development begins as well as our behavior and mental processes are intrinsically tied to our biological development. For more on the relationship between psychology and biology see Chapter 3.

The process begins after a man and woman have had sexual intercourse:

Germinal Stage (conception to 2 weeks)
1. **The sperm and egg meet, combining their half-sets of chromosomes.**

   This is *fertilization,* and it occurs in the *fallopian tubes.* The fertilization process is delicate, and a lot of things can go wrong.

2. **Twenty-four to thirty hours pass as a one-celled *zygote* (the fertilized egg) begins to divide itself.**

   This occurs in the fallopian tube as well. Through a process called *mitosis,* each chromosome makes a copy of itself and contributes the copy to the formation of a second cell. Cells continue to divide and multiply, repeating this process throughout fetal development. Fetal development is underway.

3. **Three to four days pass while the fertilized egg travels to the uterus.**

   Upon reaching the uterus, *implantation* occurs. During implantation, the fertilized egg rests against the wall of the uterus and eventually merges with and becomes implanted in the lining of the uterus.

4. **The *embryonic period* begins.**

   This occurs about 14 days after the *pre-embryonic stage,* or the *germinal period* starts. The *embryonic period* lasts until the end of the eighth week of pregnancy.

Embryonic Stage (3rd week through 8th week)

5. **Cells continue to divide.**

   The beginnings of a recognizable human take shape. The rudiments of the nervous system and other bodily systems are beginning to take shape.

Fetal Stage (9th week through birth)

6. **The *fetal period* begins and lasts until birth.**

   This begins in the third month of pregnancy. This final stage is an extremely delicate process. Psychological difficulties can sometimes be traced to problems in fetal brain and nervous system development. Mental retardation, learning disabilities, and other cognitive disorders are sometimes linked to fetal difficulties.

It's extremely important for expecting mothers to maintain proper nutrition, avoid infectious diseases, and eliminate drug, alcohol, and tobacco use. These behavioral changes won't guarantee the birth of a healthy child, but they certainly increase the odds.

The biological developments of each period are highlighted in Table 15-1.

Getting a boost

Infertility can be caused by any number of complications, including older age, endometriosis, and pelvic inflammatory disease. Fertilization is a tricky business; healthy couples in their twenties can take, on average, up to a year to get pregnant. But modern medicine can perform some pretty impressive procedures to help nature take its course. *Artificial insemination* is a process in which a physician injects a man's sperm near a waiting egg to help facilitate the meeting of the sperm and the egg. Some men have sperm that are unable to reach the egg deep inside the fallopian tube and need help making the journey. *In vitro fertilization* is a process in which a physician actually puts a sperm inside an egg, not leaving their meeting to chance.

Table 15-1	Fetal Development by Stage of Pregnancy
Germinal (Weeks 0–2): What's There?	
Amniotic sac	Placenta
Embryo	Umbilical cord
Embryonic (Weeks 3–8): What's There?	
Buds (arms and legs)	Heartbeat
Eyes and ears	Nervous system
Fingers and toes	Spinal cord
Fetal (Weeks 9–36): What's There?	
Organ systems working	Sex organs
Red blood cells	White blood cells
Fetal: What's Going On?	
Fetus is very active	Fetus is sleeping like a newborn

Going from Diapers to Drool

It's 36 weeks later, and some lucky woman has just given birth to a healthy child. Infancy is an exciting time in which both physical and psychological developments occur at an unprecedented rate. One minute, children do nothing but sleep, and the next minute they're playing peek-a-boo.

Baby disco: I will survive

For approximately nine months as a fetus, the newborn child relied almost exclusively on his or her mother for survival. This dependence doesn't end with birth. Although the infant's basic biological systems are functioning on his or her own, the maintenance of those systems requires the attentive care of a parent or primary caregiver. Sometimes, new parents can get overwhelmed with the responsibility of caring for an infant. The good news is that infants are born with a pretty impressive set of basic skills to help them survive.

In fact, nearly all of the most basic human survival skills are present at birth. When I say *basic,* I mean really basic — breathing, sucking, swallowing, and eliminating. Babies need to breathe to get oxygen. They need to swallow and suck to eat. They need to eliminate in order to cleanse their system. You nervous parents out there can rest assured that you won't have to teach your infant how to suck on a bottle or a breast. It's natural and automatic. It's reflexive.

These skills are part of a broader list of innate reflexes infants are born with that aid in their survival. Here are a few more:

- **Rooting reflex:** Turning their heads in the direction of a touched cheek in an attempt to suck

- **Moro (startle) reflex:** Stretching out their arms and legs and crying in response to a loud noise or a sudden dropping motion

- **Grasping reflex:** Grabbing on to things, such as someone's finger

Building a motor

One of the most anticipated areas of infant development for a lot of parents is their child's motor development. Parents can't wait to watch their child gain more and more prowess in his or her physical abilities. Infants have very little control over their limbs and head when they're born. It takes time for the central nervous system and the peripheral nervous system to get things coordinated. The progression of control begins with control of head movements and then turns to control of the limbs and torso. Eventually, greater fine motor control kicks in. For example, children may begin to grab things with just two fingers. Table 15-2 shows this progression.

Table 15-2	Synopsis of Motor Development in Infancy
Age in Months	*Abilities Present*
1–3	Lifting head and sitting up with support
4–8	Holding head still and balancing it; looking around; using thumb to grasp; sitting up briefly without support
8–12	Coordinating hand activities; controlling trunk and sitting without support; crawling; beginning to favor the use of one hand over the other; sitting from standing position while holding on to something; walking with help, taking simple steps
14	Standing alone and walking alone without difficulty
18	Running and tumbling

Finding out about full development

Table 15-2 is not a comprehensive list of the development of motor abilities in infancy. For a more complete discussion of these abilities and most of the other aspects of development that I mention in this chapter, I highly recommend T. Berry Brazelton's book, *Touchpoints: Your Child's Emotional and Behavioral Development* (Perseus Press). Dr. Brazelton is a well-respected pediatrician with a lot of great ideas and observations pertaining to children.

As infants turn into toddlers, their motor behavior becomes more sophisticated. They can run, kick, throw, ride tricycles, and perform a variety of other complex motor-behavior sequences. *Fine motor skills,* increased dexterity and control over the use of their fingers and hands, continue to develop as they learn to manipulate small objects like cups, crayons, and small toys.

Flexing their muscles

While infants are beginning to rely on their reflexes and developing more control over their muscle movements, their brains are developing at an extremely rapid rate. Actually, brain development begins during pregnancy and continues throughout childhood and adolescence. The progression of brain development begins with the motor areas of the brain. Without the necessary brain development in these areas, infants would not be able to respond reflexively and gain control over their bodies. The next stop on brain-development express is the *somatosensory* areas of the brain, the areas involved in sensation and perception (the olfactory, taste, pain, auditory, and visual areas). Infants are born with a good sense of hearing. They can discriminate between their mothers' voices and strangers' voices, for example, which may be a result of hearing their mothers' voices throughout pregnancy. Their senses of smell and taste are also keen. Visual acuity is less developed at birth and gradually develops over the course of their first year of life.

Scheduling time for schemata

Like a roadmap or template, children use what Swiss psychologist Jean Piaget called schemata, or mental modes of thinking, to represent, organize, and integrate experience. *Schemata* are basic ways of thinking about the world. Rather than sit passively by as the world presents them with information, children actively construct an understanding and mental representation of the world. There are three basic schemata:

✔ **Sensorimotor schemata:** These organized patterns of thought are generated from a child's direct interaction with and manipulation of the objects in their environment.

For example, when a 1-year-old takes everything off of her plate and drops it on the floor, she's not just trying to annoy her mommy and daddy. According to Piaget, she's developing a sensorimotor schema to understand the relationship between cause and effect. It's a simple representation of a basic mechanical relationship: "I drop food. Then, mommy and daddy turn red. This is fun!"

✔ **Symbolic schemata:** With the development of these schemata, a child begins to symbolically represent earlier sensorimotor relationships. He can think about the objects in his world without having to directly interact with them.

✔ **Operational schemata:** These internal, mental activities involve the manipulation of the symbolic representations of objects. Operational schemata involve the ability to think abstractly and to solve problems without actually having to physically attempt a solution. So, instead of jumping in front of a car to see if it hurts, the child can imagine jumping in front of a car and decide whether it would hurt.

Basically, the three schemata begin with concrete interactions with the world and progress to a more symbolic and abstract thinking process. This is a hallmark of Piaget's work; remember that we start out with the concrete and then graduate to the abstract. Now that I think about it, maybe that's why I never did well in Sunday school. I couldn't get past the idea that clouds didn't seem strong enough to support heaven. Wouldn't everything fall right through? I still haven't figured that one out.

Thinking things through

Cognitive developmental theory is the study of the development and maturation of thinking. A Swiss psychologist named Jean Piaget is the father and reigning king of cognitive developmental theory. Piaget began thinking about thinking as he watched his own children grow up in front of him, analyzing their behavior and theorizing about the thoughts running through their little heads. I guess having a psychologist for a parent really can be a little scary.

Piaget is considered to be a *mentalist* because his theory holds that our overt behavior is due in a large part to how we think about the world.

Piaget emphasized how we think, instead of what we know. A dictionary contains a lot of information, but can it solve the equation 2 + 2? Piaget defined intelligence as the collection of mental abilities that help an organism adapt. He also felt that intelligence involves seeking *cognitive equilibrium* — a harmonious balance between an individual's thinking and the environment. We constantly encounter novel situations and stimuli from our environment. These new experiences challenge the human mind, which leads to an imbalance. Thinking is the process that restores the balance.

We are born with two processes that help further develop thinking:

- **Organization:** Organization involves combining the different schemata we've already developed with new and more complex schemata. It's like we're constantly shifting our understanding of the world around us to create a better and more complete picture.

- **Adaptation:** Adaptation is a process of adjusting our thinking to the demands of our environments. Adaptation is accomplished by two distinct sub-processes:

    - **Assimilation:** Little kids use assimilation all the time. When little Jimmy calls a horse a "doggy," that's assimilation in progress. Children attempt to understand novel objects in their environment by drawing upon what they already know and applying to novel objects and situations, it's kind of like using a template and the child is trying to fit everything into that one template. If the child only knows one type of four-legged animal with a tail, even a horse is a "doggy."

    - **Accommodation:** Accommodation is essentially the opposite process of assimilation. Here, existing schemata are altered to fit the new and novel information. Cognitive growth, then, is the ongoing and persistent process of children applying (assimilating) their understanding to the world and making accommodations for new information. This is the overall process of adaptation, which allows for the maintenance of cognitive equilibrium between thinking and the environment.

Getting your sensorimotor running

The *sensorimotor stage* is the first stage of cognitive development, and it lasts from birth to 2 years of age. During the sensorimotor stage, the problem-solving abilities of an infant grow beyond simple reflexes. Infants extend reflexive behaviors to novel objects in their environment. An infant may suck on a little toy in addition to his mother's nipple or the nipple of a bottle. It can take some babies a few tries to get used to sucking on a pacifier until he is able apply his natural-sucking knowledge and ability to other objects.

Almost accidentally, babies discover that they can have a physical effect on the objects in the world. They gradually build on these accidental discoveries and develop intentional and coordinated responses on a simple scale. Eventually, babies progress to a type of experimentation or trial-and-error learning in which they do things to the objects around them just to see what kind of impact they can have on these objects.

The ability to imitate people also develops during the sensorimotor stage. Babies often smile when you smile at them. One of the most common forms of imitation is cooing. When an infant develops the ability to imitate, she often coos back at people who coo at her. That's so cute!

A final key development in this stage is the development of a skill called *object permanence*. If you hide something from a baby who has not yet developed object permanence, he forgets about it. But, when babies achieve object permanence, they remember that the object is still around even if it's not in plain sight — they try to look for the object when you conceal it. So, if you're going to hide things from your children, do it before object permanence develops.

Learning within the lines

Sometimes, when I'm playing with toddlers, I catch myself quizzing them and testing the limits of their knowledge. I may read them a book and ask them to point things out on each page, "Where's the ball?" This sort of toddler homework is perfectly okay, as long as I don't over do it, which I have a tendency to do.

A lot of parents begin to teach their children some of the rudiments of knowledge that will serve as the foundation for future school learning. Recognizing objects and categories of objects such as shapes, colors, animals, numbers, and letters are basic skills that all children need to possess. Although some level of pre-existing skill is present, a child's ability to recognize objects increases around the ages of 18 months or 2 years. Children love to learn stories, songs, and nursery rhymes at this time in their lives.

Play is a very important part of a toddler's learning experience. By the age of 2½, most children can play alongside their peers in both cooperative and independent activities for a sustained period of time. Prior to this age, children may engage in short sessions of independent play or interactive physical play (like patty-cake) with adults or older children. Toddlers and preschoolers prefer more natural toys such as sand, mud, and water. They invent their own games but still don't do too well with rules and regulations.

Some parents expect their children to learn how to recognize and write letters before they get to kindergarten. But, for most toddlers and preschool-aged children, these skills are too advanced, and very little retention can be expected prior to kindergarten. By the age of 5, children do begin to form letters.

Drawing, however, is a related skill that toddlers and preschoolers do demonstrate some ability in. Stanley Gardner has shown that most 2- and 3-year-olds can scribble, and by the end of this period, they can easily create straight lines, curves, and loops. Four- and five-year-olds begin to draw representations and pictures with simple designs. They can easily color within the lines.

Saying what you think

A lot of parents remember their child's first words. When their little one utters the words *momma* or *dada,* their hearts usually melt. *Ball* usually doesn't get the same reaction.

The dominant position in psychology on the development of language is that language is innate and gradually unfolds as the child's brain develops. This doesn't mean that children are born with a language, but that they're born with the innate mental capacity to learn and grasp the rules of the language community they're born into. Parents can facilitate language development by providing a supportive and stimulating environment and prompting children to use their words to communicate their needs and desires.

Our children aren't born speaking in sentences or giving speeches. Well, at least none of the children I've ever come across. We all know that children learn to talk little by little. Language develops in stages as little Johnny makes little, adorable strides over the course of his first two to three years of life. Here's a quick overview of those accomplishments that make us so proud as parents:

- Infant speech begins with *cooing.* For the first few months, infants make sounds that come naturally from the movements of the mouth (feeding, breathing, and sucking) and from crying. Making a "raspberry" sound or humming are good examples of sounds that come from natural mouth movements. The vocal behaviors associated with crying are experimented with and the use of voice begins. These sounds occur both spontaneously and in response to interaction with others. A baby may coo in response to a mother's cooing, for example. These interactions often serve as a basis for future social development as well as parent and child engaging in sound-making games and getting a feel for each other's interaction style.

- Between the fifth and seventh month, infants slightly refine these basic sounds. Around the seventh or eighth month, infants begin to form sounds that resemble syllables. In English, some syllable sounds are easier to utter than others, such as *ma* or *ba.* It's pretty hard to get a 6-month-old to utter a *th* or *l* sound.

- Around the one-year mark, infants begin to use simple monosyllabic words. Early consonant and vowel sounds are then combined to produce early polysyllabic words like *momma* or *boo-boo* or *bye-bye.* This process continues for the next few months, as new words occasionally emerge and mastered words serve as a foundation to generalize from.

- Language development explodes around the time infants reach their 18th month. According to Dacey and Travers, children learn new words at the approximate rate of one word every two hours. That's staggering!

> I've taken Spanish at different points throughout my life, and I was lucky if I could learn one word every two weeks. Pretty sad, I know. This explosion continues until children are about 3 years old. Their language skills expand beyond using one word for many things — *ball* is no longer every round object, *doggy* is no longer anything with four legs, and so on. Building upon their ability to generalize, children begin to form simple two-word sentences, and then three-word sentences, and on and on. The next thing you know, you're answering more "why" questions than you ever thought possible.

Most children have learned the greatest portion (the structures, rules, and a great deal of vocabulary) of their native language by the age of 4. By the time they're ready to enter kindergarten, kids have acquired approximately 8,000 words and learned to use language in a variety of social situations. They can also use questions and make negative statements. At this point, the rudiments of language are solidly in place, and it's simply a matter of continued learning and increased sophistication, building upon the existing foundation.

Blooming social butterflies

The earliest relationships infants have are with their primary caregivers. A parent and a baby often engage in simple visual and touching games with each other. Infants also make facial gestures at strangers. The interactions between an infant and his or her primary caregiver have been likened to a dance in which each partner takes cues from the other in a scene that almost seems choreographed. This process of using feedback from each other to gauge social interaction has been called *reciprocal interaction,* and it often depends on the primary caregiver's ability to respond to the cues given by the child.

A good connection between an infant and primary caregiver is often the result of something called the *goodness of fit* — the fit between a child's and a caregiver's temperaments and styles. I've often heard parents say that each of their children had a different temperament and that learning to respond differently to each child was a challenge at times. Some children may be very outgoing and seek social stimulation, but others can be shy and may require a lower-key style of interaction. I think part of the art of parenting is knowing how to match up with a child's temperament — it often represents a significant challenge in therapy with children.

An infant's social circle gradually expands to include siblings, and he or she begins to show signs of *separation anxiety* (fear of being left by a primary caregiver) between the ages of 7 and 9 months. From 16 to 24 months, infants are able to spend time playing and interacting with others without too much significant involvement from their primary caregivers. From the beginning of 3 to 4 years of age, children's social worlds continue to expand. Sometimes quarreling occurs as they encounter the limitations of dealing with other children.

Sharing and taking turns become more important, and simple friendships and fondness for specific children also begin to emerge.

Getting on the Big Yellow Bus

Most children enter kindergarten around the age of 5. This marks a significant turning point in child development — learning, cognitive, and social skills become increasingly important. Children leave their parents and the protective and facilitative environment of the home to begin interacting with a larger and more complex world. School-related skills, such as writing, reading, spelling, and simple mathematics, begin to occupy a great deal of their mental energy and time.

Mastering the crayon

During kindergarten, children learn to use tools and writing-related materials with greater skill. Some children may not have been exposed to such things as scissors, glue, or paint before kindergarten. They're expected to learn how to write letters, their names, and a few simple words. They also begin to acquire the basics of reading, including letter recognition and beginning phonics. As children progress through school, these skills are expected to expand with the ability to read and write larger pieces of information.

Mathematical skills begin with counting. By the age of 4 or 5, most children can count with one to one correspondence. *One-to-one correspondence* is when a child can count each object he or she is presented with. So, if I put five apples out, children at this age will count ("One, two, three" and so on) for each apple. As children progress from kindergarten through the school system, they develop concepts of addition and subtraction, and eventually they develop more sophisticated operations that extend to advanced multiplication, division, and sometimes, even fractions.

Being preoperational doesn't mean you're having surgery

The sensorimotor stage of cognitive development is followed by the preoperational and operational stages. Thinking continues to become more sophisticated, using the gains from earlier stages and applying these to more difficult problems.

The *preoperational stage* (ages 2 to 7) marks the development of symbolic thought. A child now possesses the ability to allow one object, a symbol, to represent another object. A hallmark of this is pretend play. How can a stick be used as a sword, or a bathroom towel be a superhero's cape? Symbolic representation!

The most striking features of preoperational children's thought processes are the abilities that they don't possess. They have a hard time classifying objects into two or more categories. For instance, if you ask them if there are more total balls or more red balls in a collection of four red balls and three green balls, they usually answer "red balls." They've locked onto one prominent feature of the collection of balls and cannot think abstractly to solve the problem. How much does 50 pounds of feathers weigh? A preoperational child may give some figure less than fifty pounds as his or her answer.

A classic development that sharply marks the difference between a preoperational child and a concrete operational child is called *conservation* (the ability to understand that something remains the same even though its appearance or surface properties may change).Get a tall glass of water and an empty short glass. With the child present, pour the water from the tall glass into the smaller short glass. Now, ask the child which glass had more water in it. The child will always say the tall one — that's because it's bigger. However, after the child has gotten older and progressed to the concrete operational stage, he or she can solve this problem.

The *concrete operational stage* marks the development of a child's ability to mentally represent a complex series of actions and perform relational logic. At this stage, children use a skill called *seriation,* which allows a child to arrange objects in a series of changing dimensions, like bigger to smaller, smaller to bigger, taller to shorter, and so on. Believe it or not, most children can't do this until they're about 7 years old. However, a concrete operational child still gets hung up on more abstract problems, or problems that are hypothetical. If a problem has no basis in reality, the concrete operational child has a very hard time answering the question. They balk at "what if" questions because these questions require them to abstract concrete knowledge to situations that have never happened. Luckily, they get there in the formal operations stage, which comes in adolescence.

Want to play on the swings?

The primary social-development issues for school-aged children are peer relationships and social functioning outside the home. By the time children enter school, their relationships with their parents are pretty well solidified. These relationships continue to develop, but relationships outside of the home are the primary focus between the ages of 5 and 12.

During these years, our expectations of a child's social ability grow dramatically. We no longer tolerate tantrums and less sophisticated social problem-solving techniques, such as hitting other children. We expect children to follow rules and instructions, especially in the classroom. Their affiliations with other children increase, and they start to develop a small, core group of friends.

If a child has social difficulties, these problems show up when they enter school. Problems involving getting along with the other children, joining in games, and cooperating with the routines expected of them when they're away from their parents can sometimes lead to peer rejection, emotional difficulties, or school failure.

Agonizing over Adolescence

Perhaps one of the most significant events in a child's life is his or her experience with puberty. Puberty is marked by an increase in the sexual hormones of progesterone, testosterone, and androgens. Development of secondary sexual characteristics, such as pubic hair, maturation of the genitalia, and breast development for girls, accompanies puberty. Interest in sex is markedly increased as boys begin to take interest in girls, and vice versa. Adolescents no longer think that members of the opposite sex have the cooties.

Along with these wonderful physical changes come some pretty profound changes in thinking. By the time we're about 11 or 12 years old, we can solve the "what if" problems we're faced with because we've reached the cognitive-developmental peak of formal operations. This period is called *formal operations* because the concrete thought processes of childhood are combined into more advanced concepts such as abstractions. Children and teenagers can now reason based on hypothetical questions. They don't need concrete examples or demonstrations like they did during the earlier stages of cognitive development. They've become little scientists, able to conduct mental mini-experiments instead of having to tackle problems using trial and error.

 Keep in mind that just because kids and adolescents can ask and answer these questions doesn't mean they actually do. When I was a teenager, I repeatedly failed to ask myself, "What if I get caught lying to my parents?" I should have used my formal operational thinking a little more.

Pining over puberty

Exactly when puberty begins is a questionable matter. It can come at different times for different children. But researchers have noticed that the age of onset for puberty has been gradually decreasing. On average, kids are entering puberty at a younger and younger age. This development has been dubbed the *secular trend,* and researchers believe that it's due to better childhood nutrition. According to Dacey and Travers, the average age of onset for puberty in Western countries is showing a decline of three months per decade.

The timing of puberty can have serious repercussions, depending on when it comes. Boys who develop later than others sometimes suffer from peer ridicule and social setbacks related to popularity and dating. Girls who develop too early sometimes find themselves in situations that they're mentally not prepared for because their bodies make them look older than they really are.

What about sex? A great deal of variation in sexual norms exists across societies, but whether or not a society puts strict limits on adolescent sexual behavior, sexual desire is a primary issue for members of this age group. Most of the time, teenagers learn about sex from their friends and from the media. The old birds and the bees talk doesn't come up as often as people may think.

Parents? We don't need no stinking parents!

One striking difference between childhood and adolescence is the diminished importance of parents in a teenager's life. Prior to adolescence, parents and the home occupy center stage in a child's life. During the teen years, adolescents begin to express their independence and autonomy by making friendships their top priority.

Social functions that involve parents take a back seat to teen-exclusive functions, such as dances, parties (without chaperones), and outings. Hanging out, talking on the phone, and staying the night at friends' houses are commonplace.

Peers are a major source of self-esteem, and fitting in is often more important than parental acceptance. Teenagers experiment with identity and social roles. Relationship skills and patterns laid down in childhood grow in sophistication. Romantic relationships become extremely important. Being the star of the household gives way to desires for being popular or well-liked.

Part VI
Knowing Whether You're a Nut

The 5th Wave   By Rich Tennant

BUFFETPHOBIA — THE FEAR OF MAKING INAPPROPRIATE SELECTIONS FROM A BUFFET LINE

Lime Jell-O, mashed potatoes, and a pair of opera glasses. What was I thinking...?

In this part . . .

Modern psychopathology basically began in the early twentieth century with the theories of Eugene Bleuler and Sigmund Freud. Part VI covers contemporary approaches to abnormal psychology, including neuropsychological and cognitive explanations for psychological problems. I discuss some of the major and most infamous psychological disorders, including anxiety disorders, depression, schizophrenia, and posttraumatic stress disorder. I also discuss forensic psychology, or criminal psychology. Topics related to this subject include the areas of criminal responsibility and criminal profiling, major theories of criminal behavior, and theories on treatment and correction.

Chapter 16

Modern Abnormal Psychology

● ●

In This Chapter

▶ Defining abnormality

▶ Finding reality

▶ Feeling depressed

▶ Living in fear

● ●

*T*he following vignette is based on a fictional person. Mr. Smith is not real, and any resemblance to a real person is purely coincidental.

Mr. Smith is a 30-year-old married man with two children who lives in a quiet suburban neighborhood. He works as a shipping manager for a local trucking company. Mr. Smith has been in relatively good health and is considered by most people to be a pretty average guy. About three months ago, Mr. Smith approached his wife with the idea of getting a home security system. She agreed, and they installed an alarm system. Mr. Smith then told her that he wanted to install cameras around the perimeter of their home. She reluctantly agreed. At times, Mrs. Smith began to wake up in the middle of the night to find Mr. Smith peaking out of their bedroom curtains with binoculars. He became very agitated when she questioned him about his behavior.

Mr. Smith's actions continued for several weeks, and he still would not tell his wife what was going on. Then one day she found a gun as she was cleaning out their closet. She'd never known him to own a gun, so she confronted him about it out of concern for the children's safety. When she approached him, he told her that he bought the gun to protect them from the neighbor next door. Mr. Smith said that he had been watching the neighbor for a few months, and he was convinced that the neighbor was involved in a real-estate scheme to get their home. The plot involved the neighbor hiring some criminals to break into their home and rob them, in order to scare them into moving and selling their home at a really low price. Then the neighbor would buy the house for next to nothing, tear it down, and expand his own home onto the property.

Is there anything wrong or strange about Mr. Smith's behavior? Should his wife be worried? Is he just being protective? The answers to these questions are part of the field of *abnormal psychology* — the psychological study of abnormal behavior and mental processes. But what is "abnormal behavior?"

Deciding Who's Normal

Obviously, by *abnormal* I mean not normal — something beyond the usual and customary. I've never taught a psychology course without at least one student raising a protest against the concept of abnormal behavior. "Who gets to decide what is normal and what is not?" he or she often asks. This is an excellent question. Who does get to decide what is normal and what is not? And how is a standard of normality determined?

Every society in the world has standards of behavior and conduct that delineate what are acceptable and unacceptable behaviors. Individuals, families, and even groups have *norms,* or standards. When people act outside those norms, society labels either the behavior or the person himself as "abnormal." There are at least five different ways, or criteria, to define normal versus abnormal behavior:

- **Normative criterion:** People who do things contrary to what the majority of people do or who act very differently than what is expected are acting abnormally. We are expected to live up to societal norms; we suspect something is amiss when we don't. Sometimes we use statistics to figure out who's outside the norm. If nine out of ten people act a certain way, the behavior of the one person who doesn't conform is statistically abnormal. The non-conforming behavior is considered rare.

- **Subjective criterion:** Sometimes we sense our feelings may be different than those of most other people or we may be doing something differently than the way most others do it. In this very limited sense, we're abnormal. Also, if I feel like something is wrong with me because of my awareness of my being different, then I might consider myself a suitable subject of abnormal psychology. This is a case of judging one's own behavior as abnormal.

- **Maladaptive criterion:** Does my behavior help me survive and successfully function in my society? If not, according to this criterion, maladaptive behavior is abnormal. If I have a difficult time adapting and adjusting to life's demands, my behavior is maladaptive.

- **Unjustifiable or unexplainable criterion:** Sometimes people act in ways and do things that can't be explained. We typically assume that there must always be a reason why someone acts in a certain way. If we can't come up with a reasonable explanation for these actions, we may label their behavior abnormal.

No matter what definition we use, it's pretty hard to argue that everything is normal. I realize that some people think that our lives are one big free-for-all, but in reality, every society requires a degree of order. Whether it is a family, a tribe or a nation, mores and laws are needed to enforce/maintain structure and order. I define *abnormal behavior* as maladaptive behavior and mental processes detrimental to an individual's physical and psychological well-being.

So, if someone acts abnormally, does that mean that he has a mental illness or psychological disorder? No, not necessarily. A person can act abnormally for any number of reasons. In fact, at one point in history, people believed (and some still do) that abnormal behavior was caused by demonic possession or moral weakness. What about committing murder? Isn't that abnormal? In fact, murder meets all five of the criteria we established earlier to define abnormal behavior.

The concept of *mental illness* comes primarily from psychiatry. *Psychiatry* is a branch of medicine that deals with mental disorders. During the nineteenth century, people who acted abnormally became the province of physicians. These "crazy" people were seen as sick instead of morally inept or demonically possessed. This way of looking at abnormal behavior was actually a big advance in the care of these people. When physicians began to be responsible for the care of those behaving abnormally, abnormal behavior was viewed as a medical problem and was considered an illness, to be diagnosed and treated like all other illnesses and diseases. This is known as the *medical model of mental illness*.

Compared to medical doctors, *psychologists* are relative newcomers to the field of mental illness as defined by psychiatry. As physicians tried to figure out ways to help people from a medical model perspective, psychologists eventually joined in, bringing their knowledge of human behavior and mental processes to the research, diagnosis, and treatment of abnormal behavior that was determined to be due to a mental illness.

It is important to make a distinction between abnormal behavior that is due to a mental illness and abnormal behavior that is not. A lot of abnormal behaviors are not due to the presence of a mental illness. Take slam dancing, for example. It's pretty abnormal to find enjoyment in running into people and bouncing around a pit of human pinballs. Yeah, I think that's abnormal, but do I think that this behavior is a result of mental illness? That depends, but for the most part no! Again, keep in mind that there are as many potential causes of abnormal behavior out there as there are people.

Taxonomizing Symptoms and Disorders

Over the years, psychiatrists and psychologists have worked to delineate what abnormal behaviors constitute the presence of a mental illness and what behaviors do not. This process is called *taxonomy* — the science of classification. Today, the most widely used classification system for determining the presence of a mental disorder is the *Diagnostic and Statistical Manual, 4th Edition, (DSM-IV)* published by the American Psychiatric Association in 1984. The definition of a mental disorder presented in the *DSM-IV* is "a clinically significant behavioral or psychological syndrome or pattern that occurs in an individual and that is associated with present distress (e.g., a painful symptom), or disability (i.e., impairment in one or more important areas of functioning), or with a significantly increased risk of suffering death, pain, disability, or an important loss of freedom."

A couple of key words in this definition need extra attention:

✔ **Symptom:** A behavior or mental process that is a sign or signal of a potential disorder. Symptoms are usually found within the following categories:

- Thinking or thought processes

- Mood or affect (referring to how someone feels emotionally, such as depressed, angry, or fearful) and vegetative symptoms (concerning eating, sleeping, and energy level)

- Behavior (such as violence, compulsive gambling, or drug use)

- Physical signs (such as muscle or joint pain, headaches, excessive sweating)

✔ **Disorder:** A collection of symptoms that indicate the presence of a syndrome (co-occurring groups of symptoms). In developing a taxonomy of abnormal psychological disorders, psychiatrists and psychologists look for specific groups of symptoms that tend to occur together, distinguishing one set of co-occurring symptoms that are distinct from other sets of co-occurring symptoms.

I want to make a couple of final points before we get into the specific mental disorders most commonly observed by mental health professionals today. First, it is important to realize that all behavior is viewed on a continuum of normal to abnormal. For example, crying is a normal behavior, but crying every day, all day for more than two weeks is considered abnormal. Second, everyone has experienced a symptom of mental disorder at one time or another. But simply having a symptom of mental disorder does not mean a person has the actual disorder. Remember, disorders consist of specific groupings of symptoms that define a particular syndrome. The rules for determining what symptoms constitute a disorder are complex and include specific time frames and degrees of severity.

So don't get carried away and start diagnosing everyone you know just because you see a symptom or two. It's not that simple; a symptom does not a disorder make!

Grasping for Reality

One of the most well-known examples of mental disorder is when someone seems to have lost touch with reality. What's strange about Mr. Smith in the vignette at the beginning of this chapter is that it seems like the neighbor's plot is all in his imagination. When someone loses touch with objective reality, imagining things and acting on those imagined things we say that he is suffering from a class of disorders known as the *psychotic disorders*.

The psychotic disorders, are considered possibly the most severe of all mental disorders. In addition to losing touch with reality, people who are suffering from a psychosis have severe functional deficits related to basic self-care (eating, shelter, and personal hygiene), social and occupational functioning, and thinking.

Schizophrenia

The most common form of psychosis is *schizophrenia*. Psychiatrist Eugene Bleuler used the term schizophrenia to describe people who exhibited signs of disorganized thought processes, a lack of coherence between thought and emotion, and a state of disconnection from reality. Today, the *DSM-IV* criteria for schizophrenia include:

- **Delusions:** A delusion is a firmly held belief that is maintained in spite of evidence to the contrary. One common type of delusion is a *paranoid* or *persecutory delusion,* which involves intense fear that one is being followed, listened to, or otherwise threatened by someone or something.

  In the chapter-opening vignette, Mr. Smith appears to be experiencing a paranoid delusion. He "knew" that the neighbor was out to get his house! Another common form of delusion is the *grandiose delusion,* in which a person experiences an extremely exaggerated sense of worth, power, knowledge, identity, or relationship. Someone who is grandiose may believe he can speak to supernatural beings or that he is a supernatural being himself. Or, he might just think that he's the president of the United States.

- **Hallucinations:** The *DSM-IV* defines a hallucination as a "perception that has the compelling sense of reality of a true perception but that occurs without external stimulation of the relevant sensory organ." Hallucinations can be auditory (hearing voices or sounds), visual (seeing demons or dead people), olfactory (smells), gustatory (tastes), or somatic (experiencing physical sensations within the body). Most hallucinations are auditory and often involve someone hearing a voice or voices commenting on his or her behavior.

If Mr. Smith experienced hallucinations, he may have heard voices say, "He's gonna get you!" *Command hallucinations* are a potentially dangerous form of auditory hallucination because they involve a voice or voices telling the sufferer to do something, often involving violent or suicidal behavior. "Kill yourself!"

✔ **Disorganized speech and thought:** Have you ever had a conversation with someone, and you had no idea what she was talking about? Was it gibberish? Disorganized speech and thought are characterized by verbalizations that are extremely tangential (mostly irrelevant), circumstantial (beating around the bush) or loosely associated (jumping from one unrelated thought to another). These abnormal styles of communicating may be evidence of a *thought disorder.* An extreme form of thought disorder is called *word salad* — when a person's speech is so incoherent that it sounds like another language or nonsense.

If Mr. Smith exhibited thought disorder, he might have sounded something like this: "I think the garbage came by and slipped, but he knows law enforcement, badges, peeking through." Sometimes people even make up words that don't exist called — *neologisms.* "I think the glerbage came by and sluppered the inequitised frames from me."

✔ **Grossly disorganized or catatonic behavior:** When a person behaves in a disorganized manner, she may act extremely silly or childlike, easily get lost or confused, stop caring for herself and her basic needs, do strange or bizarre things like talk to herself, or be extremely socially inappropriate. Catatonic behavior involves complete immobility, absolute lack of awareness of one's surroundings, and sometimes being mute.

✔ **Negative symptoms:** A negative symptom refers to the absence of some usual or expected behavior. The absence of the behavior is what is abnormal. Three negative symptoms are seen most often with schizophrenia:

   • **Flat affect:** When a person exhibits no emotionality whatsoever

   • **Alogia:** Describes a condition in which a person's thought processes are dull, blocked, or generally impoverished

   • **Avolition:** When a person has no ability to persist in an activity; looks like an extreme lack of motivation

When a person experiences these symptoms, he may be suffering from schizophrenia. Why do I say "may?" Someone might exhibit these signs for a lot of reasons: drugs, sleep deprivation, or some physical disease. Making the diagnosis of schizophrenia is both a complex and very serious task. Specific time frames and *rule-outs* are involved. Rule-outs involve eliminating other possible or plausible explanations.

Schizophrenia strikes about one in every 10,000 people. Generally it is diagnosed in individuals between the ages of 18 to 35. Sometimes, but rarely, it is diagnosed in childhood. It typically begins in the late teens and early twenties and is fully present by the mid- to late twenties. It can develop rapidly or gradually, and there can be periods of less severe symptoms. Other sufferers may be chronically and persistently ill. Periods of illness can be characterized by a marked inability and diminished capacity to function in everyday life, often leading to school failure, job loss, and relationship difficulties.

Don't be fooled by how easy it is to list the symptoms and describe them, they are very serious. Individuals with schizophrenia often face enormous challenges in society and sometimes end up in jail, in hospitals or similar institutions, or living on the streets because of their illness.

Revealing schizophrenia's causes

This used to be a debate that focused on the old issue of nature versus nurture. Are the causes of schizophrenia organic (biochemical/physiological) or functional (resulting from experience)? At the moment, perhaps because of the elevated status of science, the organic explanations are far more widely held, but the best answer may lie in a synthesis of the two points of view. This is still very difficult to tackle because numerous theories for the cause of schizophrenia exist, each with varying degrees of scientific support. The predominant theory in practice today is really a synthesis of two different areas of research; it's called the *diathesis-stress model.*

First, some definitions. A *diathesis* is a predisposition to a particular disease. *Stress* can be defined as any number of psychological and social factors. So, the diathesis-stress model holds that schizophrenia is the consequence of a stress-activated diathesis or predisposition.

One proposed biological diathesis for schizophrenia is an underlying problem with brain chemistry. Other researchers have found malformed parts of the brain. These biological abnormalities can lead to problems with thinking, speech, behavior, and staying in contact with reality. For the stress component, psychological factors address the matter of the reality distortion associated with schizophrenia. Why do schizophrenics make a break from reality? Generally, there is a belief that the world is experienced as so harsh, and its conflicts so intense, that a vacation from it is necessary. Research has shown that psychic trauma, such as child abuse, can be related to psychotic breakdowns. This type of trauma certainly constitutes a harsh world in need of escaping. The research, however, does not state that child abuse causes schizophrenia in all or even a majority of cases, but it has been seen as a potentially overwhelming stressor. Trauma is a form of extreme stress, regardless of the source. This stress might interact with the diathesis, the predisposition, and lead to psychotic symptoms.

A social factor related to schizophrenia that has shown promise in recent research is a phenomenon known as *expressed emotion.* Expressed emotion (EE) refers to negative communication by family members directed at the person suffering from schizophrenia. EE often consists of excessive criticism. Family members might comment on the patient's behavior, "You're crazy!" for example. EE also includes emotional over-involvement of family members that can overwhelm the patient. Let me be perfectly clear though: I am not saying that criticism and over-involvement cause schizophrenia, but only that they may contribute to the stress component of the diathesis-stress model, as many other stressors may.

You may think that you've developed schizophrenia after reading about its causes. Don't get too caught up in the detail. The bottom line is that a lot of the research out there is inconclusive. What we do know is that there are some underlying brain abnormalities in schizophrenics that may interact with certain kinds of stress in a way that produces the disorder. The devastating effects of this disorder keep researchers working hard to get to the bottom of things. We've come along way, but there's still a long way to go.

Treating schizophrenia

Schizophrenia is one of the most difficult mental disorders to treat. Its effects are often debilitating for both the individual with the disease and his family. There are numerous approaches to treating this illness ranging from the use of medication to helping individuals develop important functional skills such as money management or social skills.

- ✔ Antipsychotic medications such as Haldol and Zyprexa are typically the first line of treatment for people suffering from schizophrenia or related psychotic disorders. While extremely beneficial, these medications are known as palliatives because they don't cure disease, they merely lessen the intensity of symptoms.

- ✔ The areas of psychosocial treatment and rehabilitation have also showed some promise. Patients are taught social skills and self-care skills that can help reduce the number of stressors they face.

- ✔ Although seemingly out of fashion in recent years (too labor intensive and therefore too expensive), psychotherapy, specifically cognitive therapy, has been used in recent years to teach patients to challenge their delusional belief systems and become better "consumers" of reality.

The majority of recent research indicates a combination of medication and talking therapy is the most effective treatment intervention. Early intervention and solid social support are also factors associated with a favorable prognosis. With medication, psychotherapy, and support from family and friends, many people suffering from schizophrenia can lead productive lives. The problem is that their symptoms are often so severe they may have a difficult time achieving levels of emotional and behavioral consistency necessary to maintain jobs and conduct effective relationships. In addition, perhaps because of damaged self-esteem, poor self-image and ambivalent attitudes about relating and succeeding, schizophrenics are notorious for their inconsistent medication compliance.

Struggling with other types of psychoses

Two other forms of psychosis are *delusional disorder* and *substance-induced psychotic disorder.*

- ✔ **Delusional disorder:** Characterized by the presence of delusions that are not particularly bizarre or out in left field. A husband may be obsessed with the idea that his wife is having an affair but be unable to prove it or find any evidence. This belief may turn into a delusion if it persists for at least one month. Someone may think that the water in his home is poisoned, contrary to evidence that it is not. Another example is that an office coworker is madly in love with another coworker and keeps sending "signals" of that affection. The key thing about a delusional disorder is that the delusional person has no other signs of psychosis, like those found in schizophrenia.

- ✔ **Substance-induced psychotic disorder:** Exists when prominent hallucinations or delusions are present that are connected to being under the influence of a substance or withdrawing from a substance. People under the influence of LSD or PCP often exhibit psychotic symptoms, and it's not unusual for people who have used cocaine or amphetamines to look psychotic when they "come down" (the mimicking of psychotic symptoms). This problem can be very serious, and anyone considering using drugs, or even alcohol for that matter, should know that there's a fair chance they may experience psychotic symptoms as a consequence of their use.

Feeling in a Funk

I wonder if blues music would be around if all those musicians were psychotherapy patients. Those songs don't seem particularly sad though — they seem more pitiful than anything else. Sometimes I ask new patients if they've ever been depressed, and some of them reply, "Sure, doesn't everyone get depressed?" Not exactly.

Sadness is a normal human emotion typically felt during experiences of loss. The loss of one's job, lover, child, or car keys may trigger sadness. But that's just it — this is sadness, not depression! *Depression* is an extreme form of sadness that also includes a number of other symptoms. Most of us, well maybe some of us, have experienced being dumped by a boyfriend or a girlfriend at one time or another. How did we feel? Sad, fatigued, unmotivated, sleepless, not hungry. But all of these feelings eventually went away. We got over it. The same thing can happen when a loved one or someone who we're close to dies. We call this *mourning* or *grief.* Again, when we are grieving, we are not depressed. Depression is something different.

Major depression

When someone is depressed to the degree of needing professional attention, they experience at least a majority of the following symptoms of *major depressive disorder:*

- Depressed mood for most of the day and for most days
- *Anhedonia* (marked disinterest or pleasure in all or most activitics)
- Significant weight loss or weight gain, without trying, and decreased or increased appetite
- Difficulty sleeping or excessive sleeping
- Physical feelings of agitation or sluggishness
- Fatigue or lack of energy
- Feelings of worthlessness or excessive guilt
- Difficulty concentrating and focusing
- Repeated thoughts of death or suicide

Hopefully, most people who ask, "Don't we all get depressed?" won't have that same response after seeing all of these symptoms. If you are experiencing three or more or if you have any doubts, get thee to a doctor!

Sometimes, depression can become so severe that the sufferer may think about committing suicide. There are many myths about suicide floating around out there. One is that people who talk about suicide don't do it. This is false! In fact, talking about suicide is one of the most serious signals that someone might actually do it. All talk about suicide or self-harm should be taken seriously. If you are worried about someone or even yourself, contact a mental health professional or call a local crisis or suicide hotline.

Depression is one of the most common forms of mental disorder in the United States, occurring on average in about 15 percent of the population. Major depressive disorder can occur just one time in a person's life or over and over again, lasting for months, years, or even a lifetime. Most people who suffer from a recurring major depressive disorder have periods of recovery in which they don't experience symptoms, or they experience the symptoms in a less intense form. Depression can occur at any point in a person's life and doesn't discriminate against age, race, or gender.

Revealing depression's causes

Depending on whom you ask, the search for the causes of depression can be divided into two kinds of explanations:

✔ **Biological:** Biological theories of depression place blame on the brain and the malfunctioning of some of the chemicals that comprise it.

✔ **Psychological:** The psychological theories focus mostly on the experience of loss.

The *biogenic amine hypothesis* is the most popular theoretical explanation of the biological underpinnings of depression. According to this hypothesis, depression is a function of the dysregulation (impaired ability) of two neurotransmitters in the brain, norepinephrine and serotonin. *Neurotransmitters* are chemical substances in the brain that allow one neuron to communicate with another neuron across the *synapse* (the gap between neurons). The brain contains many different neurotransmitters, each having relative concentrations in specific regions of the brain. Specific neurotransmitters aid localized brain regions in their monitoring of particular human activities. The parts of the brain seemingly most affected in depression are those involved with mood, cognition, sleep, sex, and appetite.

Psychological theories of depression come from several sources:

✔ **Object relations theory:** Melanie Klein proposed that depression was the result of an unsuccessful child developmental process that may result in a difficult time coping with feelings of guilt, shame, and self-worth.

✔ **Attachment theory:** John Bowlby's theory gives us another view on the cause of depression. All our relationships with other people originate from the initial attachment bonds we formed with our primary caregivers as infants. When there is a disruption in the attachment relationship and a healthy bond is not formed, the child is vulnerable to depression when faced with future losses and relationship difficulties. In infancy, bonding and attachment can be disrupted for numerous reasons ranging from a drug-addicted parent to growing up in an unloving foster home. Children with poor attachment relationships are often left feeling helpless. Helplessness is a hallmark of depression.

✔ **Learned helplessness:** Many people throughout their lives have experienced failure or the inability to achieve what they've desired. Under normal circumstances, most of us just keep on keeping on. We don't give up and don't typically develop any serious sense of pessimism about the likelihood of our future successes. However, some people, because of adverse circumstances or because of a general tendency to view their efforts as worthless, may become depressed in the face of what they've experienced as insurmountable odds.

Depression drug?

Antidepressant medication is one of the most widely prescribed medications in the United States. What's going on? Are we all depressed? Well, there's a lot of public awareness about depression, and advertising these drugs on television probably doesn't hurt either. However, keep in mind that research has shown that certain forms of psychotherapy can be just as effective as medication in the short-run and perhaps more beneficial in the long-run than medication. The best "drug" for depression might not be a drug at all.

✔ **Cognitive theory of depression:** Aaron Beck's theory has become extremely popular and is well supported by research. Beck proposed that depression is a type of thinking disorder that produces the emotional outcome of depressed moods and the other related symptoms. Several cognitive "distortions" may be involved:

- **Automatic thoughts:** Automatic thoughts are statements we make to ourselves that we are not aware we say that produce depressive experiences. For example, if I get in my car in the morning and it doesn't start, I might consciously say, "Dang, just my luck." But unconsciously, I might be having the automatic thought, "Nothing ever goes right for me."

- **Mistaken assumptions and self-other schemas:** The assumptions and self-other *schemas* (beliefs about who I am in relationship to others) I assume to be true, as well as my views of the world, myself, and the future all greatly influence how I move in the world. Beck introduced the *cognitive triad* as follows:

  Each point in the triangle contains a set of beliefs that reflect a negative evaluation of oneself, a hopeless view of the future, and a view of the world as excessively harsh. A final component of the cognitive view is the cyclical nature of depressive thinking.

  An example best illustrates it. I may have the belief that I can't do anything. This belief won't exactly have me fired up, so my motivation is affected. Then, I'll obviously do nothing because of my lack of motivation, and in turn, I will "prove" to myself that I really can't do anything. This twisted and self-confirmatory bias in thinking will likely lead to the depression.

Treating depression

Several effective treatment approaches for depression exist. Antidepressant medication has been found to be effective. This course includes such famous medications as Prozac and Paxil. Psychotherapy, specifically cognitive-behavioral therapy and interpersonal psychotherapy, has been found to be effective as well. Research also indicates "activity" — staying very physically active and generally busy — can be an effective antidote to depression. Some studies indicate regular physical exercise proved as effective as medication in alleviating symptoms according to the self-reports of subjects. The common standard of practice is to utilize both medication and psychotherapy.

Bipolar disorder

Bipolar disorder is most commonly known as *manic-depression*. It can be characterized as a disorder of severe mood swings involving both depression and *mania*. Mania is a state of excessively elevated or irritable mood lasting for approximately one week and co-occurring with the following symptoms:

- ✔ Inflated self-esteem or grandiosity (coming up with a solution to end starvation and create peace on earth, all in time for dinner)

- ✔ Decreased need for sleep (feeling rested with three to four hours of sleep a night)

- ✔ Extreme need and pressure to talk

- ✔ Racing and rapid thoughts

- ✔ Extremely short attention span

- ✔ Drastically increased activity level (engaging in a lot of projects or mowing the lawn at 2:00 a.m.)

- ✔ Excessive engagement in pleasurable activities that have potentially damaging consequences (gambling your house payment, spending sprees, sexual excursions)

Someone showing signs and symptoms of bipolar disorder must have had at least one episode of mania in his or her life and currently be experiencing a manic, depressed, or mixed episode (both depression and mania). So basically, in order to be diagnosed with bipolar disorder, a person has to experience both depression and mania — hence the concept of severe mood swings. People suffering from dipolar disorder commonly have several recurring episodes. It can be a devastating illness, often because of the trouble that a manic individual can get into. When someone is manic, it's not uncommon for her to amass extremely large debts, incur broken relationships, or even engage in illegal or criminal acts.

This disorder is like being on a roller coaster of extreme emotion (sometimes sad, sometimes happy) beyond all proportion. These mood swings do not occur within a day or even within a week. Bipolar disorder refers to mood swings that occur over a long period of time, like four mood episodes (either depression, manic, or mixed) within a ten-year period. These episodes can last anywhere from one week to years. Some people, however, have what is called *rapid cycling* — they may experience four or more episodes within a one-year period. These individuals have a poorer prognosis because of how disruptive the episodes can be. There's no time to get their life back together again between episodes.

Revealing bipolar disorder's causes

The most popular theories on the causes of bipolar disorder, and more specifically mania, have been biological. Research has implicated neurochemical abnormalities in the specific parts of the brain that involve both the neurotransmitters dopamine and serotonin. There is little other conclusive evidence.

Long before biological studies, however, the psychoanalysts offered their explanation. Their proposition in its simplest form is that mania is a defensive reaction to depression. Rather than feeling overwhelmed with depression, a person's mind makes a switch of sorts, turning that extreme sadness into extreme happiness. The symbolic equivalent to this idea is laughing when someone you love dies. It's a severe form of denial. When a manic patient is seen in psychoanalytic-oriented psychotherapy, this defensive hypothesis is the main focus.

Stress too is thought to play a role in intensifying the mood episodes within bipolar disorder. Stress doesn't necessarily cause mania or depression, but it can make matters worse or speed up the arrival of an oncoming mood episode.

Treating bipolar disorder

Currently, the first line in treating bipolar disorder is medication. A class of drugs known as *mood stabilizers* is used to stabilize a person's mood and reduce the likelihood of future episodes. Common mood stabilizers are Lithium and Depakote. Supportive psychotherapy can be used to help people deal with the negative consequences of some of their manic behavior and come to terms with the seriousness of their illness. Cognitive-behavioral therapy has been used increasingly within recent years toward the goals of increased behavioral self-management and identification of early warning signs of an upcoming mood episode.

Being Scared

There are euphemisms a plenty when it comes to this next major class of mental disorders, the *anxiety disorders*. "Stress," "worry," "nerves," "nervousness," and "fear" are all terms we use every day, and we seem to think that we know what they mean. *Anxiety* can be defined as a sense of generalized fear and apprehension. When we're anxious, we're generally fearful. Fearful of what? That depends. Identifying what someone is fearful of helps determine what kind of anxiety disorder he or she may have.

Normal worrying aside, anxiety disorders are probably the most common type of mental disorder. But is worrying actually a mental disorder? Remember, all behavior and mental processes exist on a continuum of normality. Worry can be so intense or bothersome to the worrier that it could reach the level of a disorder in need of professional attention. Worried about being a pathological worrier yet? Relax, take a deep breath, and read on. There's more to cover before you start jumping to conclusions and running for help.

Some of the most common anxiety disorders include:

- **Generalized anxiety disorder:** Excessive and persistent worry about many different things

- **Posttraumatic stress disorder:** Re-experiencing traumatic events that were life threatening, including symptoms of heightened arousal and avoidance of trauma-related places and people

- **Obsessive-compulsive disorder:** Obsessions (recurring thoughts) and compulsive behavior (driven to repeat an activity like hand-washing)

In this chapter, I focus on one of the most common anxiety disorders known as *panic disorder.*

Some people are afraid to leave their homes, and it's not because they live in a bad neighborhood. The people who I'm referring to suffer from a phobia of large, open places called *agoraphobia.* Agoraphobia is typically associated with a major anxiety disorder known as *panic disorder* — a condition in which a person experiences recurring panic or anxiety attacks and a fear of future attacks.

Scared sweaterless

People can worry about or fear all kinds of things. When someone is extremely afraid of a particular thing or situation, even if he or she knows it poses no real danger, we call that a *phobia.* There are different types of phobias. Social phobia is the fear of people. Agoraphobia is the fear of being outdoors or in crowded places. Angoraphobia is fear of sweaters and heavy winter coats. I was just kidding about the last one, but hundreds of phobias are out there. Here are a few notables:

- **Acrophobia:** Fear of heights

- **Claustrophobia:** Fear of closed spaces

- **Nyctophobia:** Fear of the dark

- **Mysophobia:** Fear of germ contamination

- **Zoophobia:** Fear of animals or a specific animal

The *DSM-IV* definition for a panic attack is "A discrete period of intense fear or discomfort, in which four (or more) of the following symptoms developed abruptly and reached a peak within 10 minutes:"

✔ Palpitations, pounding heart, or accelerated heart rate

✔ Sweating, trembling, or shaking

✔ Shortness of breath, feeling of choking, or chest pain

✔ Nausea, dizziness, or lightheadedness

✔ Feelings of unreality or being detached from oneself

✔ Fear of losing control or going crazy or dying

✔ Numbness, tingling, chills, or hot flashes

A person who has recurrent panic attacks may be suffering from panic disorder if he worries incessantly about having more attacks, has unrealistic fears of the implications of the attack, or has significantly changed his behavior as a result of the attacks. A hallmark of panic disorder is the fear the panic attacks are a signal of some major illness, such as a heart attack, losing one's mind, or dying. This symptom can be very serious because it can lead to excessive stress. Worrying about dying can be pretty stressful and may well be a factor in the very illnesses actively dreaded.

The most common change in a person's behavior is the development of agoraphobia. This state involves an intense fear of being in places or situations in which it might be difficult to get away or to get help if needed. Common examples of situations associated with agoraphobia are riding in elevators, standing in a large crowd, traveling on a crowded subway car, or even driving in thick traffic.

This is only the first half of agoraphobia though. The other part involves the person avoiding these potentially trapping situations and, often, confining themselves to their homes. This symptom can be extremely stressful for the person suffering from panic disorder and for his or her family members as well. What kind of life can you have if your spouse or parent won't leave the house? Severe marital strain is not uncommon with these patients.

Revealing panic disorder's causes

There are at least two excellent explanations of panic disorder, David Barlow's *biopsychosocial approach* and the *cognitive model*.

Barlow's main idea is that panic attacks are the result of an overreactive fear response within the brain under stress. Certain individuals possess a physiological vulnerability in which their nervous systems sometimes overreact.

This biological vulnerability is paired with the psychological vulnerability caused by exaggerated beliefs that regard certain bodily sensations and the world, in general, as dangerous and the misperception (hopefully) regarding the dangerousness of the world in general.

The cognitive model (Beck, Emery, & Greenberg, 1985) is very similar to Barlow's model, but it emphasizes the person's beliefs more. The basic idea is that panic attacks are the result of a misattribution of normal bodily sensations that leads to increased fear, which in turn exacerbates the sensations, which in turn leads to more misattribution. It's like a vicious cycle. A person interprets something that he feels as life threatening or dangerous, which makes him worry and intensifies both the feeling and his fear of it.

Treating panic disorder

Panic disorder is treated with both medications and various forms of psychotherapy. Antidepressant medications known as tricyclics have been used successfully to reduce the occurrence of panic. Benzodiazapines, a class of "relaxing" drugs, also have been used successfully.

Behavior therapy has been highly successful with panic patients. It sounds kind of cruel, but behavior therapy basically involves teaching relaxation techniques and then in small-step increments, exposing patients to situations that formerly triggered panic and teaching them to endure the panic attack until it subsides. It sounds like torture, but it works. Cognitive therapy also has been used to teach sufferers to change their thinking in ways that reduce their tendency to misperceive or misinterpret their bodily sensations and blow them out of proportion. The intent is to change "what if thinking" to "so what thinking" through education regarding both physiological processes and available sources of help, if needed.

Chapter 17

Figuring Out the Criminals with Forensic Psychology

*M*any of us seem rather fascinated with crimes and criminals. I'm not basing this statement on any scientific evidence, but have you been to the video store lately? Movies about crimes and those who commit them dominate the shelves. The evening news, primetime television shows, and practically all other forms of popular media keenly focus their camera lenses on crime.

I don't know why this is. Maybe we focus on crime because of its powerful impact on the lives of everyone involved, from the victim to the perpetrator. Maybe it's just a morbid curiosity. One thing is for sure though, whether we're fascinated by it or not, crime affects everyone. Statistics show that one out of three people will be a victim of crime at least once this year. Crime has been a hot topic for politicians because of these appalling crime rates in the United States.

A lot of us are criminals actually. You don't think so? When was the last time you broke the speed limit? Yeah, I know, big deal. The crimes that hold much of our fascination are a little more exciting, horrific, or scary than barreling down the freeway. I'm thinking about murder, bank robbery, drug dealing, and many of the other crimes usually considered felonies. A *felony* is a major crime, such as murder, arson, or rape, which typically carries a punishment of imprisonment for a year or more. Psychologists also seem to have been caught up in this curiosity about crime. In fact, an entire branch of psychology is devoted to investigating crime and criminals. *Forensic psychology* is the application of psychological knowledge and science to the law and legal issues. In this chapter, I introduce you to the basic aspects of forensic psychology and cover some of the more intriguing areas in greater detail.

Consulting the Experts

Psychologists appear to be a logical choice to provide answers to questions surrounding the complexity of crime and criminal behavior. They're trained to understand and even change human behavior and mental processes. Crime may be viewed as a type of "societal illness." Most often, the "cure" for this illness is our legal system, police, district attorneys, judges, defense lawyers, jails, and prisons. The penal code of each state is like the *Diagnostic and Statistical Manual,* 4th Edition, for these societal disorders. No doubt, we spend a lot of money to prevent crime and to arrest and reform those who commit criminal acts. Each professional in the process plays an important role, and forensic psychologists come to the game with the tools of their trade, their knowledge.

Forensic psychologists typically possess a doctoral degree such as a Ph.D., EdD, or PsyD and have special training and/or experience in forensic psychology. The list of activities that forensic psychologists engage in can get pretty long. Some of the activities seem exciting, and some of them may put most people to sleep. Here are just a few:

- ✔ Predicting dangerousness or narcotics addiction (suitability for court mandated substance abuse treatment). Some people represent a danger to society due to a mental illness. Psychologists are often asked to evaluate the level of risk an individual poses as a consequence of a mental disorder.

- ✔ Competency to stand trial evaluations.

- ✔ Insanity plea evaluations. (See "Pleading insanity" later in this chapter.)

- ✔ Jury selection and witness preparation. Lawyers often consult with psychologists in selecting potentially helpful jurors. When witnesses play a key role in a case, lawyers sometimes ask psychologists to help the witnesses deal with the stress and complexity of testifying. Testifying in court can be especially stressful for children.

- ✔ Criminal profiling and consultation with law enforcement. (See "Profiling" later in this chapter.)

Some of these duties involve the court calling a psychologist as an expert witness. At other times, a prosecutor or defense attorney hires the psychologist. To gain "expert" status, a forensic psychologist usually has to be recognized by the court (a judge, in fact) as an expert. Typically, forensic experts possess a license as a psychologist in the state that they work in, have had some formal education or training in forensics, and have learned to use specialized tools and techniques for work in this area. Ultimately though, it all comes down to whether a judge thinks a prospective psychologist is qualified, and it's up to a jury to determine if it believes the psychologist's expert testimony.

Determining Why the Good Go Bad

Perspectives concerning the cause of criminal behavior range from criminality as a product of an inherent corruptness of a person's inner nature to criminality resulting from the powerful influences of a group or society. *Crime* is a legal concept that defines a legal wrong that can be addressed followed by criminal proceedings, which may result in punishment. *Criminal law* is the body of laws defining offenses and how offenders should be dealt with.

An interesting point to keep in mind is that not all societies, or individuals who make up a society, hold the same views on how criminals should be dealt with. *Penal philosophies* are viewpoints on why and how criminals should be punished.

Three basic philosophical positions are

- ✔ **Retribution:** Justice and personal responsibility for one's actions are expected and enforced by the larger society and not by individual victims. Punishment is institutionalized in the form of police, courts, and jails. If my neighbor steals my car, I don't have to confront him myself; I can just call the police.

- ✔ **Utilitarianism:** The focus here is on prevention. The moral principal of *utility* holds that the greatest happiness for the greatest number of people is ideal. Criminals disrupt this process and should be dealt with to get them back in line with this philosophy.

- ✔ **Reformation:** Rehabilitation and change is the desired end result of this position. The assumption is that crimes result from personal deficiencies and maladjustment.

Psychologists are just one group of professionals working on the problem of crime. Crime is a complex phenomenon, and it would be an oversimplification to state that all aspects of crime can be completely understood from a psychological viewpoint.

Sociological theories

A powerful sociological view of criminal behavior comes from *differential association theory.* Sociological theories approach human problems from a group and societal level whereas psychological theories tend to focus on individual people. Differential association theory is not complex. It simply states that criminal behavior is learned. Criminals themselves will tell you that they learned their "trade" from watching other people commit crimes. Some critics of prisons have even argued that prisons are just schools for learning how to commit bigger and better crimes. Go see the movie *Blow;* it covers this idea.

In differential association theory, criminal behavior is a learned behavior used to meet needs that are not being met by noncriminal means. If I can't provide for my family for example, I'll just sell drugs or rob a liquor store. How is criminal behavior learned? Do criminals go to special vocational schools that most of us are not invited to? I wonder what your SAT score would have to be to get into that school? Actually, criminal behavior is learned through social interactions within peer groups. Sometimes, it's even learned from the media. The young men who committed the horrible murders at Columbine High School in Colorado in 1999 claimed that they got the idea for their crimes from a movie.

If a peer group sees more value in breaking the law than in obeying it, they'll endorse crime, that is, they'll support the breaking of the law. Criminal techniques, motives, drives, rationalizations, and attitudes are all part of the crime curriculum, so to speak. The specific types of crime that a group endorses depend, in part, on their view of the law, in general, and their views of specific laws, as well. For example, some subgroups endorse selling drugs but don't allow armed robbery.

In 1986, Hirshci devised a theory that puts control of criminal impulses and urges at the center of understanding criminal acts. *Control theory* assigns a crucial role to *self-control* in this process. Criminal acts are often impulsive and performed on the spur of the moment. If I can't delay my need for gratification, I may just go out and get what I need now, anyway that I see fit. A crucial deterrent to criminal behavior is the bond between an individual and society. When this bond is weakened or severed, delinquency or criminality is likely. The bond between an individual and society depends upon a few factors:

- The degree to which an individual has internalized the norms of society in the form of a conscience. Should I always drive the speed limit or do so only when a cop is around? If I believe in the importance of speed laws for safety, I'll obey. If not, I haven't internalized that norm and am likely to only slow down when a cop is around.

- The degree to which an individual actually cares about what other people think. If I don't care what you think, I'll do whatever I feel like.

- The degree to which an individual is committed to normal pursuits and conventional goals in life. I may not want to graduate from high school, go to college, get a 9-to-5 job, and commute two hours a day to work and back for a measly paycheck. I may want to get my money the easy way — steal it!

Learning theories

One of the most powerful theories in all of psychology is the theory of operant conditioning. When I perform a behavior it is followed by some consequence, like a reward or a punishment. Learning occurs when I've learned that when I do A, I consequently receive B.

Jeffrey (1965) tried to explain criminal behavior by looking at what criminals get out of committing crimes. What's the payoff? What rewards follow a criminal act that might increase the likelihood that the perpetrator will do it again? If I steal, I get some money, and money is a pretty good reward. Other rewards include peer-approval, and the thrill from committing the act itself. No matter what I get out of it, the fact that I receive some reward is enough to keep the behavior going. Remember *operant conditioning* earlier in the book? (If not, check out Chapter 9.) Rats press bars to get sugar pellets. Criminals commit crimes to get whatever "sugar pellet" they get out of the criminal act.

Another version of a learning theory comes from the *social-learning* perspective. Bandura and Walters (1963) and Bandura (1986) emphasize the role of worrying about getting socially chastised for crimes as a powerful deterrent to criminal behavior. This theory overlaps with the *control theory* (see the "Sociological theories" section earlier in this chapter), but relies more on the role of learning in terms of watching other people get punished or socially punished for their criminal behavior. Social punishment often comes in the forms of guilt and social isolation. Sometimes, being shunned can be the worse punishment of all. This theory sounds a little bit like a "Bad boys commit crimes, do you want to be a bad boy?" theory. However, some research supports this idea. Grasmick and Green found that when teenagers worry about being socially punished, they're less likely to commit crimes.

Psychoanalytic theories come from the psychic determinism school of thought. All of our behavior is the direct consequence of or is determined by what is going on inside our *psyches* or minds. Sigmund Freud, the father of psychoanalysis, viewed all human beings as inherently selfish and in a state of social conflict. (You can read more about Freud in Chapter 10.) We're all born with needs that we feel must be satisfied when and where we feel like it! There's only one problem with this state of affairs; there are powerful forces working against us, namely, other people. Eventually we learn to rein in these desires and channel them into more socially acceptable means of satisfaction. We develop a conscience in the form of our *superego* to help keep our behavior in accordance with acceptable moral standards. For Freud and other psychoanalysts, criminal behavior is the result of a damaged or deficient superego and, perhaps, poor resolution of what Freud termed the developmental core conflicts: independence versus dependence, aggression versus its control, and sensuality versus its denial.

According to Stott, another view of criminal behavior is that it's a way to achieve gratification and a sense of personal power in the presence of an overly demanding superego. Sometimes the superego can be too harsh, demanding and expecting perfect morality. These demands can lead to feelings of chronic anxiety and insecurity because the individual continuously feels guilty for things that he or she didn't do. Freud felt that some criminal behavior was the physical result of a conflict between our genuine needs and our harsh superegos. We feel guilty all the time, so we seek punishment from our conscience by doing bad things. It's almost like saying to oneself, "Well, if I'm going to feel guilty, I might as well have something to feel guilty about."

Other psychoanalytic theorists view criminality less as a consequence of an overly harsh superego and more as a result of a weak one. In this case, the superego fails to provide enough pressure through our conscience to suppress our rebellious and selfish desires, leading people to do whatever they wish to meet their needs. This insufficient control over one's impulses is due to failures in child development. This theory fits with a common-sense notion that criminal or delinquent behavior is the result of poor parental control and a failure to instill good moral values in children.

The final psychoanalytic view is a "like father, like son" theory. If you're married to a career criminal, your children may say, "I want to grow up to be just like Daddy." This statement would worry you, if you believe in the theory that criminal behavior is a consequence of a child's identification with a criminal role model, desiring to emulate him or her when he or she gets older. Some psychoanalysts believe it. In this case, there's an absence of guilt associated with criminal acts because "Daddy does it." No parental or superego controls prohibit criminal behavior. In many ways, it's like having a superego that says, "Go ahead, it's okay!"

Developmental theories

Developmental theories try to account for behavior and mental processes by analyzing how they developed over a person's life span. Lawrence Kohlberg developed a developmental theory of moral development. For many people, criminal behavior and immorality are one in the same. I realize that this is not always the case, and there are times when a person's moral system may or may not be in accordance with the law. Some people advocate breaking the law in order to uphold what they consider to be higher moral principles. Martin Luther King Jr. and many others before him advocated civil disobedience, which resulted in violations of the law in the name of a greater good. Morality and criminality are not always the same, but there is considerable overlap.

Kohlberg's theory is about moral thinking or reasoning. The idea is that people who commit crimes are morally underdeveloped. Their moral growth is stunted. The more sophisticated a person's moral system, the less likely they are to commit crimes. The stages of Kohlberg's moral developmental theory are as follows:

✔ **Level 1 — Preconventional:** Morals or rules are seen as external to oneself.

- **Stage 1:** Obedience and punishment orientation. Moral behavior is carried out because of fear of punishment. Right action is only engaged in to avoid punishment.

- **Stage 2:** Instrumental purpose and exchange. If being good serves my immediate purpose, I'll do it. If not, forget it. I'm also motivated to get what I want as long as no one gets hurt. This argument is often used to promote the legalization of illicit drugs in the United States (I'm only hurting myself, and so on).

✔ **Level 2 — Conventional:** Moral behavior is a consequence of buying into the social norms and expectations of others.

- **Stage 3:** Interpersonal accord. I'll do right because I'm expected to; it's my duty!

- **Stage 4:** Social accord or system maintenance. Doing right is what's best for society.

✔ **Level 3 — Postconventional:** Social morality is distinguished from absolute or universal standards.

- **Stage 5:** Social contract. I'll do right because I've got an unwritten contract with society to do so. Not breaking the contract is the guiding principle.

- **Stage 6:** Universal ethical principles. Morality is defined by the individual's realization of the universal principles of right and wrong. Just because society sees something as right doesn't necessarily make it right. As long as society's rules are consistent with these universal principles, I'll do right. If not, I'll go by the univesal principles.

Research seems to suggest that young criminals or delinquents demonstrate preconventional levels of moral reasoning. Don't worry about Stage 6 though. Kohlberg reserved this category for such people as Martin Luther King Jr. and Gandhi. Do you obey the speed limit because it's the universally right thing to do? Or is it because of that speeding ticket you got last week? Sounds kind of preconventional to me!

Personality theories

Maybe we commit crimes because it's simply a part of who we are. Some people have the personality of a natural-born leader. Others could have made a graduation speech to their kindergarten class titled, "Born to Steal."

Hans Eysenck, a psychologist, proposed that criminality is due to an inborn disposition to perform criminal acts. A *disposition* is an inclination or a tendency to do something. Eysenck's "born bad" theory is fairly complex. He makes the argument that environmental factors (such as poverty, criminal role models, and a history of child abuse), alone, can't possibly account for criminal behavior because not everyone from a bad environment commits criminal acts. I traveled in one of the poorest nations in the world, Jordan, and I was surprised to learn that there was very little crime there. I didn't do any research, but the people left their homes unlocked, for example, and didn't seem particularly concerned with being ripped off.

- ✔ **Proximal contributions:** Consist of biological aspects of personality such as metabolic rates, hormones, and nervous system activity. Eysenck believes that people with specific abnormalities in these areas may be predisposed to criminality. A popular finding by both Eysenck and Zuckerman is that people who are under-aroused and easily bored engage in sensation-seeking behavior that may often include engaging in thrilling criminal acts.

- ✔ **Distal contributions:** Come from the genetic determinants of our personalities, our DNA. There is the idea that there exists either an inherited key gene or inherited multiple genes that account for the similarity of personality characteristics that lead to criminal behavior between parent and offspring. These causes of criminality are less close to the overt expression of criminal propensity.

Eysenck also identifies three personality types, or characteristics, that he relates to acting out in a criminal manner:

- ✔ **Psychoticism:** Individuals high in this personality type have a better chance of making the criminal cut. They tend to be more antisocial, unempathetic, creative, and tough-minded. All of these traits are consistent with many criminal behaviors.

- ✔ **Extraversion:** People who are carefree, dominant, assertive, and adventurous possess this implicated personality characteristic.

- ✔ **Neuroticism:** This dimension includes people who are irrational, shy, moody, and emotional. They too may lean toward criminal behavior.

High GNP = High crime?

An interesting bit of anecdotal support for Hans Eysenck's challenge to the environmental cause of criminality concept is that crime is directly related to wealth. Ellis and Peterson found that in 13 industrialized nations, the higher a country's gross national product (GNP) was, the higher the crime rate was. Go figure? Maybe there's just more to steal in a wealthy country. What am I going to steal in a poverty-stricken nation? Nobody has anything.

Eysenck does not go so far as to say that these personality aspects actually cause criminality, but he does state that they are powerful contributors to the risk for developing criminal behaviors.

Biological and neuropsychological theories

There has been a fairly large amount of biological and neuropsychological research on criminality. That is, a lot of scientists have tried to find the origin of criminal behavior in either the genes or the brains of people who commit these acts. That's the good news. The bad news is that a lot of the research is still inconclusive and very difficult to interpret.

Studies of the biology and neuropsychology of criminality have looked at such diverse topics as genetics, hormones, neurotransmitters, brain waves, body type, brain damage, and learning disabilities. I'm going to narrow things down a little bit in this chapter and only focus on genetics and neuro-psychological abnormalities, two topics that we think we have a pretty good handle on.

Genes

Hans Eysenck mentions genetics and other biological functions in his person-ality theory of criminality. Eysenck believes that our personalities are geneti-cally determined. Some evidence exists to support his claim that genetics do play a part in determining who might be likely to engage in criminal acts and who might not.

Genetic contributions to criminality traditionally have been investigated using the popular *twin-adoption method* of research. The logic is that if you look at sets of identical twins that are not raised together and they act in much the same way, their behavior is probably due to genetics. Why? If they're not raised together, the likelihood that they had exactly the same environmental influences is slim to none Therefore, the only things they have in common are their genes (because their genes are identical) and their behavior.

Is there a "crime gene?" That would be far too simple. Numerous studies show common criminal behaviors in twins reared together. Langein found that 71 percent of identical twin pairs reared apart had comparable criminal conviction rates. Dizygotic, or fraternal, twins in the same study only had a 12 percent hit rate. Most of the other studies have similar rates, but all have found the same higher rate in identical twins when compared to fraternal twins. The only problem is that these twins grew up in the same, or very similar, environments. Adoption studies have been less conclusive. Crowein found that 15 percent of adopted-out, identical twins of incarcerated women had a similar criminal arrest record compared to 3 percent for fraternal twins. Cadoretin found comparable arrest rates of 22 percent for identical twins versus 0 percent for fraternal twins.

An interesting qualification for most of the research findings in this area is that the percentages hold up for property crimes but not for violent crimes. Still, the propensity to commit crimes in general seems to have some relationship to our genes. The relationships are far from perfect, 15 percent and 22 percent are hardly hardcore predictors. That still leaves approximately 81.5 percent of the differences in criminal behavior not accounted for by genetics. Good thing we have all these other theories. If we relied on genetic theories alone, we'd know very little.

Neuropsychological abnormalities

Is there a "criminal" part of the brain? Well, if there is one, nobody has found it yet. Research on the roles of specific parts of the brain is more indirect than direct. In fact, much of the research on neuropsychological abnormalities in people who habitually commit crimes is inconclusive.

Moffit's theory is perhaps the best-known theory of neuropsychological dysfunction in those who commit crimes. The idea is that there is a pattern of general neuropsychological dysfunction that leads to an individual's inability to select alternative paths or behaviors to criminality. Moffit proposed that a lot of adolescents "grow out of" their criminal activities, and those who do not have these deficits. These individuals would have problems with attention, abstract reasoning, cognitive flexibility, strategic planning, use of environmental feedback, and inhibition. To this day, however, little research supports Moffit's theory. It remains a theory, and the search for the criminal brain continues.

Pinning down the "super criminals" — Criminal psychopaths

When I think of the perfect example of a criminal, a few images come quickly to mind — the criminal mastermind plotting the ultimate crime, the callous armed robber putting a gun in a bank teller's face, or the serial killer cleverly evading the police.

Each of these images represents an aspect of the stereotypic villain — intelligent but demented, cold and ruthless, violent and destructive. Batman fought against the Riddler, Catwoman, and the Joker. Superman battled Lex Luthor. All of these villains represent people who often engage in extreme criminal behavior and challenge our concept of morality. Such people have intrigued professionals for years. They're on the front page of the newspaper, and they're the lead story on the evening news. They sit in our prisons, and they're sometimes executed for their horrific behavior. These are the *psychopaths*.

There have been a lot of definitions of the psychopath. In fact, some professionals don't see psychopaths as necessarily criminals at all but rather as suffering from a clinical disorder. The title of this section may imply that all psychopaths are criminals, but, in fact, this may not be true. It is a fact, however, that many psychopaths act criminally, and when they do, they typically represent a level of seriousness unparalleled by non-psychopathic perpetrators. Therefore, for the purposes of this chapter, I focus on those psychopathic individuals who do often commit crimes or end up involved with the criminal justice system.

Robert Hare gives us a comprehensive list of psychopathic personality traits that outline the major features of this disordered personality.

- Glib and superficial charm
- Callousness and lack of empathy
- Grandiose sense of self worth
- Parasitic lifestyle (lives off of other people)
- Need for stimulation, prone to boredom
- Poor behavioral controls
- Pathological lying
- Promiscuous sexual behavior
- Conning and manipulativeness
- Early behavior problems (temper tantrums and disobedience)
- Lack of remorse or guilt
- Failure to accept personal responsibility
- Shallow affect (no deep feelings about anything or anyone)
- Revocation of conditional release (put back in jail after failing at reform)
- Lack of realistic, long-term goals
- Many short-term marriages
- Impulsivity
- Juvenile delinquency
- Irresponsibility
- Criminal versatility (good at a lot of different crimes)

Digging into deviants

If you're interested in more information, check out the following titles:

✔ *The Anatomy of Motive,* by John E. Douglas and Mark Olshaker (Wheeler Publishing)

✔ *Serial Offenders: Current Thoughts, Recent Findings,* edited by Louis B. Schlesinger (CRC Press)

✔ *Sexual Homicide: Patterns and Motives,* by Robert K. Ressler, Ann W. Burgess, John E. Douglas, and Horace J. Heafner (Simon & Schuster)

Wow, that's quite a list, I know. But this checklist has become a real standard for evaluating people in court cases, prisons, and forensic hospitals. Some of these traits seem more "villainous" than the others and are worth taking a closer look at.

Two hallmarks of psychopaths is their smooth presentation and charm. They're not easily embarrassed or even mildly self-conscious. They're calm in social situations because they couldn't care less about what other people think of them. Sometimes, they come off as if they're the hottest things since sliced bread. They're often full of themselves and see other people as inferior and easy prey. They'll lie, cheat, and manipulate to get whatever it is they want, and they'll do all of this with a coldness of heart. Psychopaths don't feel remorseful or guilty for any of their transgressions and can sometimes be so cold that they are extremely ruthless, possessing no empathy for the suffering of others. Finally, a host of crimes that they have either been convicted of or have admitted to doing represent their criminal versatility. The range is impressive, from murder to fraud, forgery, kidnapping, arson, tax evasion. . . . Get the picture?

Setting apart the serial killers

Dahmer, Bundy, Gacy, Ramirez, Jack the Ripper, Fish, the list goes on. Serial murderers represent perhaps the most serious and morbidly fascinating image of criminality. They're modern-day boogeymen. They commit horrific acts of violence and indulge in strange and perverted acts with their victims. The concept of evil comes quickly to mind when thinking of their deeds.

Psychologists, however, are not scientists of evil. They're scientists of behavior and mental processes. That doesn't mean serial murderers' behaviors and minds cannot be studied from a psychological point of view. Richard von Krafft-Ebbing is understood by many experts to have provided the seminal work on serial killers, *Pscyhopathia Sexualis* (Sexual Psychopathology), published in 1886. Many contend that much of what is known about serial homicide is contained in that work. Before we get into some of that information, however, a quick definition of serial murder is in order.

Serial murder is commonly viewed among professionals as a sexually motivated "subtype" of sexual homicide. That is, serial murder is sexually motivated. Grubin states that the sexual nature of these crimes is seen in the way a perpetrator's sexual arousal is connected to his victim's pain and humiliation. *Serial killers* are distinguished from *mass murderers* (killing a bunch of people at one location at one time) and *spree killers* (killing a number of victims at different locations within hours or days).

Krafft-Ebing identified three main components of sexual homicide that experts still focus on today.

- ✔ **Sadism:** Sexual arousal from the physical suffering, humiliation, or control of a victim is central to the serial killer's psychology. There's an absolute need to control another, weaker human being, and great sexual satisfaction is derived from this act.

- ✔ **Fantasy:** Beres defines a fantasy as a group of symbols combined into a story. It's a mental phenomenon, inside the minds of those who fantasize. I fantasize about being rich. Sexual murderers fantasize about killing and torturing their victims. Their ritualistic behaviors at the crime scenes are seen as outgrowths of their fantasy life, a way to make the fantasy real. Fledgling serial murderers begin to engage in fantasy early in their life, building on the complexity and intensity of the fantasy as they go along.

- ✔ **Compulsion to kill:** Plenty of people have kinky sexual urges and sometimes even destructive fantasies. Couture found that even normal men can have sexual fantasies involving violent and aggressive images, including rape scenes. So, just being a sadist and having a violent fantasy life does not a serial killer make. At least for now, in this society we are responsible on the level of our behavior — no "thought police," yet. Revitch and Schlesinger believe that acting out sadistic fantasies is made possible by a compulsive need to do so. A *compulsion* is like a burning and irresistible need, driving me to do whatever it is that I need to do. When I finally do it, I feel an intense, almost-orgasmic sense of relief. Revitch and Schlesinger believe that the sequence is something like this: sadism → fantasy → tension state → compulsion → action. The murderous act is, therefore, experienced as an act of release, which is pleasurable and therefore reinforcing of the prior sequence of events and make its repetition likely.

This information is powerful and very interesting. My only fear is that people will go out there and think that they've got serial killers all figured out. This discussion is a really crude introduction to the topic of sexual homicide. Some professionals have devoted their entire careers to figuring out how these people tick. It's not that easy.

Profiling

Speaking of the professionals devoted to figuring these people out, the attempt to apprehend these individuals based in part on information about their personality and mental state is called *psychological profiling*. Keppel and Walter call it *crime scene assessment*. It's an attempt to ascertain important information about the perpetrator of the crime(s), such as his physical, behavioral, and demographic characteristics, and figure out the *signature* of the perpetrator. A signature is a component of the crime that is unique to that particular killer and can be found across multiple crime scenes.

Keppel states that two very important features for developing a psychological profile of an offender are his signature and his *modus operandi*. Again, a killer's signature is the feature of the crime scene that is unique to that offender. It may be the way a rope is tied around a victim's hands or the particular way the victim is tortured. Modus operandi (MO) refers to the particular method of operation of the killer, including the object of the crime, the means, the time, and so on. The MO can change, but the signature usually doesn't.

Park Dietz is a very well-known forensic psychiatrist who sees psychological profiling as a systematic problem-solving activity with five basic steps:

1. The profiler gathers data, including crime scene photos, autopsy reports, witness statements, and forensic lab reports.

2. She attempts to reconstruct the sequence of events before, during, and after the murder.

3. The profiler tries to reconstruct what the perpetrator(s) and victim(s) were experiencing mentally and emotionally that may have led them to act this way. It's an analysis of their motivations, the "why" of their crime.

4. She uses the information that she has gathered to develop a criminal *typing* — an attempt to fit the offender into a category (sexual sadist or thrill-killer, for example).

5. The profiler tries to use the previous information to figure out what kind of person would do this — man, woman, tall, short, and so on. They even try to figure out what kinds of work he or she may do and any other activities that he or she may engage in. From this information, the expert establishes a profile and gives it to law enforcement officials to use at their discretion.

Excusing or Explaining

When someone is arrested and tried for a crime, he has several options when he goes to court. If he is competent enough to stand trial, he might plead innocent, guilty, or not guilty by reason of insanity. Forensic experts are often consulted when a defendant introduces his mental health as a factor in the crime.

Competency to stand trial

Have you ever been to court? Have you ever been a defendant in court? If so, you may have noticed how confusing the whole thing can be. I've seen judges give instructions to defendants so fast that you'd think they were speaking another language. Lawyers give you the run down and tell you to sign some paperwork that you've never seen before. Next thing you know, you're free to go. Great! But then you get a bill for restitution in the mail, and you never remember agreeing to pay any restitution. The entire court experience can be pretty confusing and overwhelming. Even people without a mental disorder can have a difficult time understanding the whole legal process. They actually have whole schools devoted to understanding the legal process. They're called law schools.

In this country, a defendant cannot be tried unless believed capable (competent) to understand the nature and purpose of the proceedings being taken against him/her and unless a defendant is also believed capable of assisting counsel in presenting a defense. Forensic experts are utilized to make this determination (current mental illness or disease and the competence to stand trial).

Competency to stand trial refers to a situation in which defendants

- ✔ Are able to understand (or totally deny) the charges against them and report the facts regarding their behavior at the time of the crime
- ✔ Can reasonably cooperate with their lawyers and assist in their defense
- ✔ Can understand the court proceedings

If a defendant can't perform any of these actions, she's typically found incompetent to stand trial for the crime that she's accused of. Forensic experts are called upon to make competency recommendations to the court. Contested recommendations regarding a defendant's competence to stand trial might even be decided by a jury. That's right, jury involvement to determine if a trial can proceed.

So, what happens to individuals who are found incompetent to stand trial? Can they just go home? The judge doesn't simply open up the doors of the courthouse and send these people on their way. Although procedures in most states differ somewhat, after defendants are found *incompetent to stand trial,* in most states, such defendants are mandated to psychiatric facilities to receive mental health treatment designed to restore them to competence for a specified length of time or for the length of time they would have served if convicted, or which ever is shorter (most states). This means that someone could be in a hospital for several years (e.g., three years in California on a felony charge). Sometimes if the hospital staff thinks competency cannot be restored, they will return a defendant to court before the expiration of the commitment term with a recommendation for the filing of a conservatorship. A mental health conservatorship is a civil procedure based upon "grave disability" designed to provide supervision of placement, treatment, and/or money management to individuals believed incapable of providing for their own needs for food, clothing, and shelter due to a severe mental illness. In some states there may also be the possibility, under certain circumstances, of establishing a conservatorship due to "dangerousness" rather than "grave disability."

The determination of conservatorship is usually done following a review of records and consultation with current treatment staff, a formal clinical interview, and perhaps some psychological testing, and contacts with family and others to determine if any alternatives to conservatorship may exist. After a recommendation to file for a conservatorship has been made, a contested hearing may be conducted in a civil courtroom with the forensic expert offering testimony in support of the recommendation to file for conservatorship. The outcome of the competency debate ultimately depends on the findings of the court and most often it is a judge and not a jury making the decision.

Pleading insanity

Every now and then, a person commits a crime, sometimes horrific and sometimes not, and his lawyer, whether it be a high-priced celebrity lawyer or his public defender, says that he was "insane" at the time the crime was committed. Most of us are familiar with this defense strategy. We've seen it in the movies, and we've seen it in real life. What counsel is arguing following a conviction or stipulated verdict ("Yeah, okay, my client is guilty as charged"), is the defendant is not guilty due to having been insane at the time of the commission of the alleged crime.

An *insanity plea* is a legal concept that states that a defendant is not legally responsible for the crime due to being insane at the time it's committed. It's a legal concept, not a clinical concept or even a logical one. Many people would see most horrible acts of murder as "insane" or that only an insane person could do such a thing. But legal insanity is different than these common-sense or clinical notions.

Each state in the United States has its own version of legal insanity, but they all basically use a standard known as the *M'Naghten rule:* The person who committed the unlawful act was "labouring under such a defect of reason, from disease of the mind, as not to know the nature and quality of the act he was doing; or, if he did know it, that he did not know he was doing what was wrong." It really comes down to whether the person committing the act knew the difference between right and wrong, and whether this confusion was due to a mental disorder or disease. If the defendant didn't know what he was doing was illegal, was this because of a mental illness?

This is the point where the forensic experts weigh in. An expert witness, like a forensic psychologist or psychiatrist, evaluates the defendant and makes a determination of whether he or she meets the criteria for legal insanity. The game is usually played with experts representing both sides, the prose-cution and the defense. It can get kind of confusing because the two (or more) experts often disagree with each other. They make their cases and are cross-examined by the opposing counsel. Ultimately, however, it all comes down to whether the jury or judge (in a court trial) believes one expert over another.

This is serious business. An expert's opinion may mean the difference between a defendant going to prison for the rest of his life, being executed, or going to a hospital for mental health treatment. You can bet that the pres-sure is on. The stakes are high, and the methods employed to make these decisions are well thought out. Three basic questions have to be answered:

- Does the defendant actually have a mental disorder or defect?
- What is the person's mental status now?
- What was the defendant's mental state at the time of the crime?

The answers to these questions only lead to more complex questions that psychologists often use psychological testing to answer.

What if someone tries to fake mental illness in order to go to a hospital instead of going to prison or receiving the death penalty? The *Diagnostic and Statistical Manual,* 4th Edition, defines *malingering* as the "intentional produc-tion of false or grossly exaggerated physical or psychological symptoms, motivated by external incentives. . . ." Can we catch a malingerer? Yes, but it's really difficult, and it's always easier if we can catch them telling someone the truth and confront them with that evidence. Malingering can be ascertained through special interview techniques and extensive psychological testing. It is, however, estimated that some significant percentage of patients remanded by criminal courts to state hospitals are, in point of fact, malingerers. There's ways to catch the liars, and forensic psychologists are on the job ever refin-ing their techniques to do just that.

Treating, Preventing, and Protecting

In addition to the more legal aspects of their work, forensic psychologists also engage in the treatment of criminal offenders, specifically those with mental illness. They also conduct "predictive" evaluations, in which they help determine if a particular person might be dangerous to the community if he or she was released from prison or a mental institution. Because professionals in this field recognize the difficulties in predicting the future, assessments of dangerousness are more assessments of identified risk factors (and the degree to which such factors can be addressed) than actual predictions of the likelihood of specific future behavior.

The Eighth Amendment to the U.S. Constitution holds that "Excessive bail shall not be required, nor excessive fines imposed, nor cruel and unusual punishments inflicted." This phrase has been interpreted to include the non-treatment of mentally ill criminal offenders while they are incarcerated. In 1978, Monahan and Steadman conducted a survey of all prisoners detained in the United States. They found that 7 percent officially were designated as mentally ill. Newer estimates range from 15 to 20 percent and rival that of the general population. Either way, the fact of the mentally ill in prison makes defenders of the Eighth Amendment nervous. They see prison as a harsh environment to begin with that can exacerbate the mental illness of a particular inmate. Ignoring such an inmate's mental health constitutes cruel and unusual punishment.

What's the answer? Provide mental health treatment in prisons and jails in the same way that medical treatment is provided. Nothing too complex there. So, in addition to the more popularly known activities of forensic psychologists, responsibility for the treatment of the mentally ill behind bars is included in their job descriptions.

Part VII
Helping You Heal

The 5th Wave — By Rich Tennant

"I'm tired of letting everyone pull my strings."

In this part . . .

Part VII starts out by introducing you to psychological testing and assessment. (Yes, this is where that famous instrument, the Rorschach inkblot test, is discussed.) Within this discussion, I deal with the most common areas of psychological assessment, such as intelligence and personality. Next, I introduce you to the traditional "talk" psychotherapies — psychoanalysis, behavior therapy, cognitive therapy, and other popular forms of psychological treatment. I give you the lowdown on the different approaches and goals of each of these therapies, and I provide a look at how each of these therapy encounters unfolds. Finally, I talk about stress and the relationship between psychological and physical health.

Chapter 18

Assessing the Problem and Testing Your Psyche

In This Chapter

▶ Taking history notes

▶ Making the grade

▶ Typing the tests

*M*any people go to a psychologist or other mental health professional because they're experiencing strong negative emotions or facing difficulties in their everyday lives. Just like visiting the family physician, a prospective patient comes into a psychologist's office with a complaint, issue, or problem. A lot of times, the individual is looking for answers because he or she is unsure about what's really going on. The psychologist listens and tries to assess the full extent of the problem, attempting to gain a fuller understanding of the patient's situation. If the psychologist gets the problem wrong, he or she won't be able to fix it. See Chapters 19 through 22 for more information on this topic.

I recently bought a new computer. I took it home, set it up, and everything seemed great. I was really excited to get on the Internet and start surfing around. When I tried to connect, it didn't work. You can imagine my frustration after I had spent over a thousand dollars on a brand new computer that wasn't working right. I spent three frantic days trying to figure out what was wrong. I changed the phone cable, I called the phone company, and I called the store I bought the computer from. Nothing I did and no one I talked to helped me fix the problem. Finally, my wife pointed out (three days later) that I had plugged a cord into the wrong jack in the back of the computer. She simply placed the cord where it belonged, dialed up the Internet, and connected with ease. I had the problem incorrectly identified and was therefore clueless about how to fix it. I figured that, because I was a scientist, I had thoroughly ruled out all possible causes and variables. Boy was I wrong.

What's the Problem?

The first step in any problem-solving endeavor is to recognize and clearly define the problem. Psychologists have specific tools and techniques at their disposal for that very purpose. Typically, a visit to the psychologist begins with an exploration of the patient's *presenting complaint* (the complaint or problem that led the patient to seek therapy) followed by a more thorough information-gathering process.

> **Psychologist:** Tell me Mr. Smith: What seems to be the problem?
>
> **Mr. Smith:** How am I supposed to know? You're the doctor.

This question sometimes annoys patients because they often don't know what's going on and expect the psychologist to have all the answers. However, without a thorough investigation of the patient's situation, any mental health professional would be engaging only in expensive guesswork. The two most common approaches to clinical assessment are formal interviews and psychological testing.

Taking down the history

There may be as many interview techniques in the psychological world as there are individual psychologists out there. Everyone has a different way of getting at the relevant information. So what is the relevant information? As I state in the previous section, most encounters begin with a discussion of the presenting problem. Very few people who come to a psychologist describe their problem according to *Diagnostic and Statistical Manual,* 4th Edition, *(DSM-IV)* criteria. Complaints are often vague or convoluted. Early communication problems between the psychologist and the patient are not necessarily because people don't understand themselves. They're often due to the fact that the doctor and patient have different vocabularies to describe the same problem. You say *toMAYto,* and I say *toMAHto.* You say you can't sleep, eat, or stop crying, and I say you're depressed.

One of the first areas in which psychological problems become evident is social functioning. During the history phase of the interview, the psychologist gathers information about the patient's family, friends, coworkers, and other major relationships. In addition to social functioning, educational and occupational functioning are assessed as well. Did the patient graduate from high school? Has she been able to stay gainfully employed?

Patients often come to therapy with a lot to say and get off their chests. They're overwhelmed and sometimes have a hard time knowing exactly how to describe their experience. Although not always so cut and dry, psychologists typically try to structure the first interview with the following steps:

1. **The presenting problem is clarified.**

2. **A history of the patient's life is gathered.**

   Is it an autobiography? In a way it is, except that only specific areas are covered. The most relevant aspect in a psychological interview is the history of the presenting problem. When did it all begin . . . ?

3. **The patient's physical health is explored.**

   An assessment of the patient's physical health and history is always important in the history-taking process. Many psychiatric or psychological problems can be the result of an underlying physical illness or condition. When was his first physical? Does she have any major medical problems? Is he taking any medications? Does she or has she abused drugs or alcohol? Does he have an altered state of consciousness that requires medical assessment or treatment?

4. **A thorough history of any psychological problems is conducted.**

   Has she ever suffered from depression in the past? Has he ever been treated for a mental disorder? Do any of her family members have a history of mental illness? Has he ever been in a psychiatric hospital or has he ever attempted suicide? Certain pieces of information are extremely important because the patient's safety could be at issue. A prudent professional always takes the time to assess the most serious aspects of a case first, and no issue is more serious to a psychologist than suicide.

Examining mental status

Throughout the interview, the psychologist looks for specific behavioral, cognitive, and emotional indicators of psychological disturbance. This is called a *mental status examination (MSE)*. Typically, the psychologist observes 11 mental status areas:

- ✔ **Appearance:** Grooming, hygiene, physical characteristics, and unusual features are observed. Grooming may be bizarre or inappropriate. He or she may be unkempt, disheveled, or unclean. A patient's weight may be a related issue, specifically being obese or severely underweight. If someone has an unusual appearance, outside of cultural or subcultural norms, it may be worth discussing.

- ✔ **Behavior:** Some of the most striking signs of disturbance come from the way people act.

  - **Body movement:** Body movements such as fidgeting, fast movements, slowed movements, or strange gestures may be relevant. Nervous individuals may fidget a lot. Depressed patients may sit slumped in their chairs. Someone with a paranoid delusion that the CIA is following him may get up and peek out the curtains every five minutes.

- **Facial expressions:** Facial expressions are important (sad, mad, immobile, or frozen expressions, for example).

✔ **Speech:** Two disorders in particular include disturbances in speech:

- **Schizophrenia:** A patient's speech may be disordered, jumbled, or difficult to understand. He or she may seem to be speaking a foreign language, using words and phrases that don't seem to make sense. I once received an anonymous phone call while volunteering at a homeless shelter. When I asked the caller if I could help him, he replied, "Stick the pin in the cushion. You called me. What do you want? The letters make me crazy . . . light bulb . . . beat the drum . . . stick the pin in the cushion . . . what do you want?" This is an excellent example of disordered speech.

- **Bipolar disorder:** The rate and pace of speech can also be abnormal. Patients currently in a manic episode can speak very fast and act as if they have to keep talking. They may jump from one topic to another.

✔ **Mood and affect:** Mood describes the predominant emotions being expressed by the patient. Is she sad, happy, angry, euphoric, or anxious? Affect refers to the range, intensity, and appropriateness of a patient's emotional behavior. Is she mildly sad or intensely sad? Does she feel anything other than sadness, or does she seem to have a full range of emotions? Another common observation of affect is called *mood liability*. How often and easily does her mood change? Is she hot one second and cold the next?

✔ **Thought content:** What people think about is relevant to any clinical evaluation. Bizarre thought content, such as delusions, can be telltale signs of the presence of a mental disorder. Less bizarre but sometimes equally disturbing thoughts, such as obsessive preoccupations and intrusive ideas, can also be signs of severe anxiety. Thoughts of death and violence are relevant to assessing suicidality and violence potential.

To each his own animal

I once saw a middle-aged gentleman wearing a pair of famous mouse ears with a mouse nose, teeth, and whiskers in a coffee shop. Now, I know it's a free country, but his appearance was unusual. Does this mean that he's mentally ill? Who knows? But there aren't a lot of middle-aged men who dress up like mice on a daily basis. When someone treats every day like Halloween, it's worth asking about. No judging or jumping to conclusions — it's just worth checking out.

✓ **Thought process:** Different ways of thinking can sometimes be clues to a disorder.

- **Tangential thinking:** Often a sign of thought disorder, tangential thinking is characterized by a wondering focus and the tendency to go off on tangents that are only minimally related to the topic currently being discussed.

- **Clang associations:** These signs are serious indicators of thought disorder. A clang association is when someone ends a sentence with a word, and the sound of that word triggers another thought, related to the conversation only by the sound of the last word uttered. "I came home from work the other day, and the car was in the driveway . . . highway's are crowded. Loud noises bother me . . . tree." This type of disordered thought is disorganized and hard to follow and doesn't make much sense.

✓ **Perception:** Perceptual problems consist of hallucinations. Patients can experience auditory hallucinations (voices), visual hallucinations, olfactory hallucinations (smells or odors), gustatory hallucinations (tastes), or somatic hallucinations (strange bodily sensations, such as feeling like bugs are crawling under one's skin). A very serious auditory hallucination is when patients hear a voice or voices telling them to hurt themselves or someone else. These are sometimes called command hallucinations.

✓ **Intellectual functioning:** This status can be casually observed by paying attention to the patient's vocabulary, general quantity of knowledge and information, and abstract thinking ability. However, trying to figure out someone's intellectual functioning based on observation alone is highly subjective and should only be used as a starting point for further assessment.

✓ **Attention/concentration and memory:** It's important to observe whether patients are distracted during the interview and have a difficult time concentrating on the task at hand. Their short-term memory can be observed by asking them to remember a few things and checking with them a few minutes later. How well they recall their history and provide historical information provides a measure of their long-term memory. Many disorders present attention problems and memory deficits.

✓ **Orientation:** Does the patient know where he or she is? The season? The time? Ascertaining whether a patient knows where he or she is in time and space is an important part of the MSE. Many serious medical conditions and neuropsychological disorders manifest signs of disorientation.

✓ **Insight and judgment:** Does the patient understand that she may be mentally ill? Does he understand the relationship between his behaviors and mental processes and a psychological disturbance? Insight is important for assessing how motivated a patient is going to be and whether any treatment compliance issues may arise in the future. Addressing a patient's judgment involves looking at the soundness of the decisions he or she makes and the degree of impulsivity and planning that goes on before action is taken. Judgment is especially important when assessing for dangerousness, violence potential, or suicide risk.

Checking Under the Hood with Psychological Testing

These days, any number of different disciplines are involved in the treatment of mental illness and working with people with mental disorders. Psychological testing, however, is considered the sole domain of psychologists. Although some professionals such as school counselors and learning disability specialists conduct psychological testing, their testing is limited in scope and to a specific problem. Psychologists are thoroughly trained in all aspects of psychological testing and are considered the primary professionals in this area.

Psychological testing is part of the entire psychological assessment process. *Assessment* is a set of scientific procedures used to measure and evaluate an individual's behavior and mental processes. Ann Anastasi defines a psychological test as an objective, standardized sample of behavior or mental processes. Tests are used to formalize data based on observations. Nearly all topics in psychology can be measured with a test.

Testing formats include surveys, pencil and paper tests, exercises and activities (like putting a puzzle together), interviews, and observation. Testing in psychology is not much different than testing in other fields. A blood test is a means of measuring an individual's T-cell count, for example. A personality test is a means for measuring some specific aspect of a person's personality. It's the same idea, just a different subject matter.

What makes a test "objective?" A test is judged to be objective if it meets acceptable standards in three important areas: standardization, reliability, and validity.

Standardizing

Ann Anastasi considers a test properly *standardized* if there is a uniform procedure for administering and scoring it. Control of extraneous variables allows for maximum accuracy. If I give a test differently to two different people, then how will I be able to trust the results? I can't. I have violated the principle of control in science.

Establishing a norm for a test is another step in standardization. A *norm* is a measure of the average performance for a large group of people on any given psychological test. For example, the average score on the *Wechsler Intelligence Test, Revised,* is 100. This average score establishes a norm or standard by which to compare people against each other. Norms are established by administering the test to a large group of people, or several groups, and measuring the average performance and range of performances, something called *variability.*

Relying on tests

A test that is not reliable is not a good test. *Reliability* is consistency. If I give the same person the same test on two or more occasions, will he get the same or comparable score? If the answer is yes, I've got reliability. A test should be found reliable before being put out on the market for use by professionals. I used to have a truck that had a totally unreliable gas gauge. I could put $10 of gas in it, and the needle would go up to half a tank. Other times, it would go up to three quarters of a tank. You may be thinking that I wasn't smart enough to do this with an empty tank and with the same price gasoline, but this wasn't like the Internet fiasco I discuss at the beginning of this chapter. I did it right. The gauge was bogus.

When it comes to psychological testing, I've often had patients object that a test was unreliable and that it didn't prove or measure a darn thing. They may have had a point, but only if the test was unreliable.

Trusting tests

How do I know that a test I am using is really measuring what it claims to measure? I may think that I'm measuring intelligence when I'm really measuring English language aptitude. This actually happens quite often when tests are improperly used with people whom the test has not been *normed* (establish its statistical properties with a large population of individuals similar to the people to whom it will be applied). Tests used with people who were not part of the group the test was normed on are highly suspect and most likely invalid.

When a test measures what it claims to measure, it's considered *valid.* The validity of a test is established by using an outside measure of the psychological topic in question to compare the test with. If I have a test that claims to measure depression, I must compare my test findings with an already established measure of depression such as the *Beck Depression Inventory.*

Keep in mind that many, if not the majority of, psychological tests measure things that are unobservable in the way other factors in other fields are. T-cells can be physically seen and therefore counted under a microscope. But can we see intelligence in the same manner? Not hardly. Intelligence is presumed to exist as it manifests itself in a measurable form on a psychological test. Therefore, the scientific basis on which psychological testing is formed is of utmost importance.

Psychological testing is a little more sophisticated than asking a few questions and counting up someone's responses. It's a scientific endeavor. Because of its complexity, most professionals argue that use of psychological tests should be controlled. Only qualified examiners should use the tests. The risk for potential over-simplification or misinterpretation is too high. If the tests were spread around indiscriminately, people would become too familiar with them, and they would lose their validity. Instead of measuring someone's intelligence, for example, we may only be measuring his or her skill at remembering what was on the test the last time that he or she took it.

Testing Types

There are numerous types of psychological testing. Five common types of testing are clinical testing, educational/achievement testing, personality testing, intelligence testing, and neuropsychological testing.

Clinical testing

Clinical psychologists typically use clinical testing as a way to clarify diagnoses and assess the extent and nature of a person or family's disturbance and dysfunction. Specific tests have been designed to assess the extent to which a patient may or may not be experiencing the symptoms of a particular disorder. I call these *diagnostic tests.* A popular example is the *Beck Depression Inventory,* which is designed to assess a patient's level of depression.

Behavioral and adaptive functioning tests are two types of clinical tests that are designed to assess how well a person is doing in their everyday lives and whether he or she exhibits specific problem behaviors. A common instrument used with children is the *Child Behavior Checklist,* which is designed to assess the extent of a child's behavior problems. Another commonly used clinical test is the *Conner's Parent Rating Scale,* which is designed to assess the presence of attention deficit/hyperactivity disorder (ADHD) symptoms.

In addition to disorder specific inventories and tests, a wide variety of tests designed for other purposes lend themselves to the diagnostic process. Intelligence tests are designed to measure intelligence, but they can also show signs of cognitive dysfunction and learning disabilities. Personality tests are designed to measure personality, but they can also provide us with good information about the types of psychological problems an individual is having.

Educational/achievement testing

Educational and achievement tests are designed to measure an individual's current level of academic competence. Glen Aylward identifies three major purposes of this type of testing:

✔ Identify students who need special instruction

✔ Identify the nature of a student's difficulties in order to rule out learning disabilities

✔ Assist in planning and instruction

A typical educational/achievement test assesses the most common areas of school activity: reading, mathematics, spelling, and writing skills. Some tests include other areas such as science and social studies. A popular achievement test in wide use today is the *Woodcock-Johnson Psychoeducational Battery, Revised.* The test consists of nine subtests, measuring the standard areas listed above but in more detail (mathematics is broken down into calculation and applied problems, for example).

Educational/achievement testing is widely used in the school systems. When a child or even a college student is having a hard time in school, it's not unusual for her to take an achievement test for a closer look at her basic skill level. Sometimes, students have a difficult time because they have a learning disability. Part of identifying a learning disability includes assessing a student's achievement level. Other times, a student struggles because of non-academic related difficulties such as emotional problems, substance abuse, or family problems. An achievement test sometimes helps to tease out these non-academic difficulties.

Personality testing

Personality tests measure a great deal of things, not just personality. Numerous tests are designed to measure emotion, motivation, and interpersonal skills, as well as specific aspects of personality, according to the given theory a test is based on. Most personality tests are known as *self-reports.* With self-reports, the person answering questions about him or herself, typically in a pencil-and-paper format, provides the information.

Personality tests are usually developed with a particular theory of personality in mind. There are tests that measure id, ego, and superego issues, for example.

Perhaps the most widely used personality test is the *MMPI-2, The Minnesota Multiphasic Personality Inventory,* 2nd Edition. Almost all psychologists are trained to use the MMPI-2, considered to be a very reliable and valid instrument. The MMPI-2 provides a psychologist with rich information about the presence of psychopathology and the level of its severity, if present. It also provides information about the emotional, behavioral, and social functioning of the test taker. A lot of psychologists use the MMPI-2 as a way to check the accuracy of their observations and diagnoses.

The test consists of 567 individual items and produces a score on 9 clinical categories or scales. If a score is over a specific cutoff, it usually gets the attention of the psychologist administering the test. Psychologists consider such scores to be of clinical significance. The MMPI-2 provides excellent information across a wide variety of areas: depression, physical complaints, anger, social contact, anxiety, and energy level to name just a few.

Projective personality tests are a unique breed of test. When most people think of psychological testing, these kinds of tests come readily to mind. The stereotype involves sitting across from a psychologist, looking at a card with smeared ink or a picture of somebody doing something on it. "What do you see here?" are the words uttered by the shrink.

These tests are unique because they're based on something called the *projective hypothesis,* which states that when presented with an ambiguous stimuli, people will project, and thus reveal, parts of themselves and their psychological functioning that they may not reveal if asked more directly. It's not like these tests are trying to trick people. The idea is that a lot of us can't really put words to or describe what is going on because of our psychological defense mechanisms. Some people are not conscious of their feelings. Projective tests are designed to get past the defenses and penetrate the deep recesses of the psyche. Sounds scary doesn't it?

Perhaps the most popular projective personality test and maybe even the most popular psychological test of all time is the *Rorschach Inkblot Test (RIT)*. The RIT consists of ten cards, each with its own standard inkblot figure. None of these inkblots are a picture or representation of anything. They were created by simply pouring ink onto a sheet of paper and folding it in half. The only meaning and structure the cards have are provided by the projections of the test taker herself.

Intelligence testing

Intelligence tests are probably given more often than any other kind of test. These tests measure a wide variety of intellectual and cognitive abilities and often provide a general measure of intelligence, which is sometimes called an *IQ* — intelligence quotient.

Intelligence tests are used in a wide variety of settings and applications. They can be used for diagnostic purposes, specifically for learning about disabilities and cognitive disorders. They're also widely used in academic and school settings. Intelligence tests have been around since the beginning of psychology as a formal science.

The most commonly used tests of intelligence are the *Wechsler Adult Intelligence Scale, 3rd Edition, (WAIS-III)* for adults and the *Wechsler Intelligence Scale for Children,* 3rd Edition, *(WISC-III)* for children. That Wechsler sure is a busy guy! Each of these tests consists of several subtests designed to measure specific aspects of intelligence. Both tests provide individual scores for each subtest and an overall score representing overall intelligence. Some examples of what the subtests measure are

✔ Attention

✔ General knowledge

✔ Visual organization

✔ Comprehension

Neuropsychological testing

Although not a new field, tests of neuropsychological functioning and cognitive ability, as a result of brain damage, are rapidly becoming a standard part of a lot of psychologists' testing arsenals. Neuropsychological tests have traditionally been used to augment neurological exams and brain imaging techniques such as an MRI, CT scan, or PET scan.

The technology of scanning techniques picks up on the presence of brain damage, but neuropsychological tests serve as a more precise measure of the actual functional impairments an individual may suffer from. Scans say, "Yep, there's damage!" Neuropsychological tests say, ". . . and here's the cognitive problem related to it."

Neuropsychological testing is used in hospitals, clinics, private practices, and anyplace else where psychologists work with patients who are suspected of neuropsychological impairment. People suffering head trauma or some other insult to their brain may be in need of a thorough neuropsychological examination.

A popular neuropsychological test is in fact not a test at all but a collection of tests called a *test battery.* The *Halstead-Reitan Neuropsychological Test Battery* consists of numerous tests measuring such neuropsychological constructs as memory, attention and concentration, language ability, motor skills, auditory skill, and planning. The battery even consists of an MMPI-2 and a WAIS-III. It takes several hours to complete the battery, and it's never done in one sitting. Going through a neuropsychological evaluation can take several weeks, and it can be costly. However, when conducted by a competent professional, the testing can yield a great deal of helpful information.

Chapter 19

Getting Comfy on the Couch

. . . .

. . . .

1've often wondered how many therapists' kids ask them to career day at school. "My mom is a therapist. She helps people, I think. She sits around with people, and they talk about their problems. Sometimes they cry, and sometimes they get mad." Some careers seem easier to describe than others. A lot of people are familiar with the concept of *psychotherapy*, or just *therapy*, even though they may have a difficult time describing exactly what psychotherapy is.

I've heard that Eskimo languages contain hundreds of words for snow, and Hawaiians have hundreds of words for surf conditions. Therapists hate to be left out — it seems like there are hundreds of definitions for psychotherapy. Lewis Wolberg defined psychotherapy as a form of treatment for emotional problems in which a trained professional establishes a relationship with a patient with the objective of relieving or removing symptoms, changing disturbed patterns of behavior, and promoting healthy personality development. The symptoms addressed are assumed to be psychological in nature.

J.B. Rotter gives another good definition, "Psychotherapy . . . is planned activity of the psychologist, the purpose of which is to accomplish changes in the individual that make his life adjustment potentially happier, more constructive, or both." I think a good conversation with friends over a pizza can promote a "happier" life, so what's all the fuss about? Psychotherapy is more than just a conversation between two people. It's a professional relationship in which one of the participants is an acknowledged healer, helper, or expert in psychological, interpersonal, or behavioral problems.

Help comes in many forms, and psychologists haven't cornered the market in helping people wade through the psychological mess that they call their lives. All kinds of people, places, and things can be therapeutic, heal us, or enhance our sense of well-being. Music, literature, great works of art, love, religion, a good movie, the birth of a child, and a beautiful sunset can all serve as forms of therapy. But psychotherapy is a unique activity specifically designed to be therapeutic or curative for psychological problems.

In this chapter and the two chapters that follow, I discuss specific forms of psychotherapy. Each type of therapy has its own goals, although all of them have a lot in common, and each of them emphasize specific psychological issues such as emotions, thoughts, or behaviors. This chapter takes a look at probably the best-known form of psychotherapy, *psychoanalysis*.

Knowing Whether One Needs It

Psychoanalysis is a type of psychotherapy that has been around for about 80 years. Different variations of psychoanalysis exist, but the basic form, *classic psychoanalysis,* was introduced by Sigmund Freud and further developed by numerous others, such as Otto Fenichel, Anna Freud, Melanie Klein, Heinz Kohut, and Otto Kernberg, to name just a few.

Psychological problems, including emotional, behavioral, and cognitive difficulties, are the general focus of psychotherapy. Psychoanalysis is no different, but it offers a unique view of the problems and a unique method of solving them. Who needs psychoanalysis? That answer all depends on how the causes of someone's problems are viewed. Therapists of different orientations and training see people's problems as stemming from different causes. A psychoanalyst might view depression as related to inner conflict, whereas a cognitive therapist may see it as due to faulty thinking. (Read more about cognitive therapy in Chapter 20.) It's pretty easy, for example, to see when people are having a hard time in their marriage. But everyone, therapists and lay people alike, have a different explanation for the causes of the difficulties. Psychoanalysts also would have an explanation based on their theory and training, specifically their theory of *psychopathology*.

Consider the following example: Bill and Teri are expecting their first child. Teri has been enthusiastic — preparing the baby's room, buying clothes, and thinking of all the things they'll do together. Bill has been a little less into it. He's been spending a lot of time away from home lately, staying late at work and coming home after Teri has already gone to bed. He seems distant and often acts irritable. He's also been complaining of having migraine headaches and fears he might have some serious medical problem. Bill's migraines have gotten so bad that he's even starting to miss work. One day while doing the laundry, Teri finds a credit card receipt for a local topless bar in Bill's pants pocket. She confronts him about it, and he confesses to drinking more than usual and going to strip clubs with his friends recently.

What's going on with Bill? He's never been to a topless bar before, and the family physician can't find any explanation for his migraines. Bill is a good example of someone who may want to seek psychotherapy. He's acting in ways that neither his wife nor he, himself, understands. Teri has taken enough psychology courses in college to realize that something is bothering Bill, and he's definitely unaware of and/or not willing to talk about it. She tells him to get some professional help. It seems that Bill is someone "who needs" therapy, but why? Maybe Bill just needs a vacation? Maybe he just needs a good kick in the pants?

People who seek help from a therapist complain of and describe any number of problems, such as

- Physical symptoms with no medical explanation
- Unusual behavior, thoughts, or feelings
- Problems with work or relationships
- A lack of motivation or enthusiasm for life

What problems would the therapist focus on if Bill chooses to go to therapy instead of taking a vacation? As in Bill's case, a lot of people go to psychotherapy because of problems with relationships or work. These are functioning and adaptation problems that center on interpersonal relationships. Bill is also experiencing physical symptoms, he's irritable, and he's socially distant, all of which can be considered symptoms of psychopathology. He could be heading for divorce at a time when his first child is on the way. It's fair to say that old Bill is not so hot.

Sifting through the psychotherapies

We're not going to pay the big bucks just for some analyst to sit there and tell us, "Yep, you're screwed up alright." That's like your family physician diagnosing your bronchitis without developing a treatment plan. So, what does a psychoanalyst contribute beyond the obvious? Bill has some obvious difficulties, but he probably has some difficulties that aren't so obvious. Discovering these not-so-obvious problems is where psychoanalysis really sets itself apart from other psychotherapies. There's more than meets the eye in psychoanalysis.

Psychoanalysts never take a symptom at face value. They assume that some reason, some psychological cause, exists for Bill's actions. Below the surface of Bill's everyday thoughts, feelings, and actions boils a chaotic brew of inner conflict. Bill's everyday problems are observable; anyone can see him screwing up. But Bill's psychoanalyst will look below the surface of his everyday thoughts, feelings, actions and awareness. The search for the internal or mental sources of his difficulties will begin in psychoanalysis.

What does going to strip clubs have to do with deep-seated mental conflict? Maybe nothing, but his psychoanalyst is going to assume that a connection is there. For instance, Bill is about to be a first-time father, and there's little doubt that the experience will be extremely stressful — getting up in the middle of the night, making emergency visits to the physician, and so on. Maybe Bill is worried, and he's just trying to unwind by hanging out with his buddies. Or, maybe Bill has some serious reservations about being a father. His wife asked him if he regretted their decision to have a child or if he was scared about the new baby, and he denied it. If Bill is worried, he may be the last one to know. Bill couldn't tell you if he was in conflict if his marriage depended on it, and it does, so psychoanalysis may not be such a bad idea after all.

Digging into the proverbial bag of tricks

Yeah, yeah, yeah, we've all got problems. It doesn't take a PhD to figure that out. But, the point of therapy is not just to pay someone to name all of your inner demons. That would be a big waste of your money and the therapist's professional training. Psychoanalysis has several goals:

- ✔ To further the development and maturation of personality
- ✔ To help the patient become fully aware of his or her inner conflicts and how these conflicts contribute to his or her difficulties in life
- ✔ To help the patient become aware of how his or her defenses operate and how he or she distorts reality, including relationships
- ✔ To help the patient experience a more meaningful life overall
- ✔ To help the patient develop more mature defenses
- ✔ To help the patient develop healthier ways and means to express his or her impulses

All of these goals have something in common, the importance of *awareness*. If nothing else, psychoanalysis is an exercise in increasing one's awareness. Awareness sits at the core of the analytic process, and it's one of the curative aspects of psychoanalysis. Change is brought about through the uncovering of unconscious conflicts so that these issues can then be consciously addressed and worked on. If you don't know what the problem is, you can't fix it. Ultimately, according to Sydney Pulver, the goal of psychoanalysis is better functioning through deeper understanding.

A neat thing about professional therapists is that they already have some ideas about what's going on before you even come to their office. They get out their little crystal ball and tarot cards and predict that a man with Bill's problems is going to walk through the door at any minute. No, that's a job for a psychic not a psychotherapist. Therapists may not have a crystal ball, but they do have a theoretical system that explains why people develop psychological problems and where their inner conflicts come from.

Problems in living like those Bill is experiencing can stem from any number of sources. The issues listed here are common underlying causes for more mundane, everyday problems:

✔ **Regression:** One source of difficulty in someone's life is related to the concept of regression — a return to an earlier stage of psychological development. Freud stated that we're all vulnerable to regression when under stress. Stress taxes our defenses, and when we increase our efforts to defend ourselves against it, psychological symptoms can emerge. Certain events can trigger unconscious impulses and memories that you've forgotten about or are completely unaware of. When this happens you may be at risk for regressing. Bill may have an impulse to leave his wife and future child for a more carefree bachelor lifestyle because he was never allowed to have fun as a child for example. When you regress you act "younger," often childish. Temper tantrums, ignoring reality, and living in a fantasy world are examples of regression. Do you stick your fingers in your ears and repeat, "La la la la la la" so you can't hear someone talk? Regression!

✔ **Impulse control:** When our impulses to seek pleasure without regard for reality are stirred, we use defense mechanisms to keep them from getting out of control. We don't want all of those powerful and primitive id impulses overpowering our more mature and reality-based personality. These impulses can boil to the top, either because we're under stress or because we haven't been able to successfully deny their power. That's when our defenses kick-in and symptoms can emerge. Psychological symptoms are the product of these defenses working against our impulses.

  • **Repression:** One of the most common primary defense mechanisms is repression, keeping those impulses out of our awareness so that we don't act on them and they don't destroy our lives. Repression requires a great deal of mental energy. Again, symptoms are produced through the intensification of our defenses, but they can also be viewed as an indirect and unconscious means of expressing of our hidden impulses.

  • **Hypochondriasis:** What defenses is our old friend Bill employing that may be producing symptoms? Bill's migraine headaches are good examples of hypochondriasis — the preoccupation with having a serious disease. George Vaillant considers hypochondriasis a defense mechanism that provides someone with an opportunity to complain and then reject other's efforts to help. Hypochondriasis allows the individual to feel "misunderstood" because no one can find anything wrong with the person and, therefore, cannot help him or her. That way, everyone looks like they're being insensitive and uncaring about his or her needs. Maybe Bill feels that no one will listen to his fears and reservations about being a father. This fear might lead to hypochondriacal complaining.

- **Acting out:** Another defense mechanism that Bill is employing is acting out — the direct expression of an unconscious impulse or desire without having to consciously acknowledge feeling a particular way. Bill may have the unconscious desire to be a bachelor again, to be free of the responsibility of parenthood. He may not be consciously aware of this, so he acts out his unconscious desire by going to topless bars, as if he were single again.

Bill's problems are the result of an inner struggle for the expression, repression, and management of impulses by his defenses and fears about having, expressing and satisfying these wishes.

Doing Analysis

What if psychoanalysis was a sport, and it had its own Monday night television show? Just for fun, imagine that it was more popular than Monday-night football. I hope I didn't lose any of you football fans — stay with me.

"Welcome to Monday Night on the Couch. I'm Dr. Clearview, and with me is my partner, Phil Good. Tonight we bring you a session of the psychoanalysis of John Smith. If you remember Phil, Mr. Smith felt pretty bad when he left his last session with the Dr. Freud. . . ."

What would these announcers possibly have to commentate on? You might be surprised. There's a lot going on in therapy. In fact, one of the ways that therapists learn how to do therapy is by watching others do it and then dissecting what they see. The therapists-in-training watch therapy training videos or observe live therapy from another room.

How would you know psychoanalysis if you saw it? It may help to think about psychoanalysis from four different perspectives: the pragmatic aspects, what the patient does, what the analyst does, and the overall process of the analysis.

Getting practical

The logistics are easy. The patient sets up an appointment, goes to the office, and meets the analyst. They work out the fees and schedule. Classic psychoanalysis involves anywhere from four to six sessions of therapy a week, but most people can't afford this many sessions. Therefore, many psychoanalysts have learned to perform a scaled down version with only one to two sessions per week. Sessions last about 50 minutes in both classic and the shorter version of psychoanalysis. After getting acquainted, the patient and analyst get to work.

Taking a load off

Of course, no discussion of psychoanalysis would be complete without discussing the *couch*. The picture of a patient lying on the couch is one of the most popular images of psychoanalysis. The analyst sits upright in a chair, out of the line of sight of the patient, for technical reasons related to the task and goals of the therapy itself. Freud used the couch but not exclusively, and today most psychoanalysts are no different. Psychoanalysis does not have to take place on the couch, but in order for it to be truly "classic," a couch is preferable.

The patient talks; the analyst listens and comments. A patient is encouraged to discuss anything that comes to mind and not to filter or edit what comes out. The analyst lets him ramble a bit but periodically will emphasize something the patient says in order to increase his awareness. The typical length of classic psychoanalysis is five years or so. Most people don't go for that long because they're involved in a variant of truly classic psychoanalysis, which I discuss in the "Transferencing to the New School" section later in this chapter.

Being (the) patient

Remember that psychotherapy, in general, and psychoanalysis, in particular, are defined by professional relationships with specific goals in mind. The roles of each of the participants are specified to bring about the desired goal of getting better. In other words, there is a certain way to behave in psychoanalysis. But it's not as strict as I make it sound.

It may seem obvious, but the patient is expected to come to his or her appointments on time and pay his or her bill appropriately. These practices are important in maintaining the professionalism of the relationship because it isn't just two good friends chatting about life.

A lot of patients come to therapy with a "fix me" or "give me all the answers" attitude, as if just showing up and passively talking about their problems is enough. That's not going to get the job done. In fact, a lot of people underestimate the amount of work that goes in to being a patient. Patients sometimes leave therapy early in the process because things get too difficult or too much effort is required or them.

It's not like a psychoanalyst is going to ask you to drop and give her 50 pushups in the middle of the session. But you are asked to think critically about the things being discussed in the analysis. Sydney Pulver provides a good summary of some of the expectations of patients:

- Notice how unconscious material arises during the session.

- Be willing to experience strong emotions and face negative memories.

- Focus on understanding the process of how the relationship between the therapist and patient produces change.

There should be a disclaimer at the beginning of all therapy stating that the therapy may not be all that fun, and it may even be downright painful. No pain, no gain I guess!

Perhaps the most important task that a patient in psychoanalysis is asked to do is *free association*. As the analysis begins, the therapist instructs the patient to lie on the couch and begin talking about anything and everything that comes to mind, no matter how absurd, silly, or embarrassing it may be. The idea is to get in touch with unconscious material by not "editing" what one thinks about and talks about. This process can be pretty difficult and sometimes takes a while to get the hang of. The only rule is to talk about whatever comes to mind, providing the patient, herself, and the analyst access to hidden conflicts and impulses.

Sometimes it's hard to remember all the things discussed in therapy. Take a pen and some paper! A lot of good information comes up during therapy, and it's a shame to forget them. Write them down. Take your own notes. This might help maintain the gains outside of the therapy room.

Getting down to analyzing

So let me get this straight — I'm going to pay a psychoanalyst, and I'm the one that has to put out all of this effort. What's the sense in that? I'm sure military recruits think the same thing when they first get to boot camp and have that tough-nosed drill instructor in their face, putting them down and challenging their commitment. The drill instructors will tell you that it's in the recruits' best interests. Psychoanalysis is a far cry from boot camp, but you are asked to believe that it's all in your best interest. Fortunately, analysts play a greater role in the process than just stating, "It's for your own good." Patients and analysts alike both have duties in therapy.

The analyst is expected to

- Be empathic and communicate a certain level of care for the patient, a professional level of concern.

✔ Be aware of his or her own inner conflicts as well. That way, the focus in the therapy session can be on the patient's problems and not on the analyst's difficulties. If the analyst's problems start to dominate the session, the analyst should seek immediate consultation with his or her own therapist, a colleague, or a supervisor.

✔ Remain objective and morally neutral with regard to the patient's problems. Classic psychoanalysts used to be expected to be a "blank screen" and to introduce as little of their own personalities as possible into the process. That way, whatever the patient free-associates about is related to the patient's inner conflicts and not a reaction to the actual person of the analyst. This is a "pure" approach, and most analysts today feel that it need not be adhered to absolutely. It's okay to be a little more interactive with the patient in order to facilitate change and give a little more personal connection than a blank screen would.

✔ Work respectfully with the patient's anxiety, not overwhelming or overstimulating the patient. When a patient comes to therapy, he may be experiencing a great deal of fear about what's going to happen during the sessions. The analyst shouldn't push the patient too hard or too fast to talk about things that he may not be ready to talk about. There's a reason that people are not aware of their inner conflicts, and a good analyst respects this, pacing her comments.

T. Reik in 1948 stated that a good analyst learns to listen with his or her "third ear," trying to find the unconscious conflict within each statement of the patient. Unconscious conflict can also be observed in the material of dreams, jokes, and slips-of-the-tongue. (Read more about those slips in Chapter 10.) The analyst is supposed to notice these signs of unconscious conflict and make appropriate comments when the timing is right. Analysts attempt to understand what is going on at all three levels of the patient's consciousness at once: the unconscious, preconscious, and conscious. For more on these levels of consciousness, see Chapter 10.

What the analyst actually chooses to comment on and when he or she comments depend on the particular conflicts of the patient. The analyst makes *interpretations,* explanations that add to the patients' knowledge and awareness about themselves and the connections between their inner conflicts and current problems. Interpretation is the primary tool in the analyst's toolbox. It's his or her best means for increasing a patient's awareness, and to many psychoanalysts, interpretation is synonymous with psychoanalysis, itself.

Analysts don't just interpret any little thing in therapy — "I noticed that you folded the tissue I gave you into fourths and not thirds. . . ." It could get pretty ridiculous if that was the case. There are specific things that the analyst finds necessary to interpret and comment on. Because the goal of interpretation is increased awareness, the analyst makes interpretations about unconscious material that is just below the surface of consciousness. Rather than just making statements that seem to come out of nowhere, the analyst attempts to push the patient toward awareness, letting her arrive at the insight on her "own," with a bit of gentle guidance. It's not as fun if the analyst gives you all the answers.

Sydney Pulver identifies at least five types of interpretation:

- **Resistance interpretations:** Pointing out the things the patient is doing to resist the process of analysis and change
- **Transference interpretations:** Pointing out when the patient relates to the analyst in a way that is similar to earlier relationships the patient has had
- **Extra-transference interpretations:** Pointing out when the patient is relating to other people in a way that is similar to earlier relationships the patient has had
- **Reconstructions:** Pointing out the patient's thoughts, emotions, and behaviors that may "fill in" incomplete memories the patient may have
- **Character interpretations:** Pointing out maladaptive behavior that seems to be a core aspect of the patient's personality

It's impossible to do justice to the process of interpretation without a thorough discussion of the overall process of psychoanalytic therapy and a more detailed discussion of such issues as resistance and the therapeutic relationship.

Overall process

The pragmatics have been negotiated (e.g., working out fees and scheduling), and the therapist is ready with a bag of tricks. Therapy begins. In an ideal world, psychoanalytic therapy is supposed to progress through a series of stages. Patients and therapists alike aren't always so accommodating, however. If things go well, the analysis progresses through these stages:

- Resistance
- Developing transference
- Working through
- Termination

Beginning

The therapist gathers information regarding the patient's history, emphasizing relationships and family interactions during childhood. The patient goes through the process of discussing his problems with the analyst, a task that may seem easier than it actually is.

A patient, I'll call him Bernie may show up to his therapy sessions and discuss how his boss is forcing him to attend therapy, constantly threatening to fire him, and just generally giving him a hard time. He may discuss his boss's bad attitude and the raise that he thinks he deserves. He may talk about anything but the "real" reason he's in analysis — his career is in jeopardy — to say nothing of the deeper conflicts that lie at the heart of Bernie's career difficulties.

As a patient continues to talk and free-associate, conflicts begin to emerge. The analyst listens for the presence of deeper conflicts. The more the patient's conflicts begin to bubble to the surface, the more the patient will work to keep them out of awareness and defend him or herself from their disturbing content. This psychological defense is accomplished, in part, by a process known as *resistance* — a form of noncompliance with the psychoanalytic process of increasing awareness and of making the unconscious conscious. All patients resist at least a little, some more than others, depending on how defensive they are. The more threatening the unconscious material, the stronger the resistance.

Resistance behavior can be as simple as missing appointments in order to avoid discussing one's problems or as complicated as developing new symptoms to keep the analyst away from the deeper material. Resistance is usually the first obstacle to the analytic cure. An analyst can count on a patient's resistance. This is because the whole theory of psychoanalysis hinges upon the idea that people's resistance of being aware of their issues lies at the heart of their problems. The analyst typically deals with resistance through the process of interpretation or commenting on the resistance. For example:

> **Analyst:** Mr. Smith, you have spent a considerable amount of today's session looking at your watch and being concerned with the time. Do you have somewhere to be or another engagement?
>
> **Patient:** I'm sorry Doc, but I told my financial advisor that I'd call her this afternoon, and I'm worried I'll miss her. Do you think we could end today's session a little early?
>
> **Analyst:** Well, whatever works best for you, but I am wondering why you told her such a thing when we've held our sessions every day at the same time for several months now. Couldn't you have made another arrangement?
>
> **Patient (acting perturbed):** I didn't think it was a big deal!
>
> **Analyst:** It may in fact not be a big deal, but I am wondering if you are somehow looking for a reason to avoid your session today or looking for a way out of it? Last session we began to discuss. . . .

This is how a resistance interpretation might be made. The analyst gently attempts to draw the patient's attention to the idea that he conveniently scheduled a phone call during his regular therapy time and the possibility of a deeper, unconscious reason for his action. Was he avoiding something in therapy? This could be a turning point in the analysis, depending on how the patient responds to the question. He could get defensive and insist that the analyst is fishing or jumping to conclusions. He could admit to the attempt at avoidance. Or, he may get angry with the therapist and accuse her of being too nit-picky. Either way, the analyst's comments are an attempt to get at something deeper than just a phone call to a financial advisor.

As the analysis progresses and resistance is gradually overcome, the patient begins to settle into the process, more easily free-associating, and *regressing* into earlier levels of psychological development. The patient begins to act in ways and speak about things from his or her earlier life, letting childhood conflicts and impulses emerge more fully in response to the interpretations of the analyst and the setting of the analysis itself (such as the couch). More and more is revealed as the analyst and patient get deeper into their archeological dig of the patient's mind.

Developing transference

Sometimes patients get angry when their analyst points certain things out. They may stop talking or accuse the analyst of being overly critical or nit-picky. Why might the patient do this? After all, isn't it the analyst's job to point things out if she thinks that they may be related to unconscious material? If the patient reacts by accusing the analyst of being overly critical, the reaction may be something slightly more complex than just a simple act of resistance. The patient may be engaging in *transference*.

Transference occurs when a patient begins to relate to the analyst in a way that is reflective of another, typically earlier relationship of the patient. It's a distortion of the real relationship and interaction between the patient and analyst.

Most of us have had some experience with the concept of transference. Ever heard of the term "baggage?" In today's usage, it commonly refers to bringing relationship problems and issues from previous relationships into new ones. Say you're out on a first date and you run into a coworker at a restaurant. He or she stops by the table and says hello, you introduce your date and the coworker to each other, and then say you'll see the person tomorrow at work. Your date then proceeds to question you about who that person was and whether you have been intimate with him or her. He or she generally acts jealous and insecure about your friendly interaction with this person.

It's pretty clear that your date is overreacting, and because it is your first date, you're probably a little confused as to where all of this jealous behavior is coming from. Luckily for your date, you've just read *Psychology For Dummies* and understand that his or her behavior is probably a type of transference from a previous relationship. However, you're on a date, not in a therapy session, so you make a mental note to lose this person's phone number the first chance you get.

When a patient starts acting toward an analyst in a similar way, the analyst interprets the behavior as representing a kind of reenactment of some other relationship. The analyst points out the distortion, helping the patient become aware of when it happens and how it influences his or her perceptions of people. This process is intended to help patients become fully aware of their distortions, how they relate to people based not on the people themselves but on their own "baggage."

An interesting thing can also happen on the other side of the couch. An analyst also can be guilty of transference toward the patient, relating to him or her in a distorted way based on the previous relationships of the analyst — *countertransference*. When a patient gets angry with his analyst, accusing her of being too nit-picky, the analyst may get angry in return, accusing him of being an avoidant jerk. The analyst may have had a father or husband who avoided responsibility and then called her a nag when she reminded him of things he needed to do. Or, she may have witnessed her mother doing that to her father, and her father accusing her mother of the same. Either way, the analyst is out of touch with the reality of the current analytic relationship and should seek consultation in order to get this situation under control. After all, patients are not paying their analysts good money for them to work out their own relationship problems at the patient's expense.

Working through

Transference and the analyst's interpretation of it comprise the core of psychoanalytic therapy. This process happens over and over again, and each time the analyst interprets it with the goal of awareness in mind. As episodes of transference occur and reoccur, the analyst and patient work them out in a stage of therapy known as *working through*. Old conflicts are brought to light and worked out by the patient, learning how to recognize these incidents and relate to the analyst in a more realistic and non-distorted way. The reality of the patient-analyst relationship is not interfered with by transference, and the patient will be well on the way toward ending his or her analysis.

Terminating treatment

As the distortions diminish, awareness increases, and symptoms subside, a date for terminating the therapy is decided on. This involves another layer of working through that focuses on addressing thoughts, feelings, and distortions related to separation in relationships. Saying goodbye is hard for some people, but even harder for others. If a patient has significant conflict with being separated from her parents or other important relationships, there may be more resistance, transference, and working through in order before the analysis can finally end.

Transferencing to the New School

Much of what I've talked about in this chapter applies to classic psychoanalysis. However, very few people practice classic psychoanalysis today. Numerous revisions and adaptations have been made to this classic form, even though the basic process and mechanisms remain at the core of conducting psychoanalytic therapy. The main difference between the newer forms of psychoanalytic therapy and the classic form is the emphasis on the relationship and the interpretation of transference.

Harry Stack-Sullivan introduced an *interpersonal* focus to psychoanalysis in the 1920s that emphasized the real relationship dynamics between patient and analyst. Freud emphasized what was going on inside the patient's deep unconscious, but the interpersonally-oriented analysts instead began to focus on what happened in the relationship. They viewed and interpreted incidents of transference as deriving from the interaction, not solely from within the patient. The analyst may actually act in certain ways that remind the patient of earlier, conflicted relationships, thus setting the wheels of transference in motion.

The key for the newer psychoanalysts is the relationship between the therapist and the analyst and how the patient interacts with others in relationships — reenacting earlier conflicts in their styles of relating to others. Alexander introduced the concept of the *corrective emotional experience* to depict a situation in which the analyst relates to the patient in a manner that the patient did not experience growing up, helping the patient to overcome his developmental impasse. If a patient's conflicts are assumed to be the consequence of poor parenting, the analyst's job is to "re-parent" the patient, in a sense. Therapy, then, is a new type of relationship, one that the patient has never had and one that will help him or her relate to people in a healthier and more mature manner.

Shorter versions of psychoanalytic therapy, known as *brief dynamic therapies,* also exist. The process is much more active, and the therapist attempts to push the process along by being more targeted in his or her work. More specific goals are established that focus the therapist and patient on a specific interpersonal problem and practically change the problematic circumstances that a patient finds him or herself in. Instead of talking about relationships in general, they target a specific relationship such as spouse to spouse or parent to child.

Are We There Yet?

Does psychoanalysis actually work? Do people get better, or do they end up going to their analysis indefinitely? A large study conducted by *Consumer Reports* in 1996 found that people who go to any form of psychotherapy all report feeling generally better as a result, regardless of the type of therapy. But psychoanalysis is typically a long form of therapy, and today, many people don't have the time or the money to invest in such a long and expensive enterprise. Some studies show that people do get better with psychoanalysis when compared to people who get no help at all.

However, psychoanalysis is not recommended for certain problems, such as schizophrenia, and patients, such as individuals who are developmentally delayed or who have significant language difficulties. There are, however, forms of therapy for people with schizophrenia, people with cognitive limitations, or those who have limited funds or inadequate insurance coverage. That therapy is generally shorter and thus cheaper, such as cognitive therapy. (See Chapter 20 for more on cognitive therapy.) I guess the thing to keep in mind is how much time and money you have at your disposal.

Insurance can drive you crazy

Insurance companies and employee assistance programs (EAPs) do not typically pay for long-term therapy but instead offer a scaled-down version that, in my professional opinion, rarely gets the job done. This is not to say that short-term therapy is ineffective, but to expect change from two to six sessions of any form of therapy is ridiculous. Short-term therapy is typically anywhere from 12 to 18 sessions. Serious mental problems cannot be addressed in such a truncated format.

Chapter 20

Changing Behavior, Changing Thinking

● ●

In This Chapter

▶ Learning better behaviors

▶ Thinking better

▶ Combining two approaches

● ●

*T*here are few things in life that I hate more than shopping for a car. It wouldn't be so bad if I could walk onto a car lot, look around for something I like in my price range, and talk business. Unfortunately, salespeople seem to have something else in mind. If I'm looking for a blue, two-door, compact pickup, they'll show me a white, four-door model. If I want a sports car with front-wheel drive, they'll show me the latest, greatest, four-wheel-drive sports utility vehicle. It's like I walk onto the lot thinking that I know what I want, but somehow I leave thinking that I now want something that I originally didn't have in mind. "I didn't know that I wanted a white, four-door, four-wheel-drive sports utility vehicle."

Now imagine a similar experience in the context of going to a therapist. Mr. Ramirez is having marital problems, and one of his children is acting up at school. He knows that he wants help with his marriage and his child. But, when Mr. Ramirez meets with the therapist, something strange happens. He wants to talk about his marriage, and the therapist wants to talk about his childhood. He wants to talk about his kid, and the therapist wants to talk about his dreams. This guy may walk away from the encounter with "car-shopping disorientation disorder," not knowing which way is up and what he really came to therapy for.

Jay Haley criticized therapy approaches that ignore a patient's real concerns and insist that his or her real problem is something else that's related to some underlying or hidden issue waiting to be uncovered and analyzed. Psychoanalysts, for example, might be criticized as seeing the unconscious as the cause of any problem, even if it's fear of flying. "The power of the airplane and your fear of flying represent your father and an unresolved Oedipal complex." Say what? Do I really need seven years of psychoanalytic therapy to get over my fear of flying? I'd rather take the bus.

The therapy approaches discussed in this chapter can probably pass the "Haley test." *Behavior therapy* and *cognitive therapy* are two very widely used forms of therapy that have a simpler view of psychological problems. Behavior therapy focuses on behavior. Pretty simple, huh? So, if Mr. Ramirez went to a behavior therapist, the focus would be on the behaviors occurring within his marriage. Cognitive therapy focuses on thoughts, so a cognitive therapist would focus on the thoughts that Mr. Ramirez is having about his marriage and his kid. Both approaches take a simpler and less mysterious approach to patients' difficulties than psychoanalysis for example.

Weeding out Bad Behavior with Behavior Therapy

Behavior therapy emphasizes the current conditions that maintain a behavior, the conditions that keep it going. This form of therapy focuses on the problem, not on the person. A psychology professor who I once had, Elizabeth Klonoff, likened behavior therapy to a weed-pulling process. Psychoanalysts attempt to pull the weed up by its roots so that it'll never come back, but behavior therapists pluck the weed from the top, and if it grows back, they pluck it again. The origins of a problem are not as important as the conditions that keep it going. Who cares how you started smoking. The important part is the factors that keep you smoking.

Behavior therapy is based on the learning theories of Ivan Pavlov's *classical conditioning,* B.F. Skinner's *operant conditioning,* and Albert Bandura's *social learning theory.* All behavior is learned, whether it's healthy or abnormal. *Learning,* in the classical-conditioning sense, refers to associations formed between events or actions. *Learning,* in the operant-conditioning sense, refers to the process of increasing the likelihood of a behavior occurring or not occurring based on its consequences. "Learning" in the social learning theory sense refers to learning things by watching other people. For more on learning theories, see Chapters 8 and 9.

These days, it's pretty hard to argue that smoking is not bad for a person's health. I think most people now accept the unhealthy aspects of smoking as fact, but some just choose to ignore this information. Smoking is a good example of an unhealthy behavior that is learned. Cigarette advertisements associate sexy people and having fun with smoking (classical conditioning). Nicotine gives a pleasurable, stimulating sensation (operant conditioning). Teenagers sometimes learn to smoke by watching their parents, older siblings, or peers smoke (social leaning theory).

Classical conditioning and behavior therapy

Behavior therapy treats abnormal behavior (see Chapter 16 for more on abnormal behavior) as learned behavior, and anything that's been learned can be unlearned, theoretically anyway. The classic case cited by proponents of behavior therapy to support this approach is the case of *Little Hans*.

Little Hans was a boy who was deathly afraid of horses. A lot of children like horses, so his fear seemed at least a little strange. Why was Hans afraid of horses? According to psychoanalysis, Hans's fear of horses was a displaced fear of his powerful father. The behaviorists had a simpler explanation.

Hans had recently witnessed a number of extremely frightening events involving horses. On one occasion, he saw a horse die in a carting accident. This event made Hans very upset, and it scared him. The behaviorists proposed that the fear Hans developed from watching the horse die and from witnessing the other frightening, horse-related events had become classically conditioned to horses. He had associated fear with horses.

Remember how classical conditioning works? Here's a little review, but check out Chapter 8 for all the details.

Unconditioned Stimulus (Accident) → Unconditioned Response (Fear)

Conditioned Stimulus (Horse) + Unconditioned Stimulus (Accident) → Unconditioned Response (Fear)

Conditioned Stimulus (Horse) → Conditioned Response (Fear)

What do we get? Fear of horses à la classical conditioning. The beauty of this explanation comes from its implications for treating Little Hans's horse phobia. According to behavior therapists, if he learned to be afraid of horses, he could learn how to not be afraid of horses. This type of result can be accomplished with a behavior therapy technique called *systematic desensitization,* which I cover in more detail in the "Exposure-based therapies" section later in this chapter.

Operant conditioning and behavior therapy

What about operant conditioning? What role does it play in behavior therapy? Take a look at anger, for example. If I get my way every time that I get angry, I'm being positively reinforced for that behavior; therefore, I'm more likely to keep using anger in this way. This is a common explanation for a child's behavior problems. If a child behaves in a manner that is not acceptable, her parents may reinforce that behavior by providing attention to her that they may not provide in any other way. An example of a negatively reinforced behavior is seen when an individual gives in to peer pressure. The ridicule a teenager endures for not going along with the crowd can be hurtful. He may give in to peer pressure just to put a stop to the ridicule (the removal of a painful stimuli).

Having a difficult time being assertive is a great example of a behavior, or the lack of that behavior, that is maintained through punishment. If I live in a home where I'm laughed at or otherwise punished for being assertive and speaking my mind, I'm far less likely to be assertive in other situations. I've been punished for being assertive. Lacking assertiveness can be a serious problem, and it often leads to feelings of victimization and resentfulness.

Social learning theory and behavior therapy

A lot of what we learn we learn by watching other people. A common problem in marriages involves fighting over money. This is sometimes a consequence of watching our parents fight over money. *Modeling* is a form of behavior therapy that is used to teach people new behaviors by showing them how to behave in a healthier way. I might ask that the husband begin a conversation with me about money and I can model, or show, the couple how to discuss money in a healthier manner. This only works, however, if the therapist knows how to model healthy behavior!

Don't take any wooden nickels

One of the more advanced forms of reinforcement-based therapy is the creation of a *token economy.* A token economy is a structured system of reinforcement that uses *tokens,* symbolic reinforcers that represent more tangible reinforcers, to increase the likelihood of a target behavior occurring. The best example of a token is money. Money in and of itself is useless, except maybe for the paper it's printed on. (The paper can start a nice fire or be used as pillow stuffing.) The power of money comes from what it can bring us or what it represents — the ability to purchase tangible goods.

Token economies are often used in situations that require individuals or groups to follow a particular set of instructions or rules. Patients in a psychiatric hospital, for example, are often given points or other tokens for following institutional rules or performing one of their patient-specific target behaviors. In many cases, these tokens can be redeemed once a week at a snack or gift exchange. Some systems use tokens to help patients work toward leaving the hospital on small trips or excursions with the eventual goal of discharge in mind. This form of therapy is an excellent example of shaping.

Assessing the problem

The simplicity of the behavioral approach to psychological problems is made possible with an equally simplified (but not easy!) set of practices. Behavior therapists put a lot of emphasis on the scientific method and its focus on observable changes and measurement. The therapy techniques and activities are well planned out, highly structured, and systematic. The therapist is viewed less as a holder of some divine truth and more as a collaborative partner in the behavior-change process. The patient is expected to pull his or her own weight outside of therapy, as well as in the therapy session itself, by completing homework assignments designed to change behavior in the real world and to further the progress made during each session.

In keeping with a systematic and scientifically based approach to psychological disturbance, behavior therapists begin by conducting a thorough assessment of the patient's problem. Here's a simple outline of the basic steps of *behavioral assessment:*

1. **Identify the target behavior.** Step one involves taking a thorough look at the *target behavior* — the problem that the patient originally presents to the therapist. Behavior therapists use a special technique to analyze the initial problem called an *ABC analysis.*

    ABC analysis: Behavior therapists use a simple model called an *ABC analysis* to approach the analysis of the patient's initial complaint. Spiegler and Guevremont describe the ABC analysis as an evaluation of the events that happen before, during, and after a *target behavior* (the patient's problem behavior).

    A. Stands for the *antecedents* of a particular behavior, the things or events that happen just prior to the target behavior. A common problem that behavior therapists encounter involves couples that argue excessively, so it serves as a good example. The particular antecedents of interest in the case of such a couple may be the time, place, and surrounding circumstances that immediately precede each argument.

    Time: When each of them gets home from work

    Place: Dinner table

    Circumstances: Talking about each other's day at work

    B. Stands for behavior, as in the target behavior. In the case of the bickering couple, the target behavior is the act of arguing, itself.

    C. Stands for the *consequences* of the behavior, or the events and general circumstances that occur after and are a direct result of *B*. In the case of the arguing couple, the *Cs* may be that both individuals get mad and stomp off, the man goes out for a drive, or the woman leaves the house to take a long walk.

2. **Identify the present maintaining conditions.** Spiegler and Guevremont define the *present maintaining conditions* as those circumstances that contribute to the perpetuation of the behavior. They identify two specific sources:

> **Environment:** Conditions from the environment include time, setting, reactions from others, and any other external circumstances. This would be the who, what, when, where, and how of our arguing couple.

> **Patient's own behavior:** The patient's contribution includes his or her thoughts, feelings, and actions. This would be what each partner is thinking, feeling, and doing before, during, and after the arguments.

3. **Establish the specific goals of therapy in explicit terms.** The original therapy goal may be to stop arguing. However, this description is a little too vague for a behavior therapist's liking. A more precise measure of the target behavior may consist of identifying specific numbers, occurrences, or lengths of time of the arguments. So, instead of the couple simply trying to stop fighting, a more fitting target behavior is to reduce their fighting to once a week.

Trying different techniques

Two of the nice things about behavior therapy for both the patient and the therapist are its clarity and structure. Behavior therapists can use a variety of highly structured treatment techniques to approach their patients' problems. Spiegler and Guevremont identify three classes of behavioral therapy techniques: *reinforcement-based therapy, decelerating therapy,* and *exposure-based therapy.*

Reinforcement-based therapy

Reinforcement-based techniques of behavior therapy are based on the principles of operant conditioning, specifically the use of positive reinforcement.

After a thorough behavioral assessment, the therapist and the patient(s) follow these steps when participating in reinforcement-based therapy:

1. **Identify a list of reinforcers to be used in the therapy.**

   This is a crucial process. Anything that's likely to increase the probability of a desired behavior occurring again can be used as a reinforcer.

2. **Determine how and when to administer the reinforcers.**

   Remember the schedules of reinforcement from Chapter 9? Continuous reinforcement is the best way to get a quick jump on changing a behavior. Continuous reinforcement involves the patient receiving reinforcement every time he or she performs the target behavior. When the patient begins to consistently perform the new behavior, the reinforcement can be *faded* and only given once in a while, even randomly. This is the best way to keep a behavior going.

3. **Begin shaping.**

   Shaping is a procedure in which successful approximations of the target behavior are reinforced in order to "shape," move, or guide the patient toward the desired target behavior.

   If the problem is studying and the target behavior has been identified as studying two hours a night without interruption, the student may be reinforced after studying for increasingly longer intervals leading up to the two-hour mark (20 minutes, then 30 minutes, then one hour, and so on) during the shaping process.

4. **Create a formal contract that outlines all of the agreed-upon features of the treatment plan and clarifies when, how, and where the target behavior is to occur.**

5. **Conduct periodic reassessments throughout treatment to monitor the patient's progress toward the goal.**

   Adjustments are made, as necessary, in the reinforcement procedures.

6. **End therapy.**

   When the patient achieves the target behavior and maintains it for the desired length of time, therapy ends.

Bribing for basic school skills

I worked with autistic children for a few years using a reinforcement-based treatment approach, and one of the most challenging aspects of the therapy was finding reinforcers. The treatment consisted of using reinforcement to increase the children's functional behaviors, such as communicating, socializing, playing, and learning basic school skills (recognizing letters, numbers, and colors, for example). The process consisted of teaching the target behaviors and reinforcing the children when they successfully performed them. But if the reinforcers had no reinforcing value, forget it.

Some children liked certain kinds of food or candy, so that's what we used for them. Some liked certain toys or other objects, so we used those items too. If it improved their functioning, we used it. Some days candy worked; other days it was toys. One child liked it when I pretended to bonk my head on the table, so I used that as a reinforcer. Hey, whatever works right?

You may be thinking that all of this sounds like bribery. It is in a way. Sure, we "bribed" the kids to perform the goal behaviors, but think about the alternative. If we didn't use reinforcement, the kids wouldn't have learned these skills that have the power to improve the quality of their lives. I'd choose bribery over neglect any day.

Time-out tips

I've heard a lot of parents say that time out doesn't work, but I often wonder if they're actually doing it right. Spiegler and Guevremont point out four conditions that help make time out more successful:

✔ Time-out time periods should be brief (five minutes or less), and the child should know how long the time period will last. A lot of parents leave their children in time out for too long. Younger children only need about one minute of time out for every year of their age — 4 years old: four minutes. Simple.

✔ No reinforcers should be available during the time-out period. Using the playroom as a time-out area is not recommended. That's

like suspending a kid from school who hates school to begin with. Thanks!

✔ Time out should end when the time is up and the child is behaving appropriately. If he or she is still acting up, extend time out for another designated time period.

✔ Time out shouldn't be used by kids as an escape to get out of doing things that they didn't want to do in the first place. It requires some skill to determine when a child is manipulating the use of time out for this purpose. If children attempt to pull this trick, make them do whatever they were trying to avoid when they get out of time out.

Deceleration therapies

Never cry wolf — most of us are familiar with this ancient warning. If I yell out for help too many times when I don't need it, I won't get help when I really do need it. But how long does it take for people to realize that I'm full of it? Don't they know that I only keep crying wolf because they keep running to help? Basically, their response reinforces my crying-out behavior. It's all their fault! All they have to do is ignore my pleas and stop running to my aid. That'll get me to stop.

The process of withholding or eliminating reinforcement, thus eliminating the response, is known as *extinction*. A long time ago, behaviorists figured out that a behavior stops when reinforcement stops.

Spiegler and Guevremont classify treatments that utilize the phenomenon of extinction as *deceleration therapies*. When the reinforcer that maintains a behavior is either withdrawn or withheld, the behavior eventually extinguishes. Deceleration therapy is conducted in much the same way as reinforcement-based therapy: Target behaviors and reinforcing conditions are identified. The main difference between the therapies is that reinforcers are withheld instead of given.

One of the best-known examples of deceleration therapy is the dreaded *time out*. Time out has become one of the most widely used disciplinary techniques by parents. The idea behind time out is that the undesirable target behavior of a child (or anyone for that matter) is being maintained by either the reinforcing social attention the child receives as a result of the behavior or some other reinforcer inherent in the situation itself such as getting a toy away from another child.

When little Johnny performs the target behavior, he's taken to a designated time-out area, thus removing him from whatever reinforcers are present in the situation. Also, no potential reinforcers should be present in the time-out area that could provide the child with reinforcement while on time out.

Exposure-based therapies

There are several different types of therapy known as *exposure-based therapies* that involve "exposing" a target behavior to new conditions in order to reduce it's occurrence. *Exposure* is another word for reassociating or relearning a target behavior with another behavior that results in the cessation of the target behavior.

Have you ever tried to smoke a cigarette while in the shower? It's pretty hard to do. I once worked with a guy who managed to come up with a way to pull it off. (Interested? I won't support that habit by giving you the details.) Anyway, I'm guessing that most of us find that smoking and water don't mix. These two actions are incompatible. Finding a behavior that interferes with a target behavior is a good way to stop the target behavior from occurring.

Jacobsen and Wolpe both developed therapy techniques that made use of this incompatibility concept. When two behaviors occur at the same time, the stronger behavior prevails. Water always wins over cigarettes. The behavior-therapist jargon for this concept is *reciprocal inhibition* or *counterconditioning*. Therapy that makes use of reciprocal inhibition or counterconditioning is designed to weaken the classically conditioned, negative target behavior. When you "expose" cigarettes to water, smoking is pretty hard to pull off! *Counterconditioning* is the operative mechanism of all exposure-based therapies.

Perhaps the best way to explain how counterconditioning drives exposure therapy is to talk about one of its most popular forms of exposure therapies, *systematic desensitization (SD)*. SD is most commonly used to treat phobias, like fear of public speaking, social phobia, or some other specific phobia. Therapists have also used it to successfully treat panic disorder accompanied by agoraphobia. There are several types of exposure-based therapies based on the systematic desensitization principle:

- ✔ **Covert sensitization (imaginal exposure):** The "learning" or associating is only occurring in the patient's mind and not in real life.

  The procedures that Wolpe and Jacobsen developed are very similar. Therapists teach patients how to enter a state of deep relaxation. Then they ask the patients to imagine themselves in the fear-producing, phobic situation, while maintaining their state of relaxation. When a patient's anxiety level gets too high, the therapist asks the patient to let go of the image and continue to just relax.

When this process is repeated over and over again for several sessions, the fear response to the situation is diminished because the state of relaxation is competing with the original fear of the situation or object. Instead of fear, the patient now associates relaxation with the fear-inducing situation or phobic object.

✔ **Graduated-exposure therapy:** When a patient learns to perform his or her feared behavior in a real life situation, he or she is engaging *in vivo sensitization*. Usually, this form of desensitization is done gradually, and hence its name. If I'm afraid of flying, my therapist might start with me watching movies about flying. Then I'd go to the airport; then I'd sit in the terminal; then on an airplane. There's a gradual move toward the eventual goal of flying, but not until I've done a lot of preparatory work and learned to relax during subsequent stages.

✔ **Flooding:** This form of therapy involves exposing a patient to his or her fear-inducing situation or object for a sustained and prolonged period of time. The patient's anxiety goes through the roof, so this can kind of sound like torture. If you're afraid of snakes, jump into a tank full of them. You'll either die or get over your fear of snakes! There's no gradual exposure here. Just jump into a pit of snakes and get over it already!

It gets better! The patient is not only exposed to his worst fears, but he's prevented from running away, leaving, or engaging in whatever escape behavior he's typically used in the past to avoid the fear. This is called *response prevention.*

Flooding sounds horrible, but it's actually one of the most powerful forms of behavior therapy. If a patient trusts his or her doctor, it can be a quick way to get over some powerful and debilitating phobias. It may seem cruel, but patients must consent to all treatment, and typically, people aren't forced to go to any kind of therapy, unless it's by the courts. (For more on the role of therapy in the criminal justice system, see Chapter 17.)

Applying Some Soap to Your Mind with Cognitive Therapy

Alcoholics Anonymous uses the term "stinking thinking" to describe the kinds of thoughts that a recovering alcoholic has when he or she thinks negatively and contemplates taking a drink. The simplicity of this statement should not be mistaken for a lack of wisdom. The power of thought should never be underestimated.

Getting in good with germs

A good example of flooding (see the "Exposure-based therapies" section in this chapter) comes from treating people with germ phobias. Let's say that I was afraid of germs and catching diseases from trashcans. I managed to fill my entire apartment with garbage because I was too afraid to touch the trash in order to take it out. It was getting pretty rank in there, and my landlord was threatening to evict me. Luckily, I found a good behavior therapist in the neighborhood, and he agreed to help me.

When I met the therapist, he told me that he was going to do the therapy in my apartment. I thought that was pretty cool. When the therapist showed up, he explained that he was going to cure me of my germs-from-trash phobia. He pointed out a pile of trash and told me to jump in it. "Say what?" I said. "You heard me," he replied, "jump in it!" The rest is history. I jumped in the pile of trash and began to roll around. After my garbage swim session, the therapist refused to let me take a shower until the next day. I complied, and I no longer fear trash.

Keep in mind that this is not a true story, and it's a pretty extreme example of flooding, but it's not that far from the truth. Therapists who use flooding ask their patients to completely expose themselves to the things they fear the most. Believe it or not, it actually works!

Cognitive therapy is a popular and well-researched form of psychotherapy that emphasizes the power of thought. From the perspective of cognitive therapists, psychological problems, such as interpersonal difficulties and emotional disorders, are the direct result of "stinking thinking." In other words, maladaptive thought processes or cognitions cause these problems. "Stinking thinking" can have a tremendous impact on our psyche because we analyze and process information about every event that occurs around us and our reactions to all of these events. It can look something like this:

A (losing my job) → B (my thoughts about getting fired) → C (my emotions thought processes about the event)

Our reactions are the product of how and what we think about a situation or event. In many situations, such as the experience of loss, an insult, a failure, or encountering something scary, it's only natural to feel some negative emotion. Negative reactions are not necessarily abnormal. It's only when our emotional and behavioral reactions become extreme, fixed, and repetitive that we start down the path of psychological disturbance.

Sometimes our thinking can be biased or distorted, and this can get us into trouble. Cognitive therapy approaches reality from a relativistic perspective, an individual's reality is the byproduct of how he or she perceives it. However, cognitive therapists don't view psychopathology as simply a consequence of thinking. Instead, it's the result of a certain kind of thinking. Specific errors in thinking produce specific problems.

TIP

Peale is so positive

Norman Vincent Peale's *The Power of Positive Thinking* (Ballantine Books) is now one of the most famous self-help books on the market. Peale's basic idea is that positive thinking produces positive results in people's lives. Peale is not the only person who believes that our thoughts play such a central role in the production and maintenance of behavior.

Aaron Beck identified six specific cognitive distortions that lead to psychological problems:

- **Arbitrary inference:** This distortion occurs when someone draws a conclusion based on incomplete or inaccurate information. If a couple of scientists are asked to describe an elephant, but all they can see of the elephant is what's visible through a small hole in a fence, each scientist's elephant description will probably be different. One scientist looks through the hole and sees a tail. Another looks through and sees a trunk. The first scientist describes an elephant as an animal with a tail, and the other says that it's an animal with a trunk. Neither one of them has the complete picture, but they both think that they know the truth.

- **Catastrophizing:** My grandmother used to refer to this distortion as "making a mountain out of a molehill." Beck defined it as seeing something as more significant than it actually is.

- **Dichotomous thinking:** Most of us know that thinking only in terms of black and white, without considering the gray areas, can get us into trouble. When we categorize events or situations into one of two extremes, we're thinking dichotomously. While working in prisons, I've found that inmates often separate people into two groups, — friend or foe. "If you're not my friend, you're my enemy."

- **Overgeneralization:** "My boyfriend dumped me; no one loves me." This is an example of overgeneralization — when someone takes one experience or rule and applies it across the board to a larger, unrelated set of circumstances.

- **Personalization:** One of my favorite movies is *The Tempest.* Toward the end of the movie, the main character thinks that he summoned a storm that capsized his enemies' boat. Personalization occurs when someone thinks an event is related to him or her when it actually isn't.

- **Selective abstraction:** I once knew a guy in college who believed that women always laughed at him when he walked by them on campus. Little did he know that most of the women probably didn't notice his existence. They were most likely laughing at a joke or some other funny situation that had nothing to do with him. He arrived at a conclusion by taking their behavior out of context.

As with behavior therapy, the theory underlying cognitive therapy is beautiful in its simplicity. If psychological problems are the products of errors in thinking, therapy should seek to correct that thinking. This is sometimes easier said than done. Fortunately, cognitive therapists have a wide range of techniques and a highly systematic approach at their disposal.

The goal of cognitive therapy is to change biased thinking through the use of logical analysis and behavioral experiments designed to test dysfunctional beliefs. Many thinking errors consist of faulty assumptions about oneself, the world, and others. Cognitive therapy usually goes something like this:

1. **The therapist and patient perform a thorough assessment of the patient's faulty beliefs and assumptions and how these thoughts connect to specific dysfunctional behaviors and emotions.**

   Christine Padesky and Dennis Greenberger, in their book *Mind Over Mood* (Guilford Press), provide the patient with a system for identifying these thinking errors, which cognitive psychologists commonly call *automatic thoughts* — thoughts that occur automatically as a reaction to a particular situation. The patient is asked to keep track of specific situations that occur between therapy sessions and to identify and describe in detail his or her reactions to those situations.

2. **The therapist and patient work together, using the automatic thought record, to identify the cognitive distortions mediating between the situations and his or her reactions.**

   This often-difficult process can take anywhere from several weeks to several months, but at the end of the process, the distortions have been thoroughly identified.

3. **The patient and therapist work collaboratively to alter his or her distorted beliefs.**

   The therapist and patient collaborate in a process of logical refutation, questioning, challenging, and testing of these faulty conclusions and premises. This effort attempts to make the client a better thinker and break him or her of the habit of poor information processing.

More than pessimism

Certain mental disorders (see Chapter 16) are the consequence of distorting reality through biased thinking. If I lost my job, it would be natural to think, "I need to find another job." But I would be distorting reality if I thought, "I'm never going to find a new job." This kind of pessimistic thinking is bound to produce a stronger than usual negative emotional reaction. There's a world of difference between "I need a new job" and "I will never get another job."

Playing Together Nicely: Behavior and Cognitive Therapies

Albert Ellis is the founder of a combined form of therapy that borrows from both behavior therapy and cognitive therapy. *Rational emotive behavior therapy,* or REBT, is built on the premise that psychological problems are the result of irrational thinking and behavior that supports that irrational thinking; therefore, they can be addressed by increasing a patient's ability to think more rationally and behave in ways that support more rational thought.

Ellis is a charismatic psychologist whose style and personality accentuate the main ideas of REBT. Rational emotive behavior therapists believe that most of our problems are self-generated, and that we upset ourselves by clinging to irrational ideas that don't hold up under scrutiny. The trouble lies in the fact that most of us don't scrutinize our thoughts very often. We make irrational statements to ourselves on a regular basis:

"I can't stand it!"

"This is just too awful!"

"I'm worthless because I can't handle this!"

Depressing thoughts

One of the best-known applications of cognitive therapy comes from Aaron Beck's *Cognitive Therapy of Depression*. Beck proposes that depressive symptoms, such as a sad mood and a lack of motivation, are the result of cognitive distortions based on three very specific beliefs that the patient holds about himself, the world, and the future. Beck called these beliefs *depressogenic assumptions,* and they exist in a *cognitive triad.* The cognitive triad of individuals suffering from depression consists of the following basic beliefs:

✔ I am inadequate, deserted and abandoned, and worthless.

✔ The world is an unfair and harsh place. There's nothing in it for me.

✔ There is no hope for the future. My current troubles will never go away.

These beliefs interfere with reasonable and healthy adaptation and information processing concerning events in the patient's life. The challenge for both the patient and therapist is to come up with ways to identify, challenge, and alter these beliefs in order to reduce their impact on the patient's emotions and motivations.

These are examples of irrational thinking. Rational emotive behavior therapists define these statements as irrational because they argue that people can actually handle or "stand" negative events. These events are rarely, if ever, as bad as people think they are. Also, we often hold ourselves to rules of "should" that increase our guilt for being overwhelmed, sad, anxious, and so on. "I shouldn't get angry." "I shouldn't care what she thinks." "I shouldn't worry about it." Ellis used to call this "shoulding all over yourself." REBT therapists vigorously challenge statements like these.

The challenging posture of REBT should not be taken as harsh or uncaring. REBT emphasizes the same levels of empathy and unconditional acceptance as many other therapies. REBT therapists are not necessarily trying to talk patients out of feeling the way that they feel. They're trying to help patients experience their emotions in a more attenuated and manageable fashion. There are healthy levels of emotion, and then there are irrational levels of an emotion. The goal of therapy is to help the patient learn how to experience her emotions and other situations in this more rational manner.

The behavior-therapy aspects of REBT involve the patient engaging in experiments designed to test the rationality or irrationality of his beliefs. A therapists may ask a patient who is deathly afraid of talking to strangers to approach ten strangers a week and strike up a conversation. If the patient originally thought that he was going to die from embarrassment, the therapist might begin their next session with, "Nice to see you. I guess talking to strangers didn't kill you after all, did it?"

REBT takes the position that two approaches can bring about changes in thinking — talking with a therapist and rationally disputing irrational ideas and engaging in behaviors that "prove" irrational ideas wrong. Ellis states that people rarely change their irrational thinking without acting against it. Their thinking won't change unless their behavior changes.

Chapter 21

Being a Person Is Tough: Client-Centered, Gestalt, and Existential Therapies

A 35-year-old woman, I'll call her Mrs. Garcia, had recently attended her mother's funeral and was having a difficult time going back to work and interacting with her family. She went to her family physician for fear that she may be depressed. Instead of putting her on medication, her family physician referred her to a psychologist.

Consider the following opening exchange between Mrs. Garcia and the psychologist:

Therapist: Hello Mrs. Garcia, nice to meet you. Dr. Huang had mentioned that you've been having some trouble going to work and that you recently attended your mother's funeral. Please, sit down.

Patient: Thanks. First of all, I want to say that I'm a little uncomfortable with this. I've been through psychoanalysis before, and I didn't like it. My doctor was too impersonal and cold.

T: I'm sorry that you had a bad experience. Just so you know, I'm not a psychoanalyst. Would you like to talk about that experience?

P: Not really, not now anyway. I've been feeling pretty bad lately, really ever since my mother became ill. I'd go and help my sister take care of her and leave feeling this sense of doom and gloom.

T: Doom and gloom? Like sadness? Was it related to your mother's condition?

P: Yes to both. But I didn't really feel sad about the fact that she was dying; she had suffered for a long time, and I accepted that her death would probably be a relief. It was her life, not her death, that seemed to be bothering me.

T: Her life was bothering you. You had accepted her death. Tell me more.

P: Here was this 68-year-old woman who had worked as a maid since the age of 16. She was a loving mother and a devoted wife, and I felt almost ashamed of her. It's horrible to say, but that's how I felt.

T: You did not approve of her lifestyle?

P: Kind of. It was like she was living for everyone else, the boss, my father, us children, the grandchildren. I felt really bad about judging her, especially when I began to realize that I was living the exact same life.

T: You've been living the same way as your mother?

P: Not exactly, but close. Doctor Cash, I spend four hours a day on the freeway going to and coming from a job where I feel unappreciated. I need the money. When I get home, I have to cook dinner and take care of my son. My husband gets home and expects dinner to be ready. I know it sounds selfish thinking about my own life when mother was dying, but her sickness and death led me to reflect on my own life, and I didn't like what I was seeing.

Mrs. Garcia's feelings and experience are illustrative of the kinds of issues that theorists of these types of therapy are concerned with. She's questioning her life, her very identity, her sense of self. Who is she really living for? Is she being true to herself?

Although each of them made unique contributions to the theory and practice of psychotherapy, Carl Rogers, Fritz Perls, Rollo May, and Irvin Yalom all had one thing common. Each of them saw great potential in all of us. They believed that all people strive for maximum development of themselves and their potential and take responsibility for their lives.

Many of the forms of psychotherapy I introduce in this book (psychoanalysis in Chapter 19 and behavior and cognitive therapies in Chapter 20) have been criticized for being too technical, sterile, or out of touch with the real experience of the patient or client. There's been little room for the *real person* in a lot of these theories. The therapies discussed in this chapter all have the "personhood" of the patient seeking help as a central theme.

Shining in the Therapist's Spotlight

Take a minute to do a little exercise. Get a piece of paper and a p
a list of all the people you admire and hold in a positive light. W
list — teachers, spouses, celebrities, parents? What about yours
on your list of people you positively regard? Would you be a mer
own fan club?

In this big, chaotic world of over 6 billion people, sometimes it s
don't matter, like my individual identity is so small, so insignifica
us walk around with the sense of being an individual. Sometimes
independent that we actually feel lonely and isolated, like no one
us. "What about me? Don't I matter?"

Carl Rogers cared. His influence on psychotherapy has been pro
put the person back into the process, attempting to understand
each of his patients as unique individuals with real problems and
abstract theories and models. You can say one thing for sure abc
Rogers's *client-centered therapy* — it placed great value in the "hu
each and every patient. Rogers believed that all humans inheren
toward the fullest development of their capacity to maintain an c
of survival. It's kind of like the U.S. Army slogan, "Be all you can l

All of us begin life with the humble need to have our basic needs
shelter, and protection met. From this foundation, we seek to enh
lives and expand our abilities to their fullest extent. *Growth* is a b
for client-centered therapists. A patient's personal growth is fore
therapist's mind and central to the therapy process. Every time I
thing from a client-centered perspective or something that Carl R
I start reflecting and asking myself, "Am I growing?" If you count r
the answer is definitely yes. As far as that personal growth and e:
abilities stuff. . . .

What does Carl Rogers's belief in the inherent worth of each of hi
have to do with helping them get better? Are client-centered ther
paying for someone to like them, to value them? Kind of, but that
gross oversimplification. It's a little more than a "I'll love you unti
love yourself" therapy or "I'll accept you until you can accept you

The healing or helping mechanism in client-centered therapy is fc
process of the therapist working to understand the patient's uniq
ences, thoughts, behaviors, and feelings. As the therapist strives t
stand where the patient is coming from, the patient learns to expe
herself in a new, and more productive, life-enhancing way.

Theory of the person

Why would Carl Rogers think that making a genuine connection with his patient and really trying to understand what it's like to be that particular individual has a helping or healing effect? The answer to that question may seem obvious: All of us like to feel understood. (See Chapter 13 for more on the importance of relationships.) Having people "get" what we're about seems to give us a sense of well-being, a feeling of being more alive and present against the backdrop of a dark and uncaring world.

Although he's not considered a client-centered therapist, Eric Fromm introduced a concept that attempts to explain why being understood is so important to all us. Fromm believed that we all make constant attempts to check our perceptions and experiences against the perceptions and experiences of others around us, particularly people whose opinion we value. You may have heard of the concept of a *reality check* — like asking someone if he or she just saw the UFO land in the field next to the highway. "Did you just see what I just saw?" If the other person saw it too, you experience something Fromm called *validation.* Validation is the experience of having someone concur or support your experience of reality. Validation gives us a sense of presence; it makes us feel like we *exist.* According to Fromm, we would feel as if we didn't existence without validation.

So, being understood seems to be central to feeling like we actually exist — that we're alive! Have you ever talked to someone when she wasn't getting what you were trying to say, like she didn't understand you? This type of experience can feel pretty bad. In situations like this and many others, we can feel disconnected and, in extreme cases, isolated.

Why is being understood or understanding others so difficult at times? Rogers believed that each and every one of us has a unique frame of reference from which we experience the world. Think about it. Someone else in this world may look just like you, have the same name, and be exactly like you in almost every other way. Biologically, identical twins even share the same genetic code! But according to Rogers and the client-centered therapists, even identical twins are not exactly alike. They are, in fact, two separate people. I like to look at it this way. No other person can occupy the same physical space that I occupy at the same time I occupy it. And they can't occupy the same mental space either! People can abstractly "walk a mile in my shoes," but only when I'm not wearing them.

You're unique! Our individual experience is specifically separate from others, and as we differentiate our experience from the experiences of others, we begin to develop a sense of self, a sense of who we are. Our sense of self depends first, however, on how other people see us and relate to us. As children, our experience is intertwined and merged with the experiences of our parents, families, and caregivers. They serve as an experiential guide of sorts, providing us with our first models of understanding and experience in the world. Later, we begin to differentiate our experience from the experiences of others.

This *experience-differentiation process* is only possible, however, within an environment of positive regard and support from those around us. If I see a UFO and the other person doesn't, he may still support me in my experience by saying that he doesn't see the UFO, but that doesn't mean I didn't see it. If he wasn't supportive, he might say, "You're crazy! You don't see a UFO!" More realistically, I've often witnessed a young child who gets hurt or upset and goes to a parent for comfort only to have the parent say, "You're not hurt. You're okay." This situation is the opposite of validation; it's an *invalidating* experience. The child may get confused, thinking, "I feel hurt, but Daddy says I'm not. Am I really hurt or not?" Pretty confusing stuff for a kid.

Rogers called our experience of ourselves, as it depends on the views of others, our *conditions of worth*. As long as we continue to meet the conditions of worth set up by others, we'll do fine. But when we don't receive uncondi-tional acceptance, we can get into trouble. We may then start seeking the *conditional acceptance* of others because we've yet to experience their *uncon-ditional acceptance.* When seeking conditional acceptance, we live a lie of sorts, adopting a confusing and undifferentiated experiential approach to living. If our experiences are different than the experiences of those around us, we may distort our own thinking, feelings, or behavior in order to be in line with theirs. We walk around with a belief that, if we think, feel, and behave in accordance with the people around us, we'll get the positive regard we long for.

Even if we don't receive unconditional acceptance, we still have this underly-ing sense of individuality and uniqueness. When there's a disconnection or inconsistency between my experience of my self and my experience of my self as I distort it to be in line with other's views, I'm *incongruent.* This involves having two views of yourself: how you actually are, and how you think others think you are. Rogers believed that what lies at the core of psychological mal-adjustment is the incongruity between my total experience and my distorted self-concept. This incongruity leads to feeling estranged, disconnected, and not whole. We're then only living out part of our full being, and therefore, we're not fulfilling our basic need to experience, enhance, and expand our being.

As we travel along this compromised path, we use different defense mecha-nisms to keep up the act. We selectively process information about ourselves, others, and world around us so as not to overturn the apple cart of reality. For example, a lot of families have a black-sheep member who stands out. At times, this person may deliberately do something that goes against the grain in order to stay in line with his family-derived self and the image that everyone has of him. Sometimes, we can stick to this plan in such a rigid manner that we may actually lose touch with reality. Have you ever been in a situation where something happened and everyone tried to pretend that it didn't? I call this a "Twilight Zone experience." Everyone seems to know what's going on, but no one is willing to acknowledge reality.

Reconnecting in therapy

One of the main goals of client-centered therapy is to help the patient reintegrate these different versions of the self. At the center of this process is perhaps Rogers's most important contribution to psychotherapy — *unconditional positive regard*. This involves accepting the patient as a person without judging his or her experiences, feelings, thoughts, or behaviors in a moral sense. The therapist does not want to repeat the invalidating experience that the patient probably went through growing up or continues to go through.

Client-centered therapists engage in what Rogers called *reflection* — communicating to the patient that they hear what the patient is saying and that they're trying to understand where the patient coming from. Rogers emphasized *accurate empathy*. Therapists who adopt this concept stay away from imposing their own understandings and structures on the patient's experience. This helps patients begin to see how they've distorted their own experiences without introducing any new distortions in relation to the therapist's expectations.

The therapist "reflects" you back to yourself by being attentive and describing to you the self that you're presenting to him. During this process, your self-awareness increases, and you start to see yourself in a way that you've never been able to before. The client-centered therapist is kind of like a mirror or a "self-amplifier." Anderson and Wexler viewed this process as therapists helping patients attend to and better organize their own experiences and thoughts.

Another huge contribution Rogers made to psychotherapy was the introduction of his six *necessary and sufficient conditions* that must be in place for therapy to be helpful:

- ✔ A professional, respectful, and accepting relationship formed between the client and therapist.

- ✔ Patient's willingness to be vulnerable and to experience strong feelings, such as anxiety, and the therapist's ability to motivate the patient to seek and stay involved in the therapy relationship.

- ✔ Genuineness — the client is expected to be "freely and deeply" herself, not distorting how she feels or what she thinks.

- ✔ Unconditional positive regard.

Yeah, but does it work?

Rogerian, or client-centered, therapy has been around in one form or another for about 50 years now. The ultimate question for any form of psychotherapy, psychological intervention, or medication is whether it works or not. Research into the effectiveness of client-centered therapy has typically investigated the specific "necessary and sufficient" conditions.

Most studies, including one conducted by Beutler, Crago, and Arezmendi, have shown that three of the six conditions, empathy, genuineness, and prizing (unconditional positive regard), are valuable but not necessary or sufficient (on their own) to bring about therapeutic change. That is, a therapist doesn't have to possess or do these things in order to be helpful.

Orlinsky and Howard, however, found that warmth, empathy, and genuineness facilitate the therapy process. That is, therapy may go a little better if the therapist creates these conditions. It doesn't seem to hurt, so why not?

- Accurate empathy.
- Perception of genuineness — the therapist has to be a real person (with feelings, thoughts, and behaviors of his own), not just a person playing a role, acting, or pretending for the sake of the client.

Getting It Together with Gestalt

I want to start out this section with a little philosophical conundrum. Do you remember the "beaming" transporter in the television show *Star Trek?* As of now, you're a crewmember on the starship *Enterprise.* You're on an extremely dangerous mission to the planet Rumalian, and things start to get really out of control, so you radio Scotty to beam you back to the ship immediately. Ol' Scotty beams you up, and you're scheduled for mission debriefing with Captain Kirk. But first, you have get medical clearance from Bones, the ship's doctor. You go to the infirmary for your examination.

During the course of Bones's examination, you hear him say "Uh oh!" He tells you that, during the computerized mind-mapping scan, he's discovered that part of your brain is missing. He explains that the beaming process has been known to fail in reconfiguring some body parts, and sometimes things get lost.

"How often does this happen Doc?" you ask.

"The chances are one in a million. Don't worry though; it's not a very important part of your brain. You won't even miss it," Bones replies.

At that moment Dr. Spock enters the infirmary.

"Hold on a minute Bones. Don't tell her that it doesn't matter. She'll never be the same person again." Spock says.

"Of course she will," Bones replies. "I've got prosthetic brain section 45 ready to install. She'll never know it was gone."

"Yes she will," Spock adds. "Have you ever heard of the concept that the whole is more than the sum of its parts? Even if you replace that missing brain part, she'll never be the same person because the original person that she was had been more than the sum of a bunch of body parts."

At this point, you're thoroughly freaked out. Is Spock right? Who are "you" with that missing part? Will you still be "you" when Bones replaces the part? Will the new "you" with the new parts be the same "you" as the old "you" with the old parts?

It seems that Dr. Spock has been reading some Gestalt psychology. *Gestalt psychologists* believe that the human mind organizes the world into meaningful wholes, called *Gestalts,* and that the organized whole is essentially different than the sum of its parts.

Wholly in need

I was a late-night snacker. It never failed — every night around 10:00, I got a craving for something. Sometimes it was a peanut butter and jelly sandwich, and sometimes it was a frozen burrito. Then, I heard something one day that really blew me away. I heard that a lot of people mistake dehydration for hunger. So, the next time I felt that late-night craving for food, I drank a bottle of water instead. It worked! I wasn't "hungry" anymore. What's the moral of this story? There isn't one; I just thought I'd tell you about my late-night eating binges. Actually, that's not true. There is a moral to this story — I was out of touch with what my body needed, and I mistook one need for another. How could I mistake hunger for dehydration?

Gestalt therapy, founded by Fritz Perls, although not specifically concerned with my PB&J problem, focuses on patients being out of touch with their needs as a living organism. Each of us is a living, breathing, eating, and pooping organism that exists in an environment. We are self-regulating organisms. We inherently know what our needs are, and when we're free of obstacles, we satisfactorily meet those needs naturally.

Our biological needs lie at the core of all our behaviors, and as Fritz Perls emphasized, we are biological entities. Perls called these biological needs *end-goals* — our basic needs for food, water, sex, shelter, and the ability to breathe. Everything else that we do and all the other needs we satisfy are connected to serving these basic needs. These needs are the means to the end of biological existence. When a need arises out of deficiency, we feel an urge or drive to restore our natural balance, our wholeness. This need dominates our consciousness until it is met.

So far, it seems that Gestalt therapy is concerned with organization, and by that I don't mean that Fritz Perls was a neat freak. The Gestalt point is quite simple: We organize our lives, behaviors, thoughts, feelings, and activities around our needs. Our end-goal needs and those means by which we try to meet them lie at the center of our personal organization.

I'm a bunch of parts organized around a need (basic needs and secondary needs). To the Gestalt psychologists concerned with human perception, when something is central in our perceptual field, it is called *figural*. It becomes a well-defined "figure" set against a less clear and ill-defined background called the *ground*. At any particular point, I have a need that is figural, set against a ground. My life is organized around what is figural to me. Perls and the Gestalt therapists called the figure and ground together, including all the various parts of the person and the environment, the *field*.

In order to try and understand how this figure-ground concept works, try the following exercise. In Chapter 5, I discuss how perceptual wholes consist of figural percepts set against a backdrop or background. Sometimes, we focus on the figure, and sometimes we focus on the ground. Try it. Hold a pen or pencil about 10 inches from your face. Focus on it. Then focus on the things behind the pen. Shift back and forth to get the idea of figure and ground. The same concept applies in a metaphorical sense to our needs. Some needs are in focus, and others are not.

The field is separated into figure and ground based on the need that most demands satisfaction (figure) and those needs that are already satisfied (ground). In a process called the *cycles of experience,* a need stays figural until it's satisfied, and then it fades into the background, permitting the next-most pressing need to emerge. According to Clarkson and Mackewn, the cycle looks something like this:

1. **Fore contact:** An organism (that's you and me) becomes aware of a need.

2. **Contacting:** Resources are mobilized and utilized to meet the need, as the organism takes action to overcome anything standing in its way.

3. **Final contact:** The organism becomes fully invested in the process of need fulfillment. Any non-figural needs fade into the ground, and the organism's current, most-pressing need sharpens and brightens in its field.

4. **Post-contact:** Satisfaction is achieved, and the figure fades.

Gestalt therapists are big on being aware. Perls defined *awareness* as being in touch with the whole field, which includes both what is figural and what is ground. Gestalt therapists call being aware of the whole field, being in *contact* — the process of continual interaction and adjustment between an organism and its environment. We grow and mature through contact.

Perls often used eating as an example. Eating is a process of feeling hungry, searching for food, taking in the nourishment, and growing from its benefit. As we connect and maintain contact with the world, including ourselves, we take in what is nourishing and reject things that are poisonous or toxic. Contact is not an indiscriminate process. All food needs to be broken down, chewed, and digested in order to be useful, and we can't go stuffing our mouths with everything we see. So stop eyeballing that Oleander bush — it's not edible, no matter how figural your need to chomp on its pretty pink flowers is.

Perls seemed to have great respect for the self-regulating capacity in all of us. He expected his patients to strive toward integration and maturity, avoiding unnecessary dependence on others. He expected and respected each individual's independence and autonomy. His famous Gestalt mantra says it well:

I do my thing, and you do your thing.

I am not in this world to live up to your expectations,

And you are not in this world to live up to mine.

You are you, and I am I.

If by chance we find each other, it's beautiful.

If not, it can't be helped.

Healthy Gestalts

Gestalt therapists don't typically use traditional diagnoses and categories of psychopathology, which doesn't mean they think that nothing is wrong with the patients seeking help. With all of these parts, needs, figures, and grounds floating around, it may be easy to see how someone's life could get messed up.

Some of the problems Gestalt therapists identify in a typical patient follow:

- When we stop growing and maturing, and we cease to function as effective need-meeting organisms, we have a *growth disorder*. The normal process of figure-ground formation is disrupted, and instead of real satisfaction, all we have is a bunch of unresolved needs.

- When a need isn't met, it stays figural and is referred to as *unfinished business*. The gestalts for each of these different needs all push for completion. Everything we do, say, feel, think, and so on becomes interpreted with respect to this piece or these pieces of unfinished business.

It's like the old saying: When all you have is a hammer, everything looks like a nail. Well, when all I've got is unfinished business, everything looks like a business opportunity.

Here's an example: I recently interviewed for a new job. The people I interviewed with told me that they would either send me a letter or call me within two weeks of the interview. I couldn't get the "call me or mail me" thought out of my head. I incessantly went to the mailbox and answered the phone thinking it was the potential employer! My need to get the job was organizing my experience. As I write this, it's still unfinished business; they still haven't contacted me.

✔ We have two strategies to try to deal with this unmet need: *forgetting about or suppressing the need.* Perls believed that suppressing an unmet need exacts a toll on our vital life energy. It can sap us of our strength. We become un-centered and unaware of the field through the process of suppression.

✔ Another way of dealing with unmet needs is to *create substitute or replacement needs.* This process may serve to satisfy some part of us, but it never really quite does the job. We find ourselves stuck in a *fixed-gestalt,* where no figures fade and no new ones emerge.

We're never quite satisfied by either suppression or replacement. Our unfinished business always comes back to haunt us. Reminds me of the Rolling Stones's song "(I Can't Get No) Satisfaction."

✔ We reach an *impasse,* or a block in our growth, the natural cycle of experience is disrupted and contact is interrupted. We're stuck with compromised solutions to unfinished business.

Perls and the Gestaltists proposed five different layers of being stuck. That's five different ways that are growth stops as we live an out-of-touch, inauthentic life. When we're at this stuck point, we've adopted a compromised and ineffective approach to meeting our organismic needs. We're out-of-touch with our truest cycle of experience. Here are the layers:

- **Phony layer:** This is the level of functioning in which we construct an unreal self in order to engage with the world. We adopt roles and identities that are not reflective of our truest needs. We strive to fulfill a concept of who think we are, not who we actually are.

- **Phobic layer:** Here, we're afraid of who we really are, underneath the phony layer. We fear that if we show who we really are, everyone will run away in horror. No one could possibly love the real me!

- **Impasse layer:** This is the point where we get stuck. We start giving up on getting our needs met because we think that we're incapable of going on or providing our own solutions. Often, a fear of independence is involved.

- **Implosive layer:** This is an experience of detachment from various parts of our self that we've disowned or denied. It's as if we're frozen with fear of moving on with life. We're almost paralyzed.

- **Explosive layer:** This is a release of all that imploded and pent up energy. Some patients describe this as a feeling of having a weight lifted off their backs. They feel energized, and there's a huge gain in energy.

Each of us has a variety of defense mechanisms that disrupts contact. Remember that contact is the utilization and mobilization of resources to meet a need and being in touch with the entire field. We use these defense mechanisms to survive, even though we survive in a compromised position. These are called *boundary disturbances:*

- **Introjection:** This is a process of taking information in from the environment without assimilating it into our personalities. It's like swallowing food whole without chewing it up first. You get a belly-full of indigestible goop. If nothing is digested, its nourishment can't be extracted. This can happen when we feel overpowered or overwhelmed by our environment. If I've introjected my domineering father's opinion that I'll never amount to anything, I'll grow up believing this.

- **Projection:** Have you ever felt guilty about something? Of course you have. Did you ever accuse someone else of doing the thing that you knew you were guilty of? If so, you were guilty on two counts — guilty of doing whatever it is that you did and guilty of projection. Projection is more than blaming. It's the process in which we attribute something about ourselves to someone else. Sometimes, projection occurs when we think, feel, or experience something that is "unacceptable" to us or to the people who are important to us. Projection allows us to avoid responsibility. "I didn't do it, I swear. You did!"

- **Confluence:** If we fail to make a distinction between our own contact boundary and someone else's contact boundary, we can avoid contact all together. Contact results from friction. If there's no "you" and "me," then there's no friction and thus no contact. We're mixed up, not knowing where I begin and you end and vice versa. This kind of sounds like a smooth process, and it is. Gestalt therapists are not big on smooth relationships because they believe that peoples' needs aren't optimally met under these conditions.

- **Retroflection:** The retroflection proclamation: "Do unto yourself what you want to do to others." This is a process of turning outward-going feelings, thoughts, and behaviors back toward oneself. Instead of being angry with my parents, for example, I may start to be angry with myself. Retroflection also describes the process of doing to yourself what you want others to do to or for you. Remember Stewart from the movie *Stewart Saves His Family?* He would sit in front of a mirror and give himself positive affirmations. "You're good enough, you're smart enough, and gosh darn it, people like you!" If nobody else will love you, love yourself!

- **Desensitization:** We numb ourselves to the world around us through the desensitization process. Remember the Pink Floyd song, "Comfortably Numb"?

- **Egotism:** This is when we're paralyzed by extreme self-analysis. We attempt to control the chaos of our worlds by being perfect and making all the "right" decisions. Analysis is paralysis in this case.

Hopefully you haven't become hopeless after hearing about all those impasses and defense mechanisms. If you have, that's alright. Gestalt therapists have their own unique approach to therapy that addresses being stuck and out of contact.

Doing it in therapy

I realize that I'm out of touch with my needs and that I've adopted all kinds of defensive maneuvers and layered adaptations. Now what? Gestalt therapy here I come. Does Fritz Perls show me the error of my ways, pointing out where I cut off, shut down, and missed the mark? Well, not exactly. If I go to a Gestalt therapist looking for him or her to be the "doctor" while I sit passively by and play the role of the "patient," I've got another thing coming.

Gestalt therapists begin therapy with some very basic expectations. Patients are responsible for

✔ Guiding the process

✔ Deciding when they're feeling better

✔ Finding their own solutions

At this point, you may be wondering, "So what's the patient paying for then?" Gestalt therapists provide a collaborative relationship, which is accompanied by expertise in Gestalt personality theory and psychopathology as a means to guide the patient toward a more thorough awareness of himself and his needs. The therapist and patient are expected to be on a more equal ground than other forms of therapy (psychoanalysis emphasizes the doctor-patient roles, for instance). The patient doesn't lie on a couch — the therapist provides more human contact than that. The therapist is expected to be as genuine and real with the patient as appropriate. The two main goals of Gestalt therapy are to

✔ Improve the patient's awareness of the entire field

✔ Restore a healthy cycle of experience

The Gestalt therapist points out the patient's unfinished business as it emerges through both the content and the process of the therapeutic relationship. The therapist directs the patient to focus on his or her immediate experience, in an attempt to help the individual reconnect with his or her discarded needs and break out of old behavior.

One of most unique contributions to therapy by the Gestaltists is their use of "experiments" and special awareness-enhancing techniques. These experiments and techniques help patients to see how their currently compromised means for meeting their needs have gone from a technique of trying to get needs met to an obstacle in getting needs met.

The *empty chair technique* is an excellent example. If a patient has a conflict with a particular individual that qualifies as unfinished business, the therapist asks the patient to imagine that the person is sitting in an empty chair in the room. The patient then talks to the individual, saying whatever it is he or she has always wanted to say. Here are a few more experiments and techniques used by Gestalt therapists:

- ✔ **I take responsibility:** Asking patients to end everything they say with "... and I take responsibility for it"

- ✔ **Playing the projection:** Asking patients to play the role of the person they project upon, such as a spouse playing the other spouse

- ✔ **Reversals:** Asking patients to act in the exact opposite manner of the way that they usually act in order to explore hidden and unknown aspects of themselves

Gestalt therapists expect the patient to stay in the *here and now,* not spending too much time reminiscing on the past or worrying about the future. Perls was famous for aggressively challenging his patients to stay in the moment and own their experience. Gestalt therapists may repeat something over and over again until the patient faces the issue, or they may exaggerate a point to increase the energy of a session.

Ultimately, Gestalt-therapy patients leave therapy with a renewed sense of energy and purpose. They're able to more effectively meet their needs and take a more experimental approach to life. Most of all, they're more aware — the Gestalt key to the good life!

Being at Peace with Your Being: Existential Therapy

In the 1960s, the *Tibetan Book of the Dead* became really popular among members of the counterculture (you know, hippies). The book is a Buddhist instruction manual for what to do when you die — go toward the light, don't

TIP

Getting into nothing

If you ever want to take a road trip into hardcore philosophical obscurity concerning the issue of being or not-being, read Jean Paul Sartre's *On Being and Nothingness*. It's like a computer instruction manual for existential philosophy.

go toward the light, that sort of thing. The book and its subject matter captured a lot of people's imaginations, as death always seems to do. Death seems to have a profound effect on the quality of our lives. Whether we're facing death ourselves or dealing with the loss of someone important to us, the looming presence of death almost invariably stirs up strong emotions.

A group of psychologists from the school of *existential psychology* place death center stage among the most important issues to discuss in psychotherapy. In addition to death, they view some issues (anxiety, freedom, and choice) as very basic to our existence and at the core of much of what we call *psychopathology* (psychological problems). In a way, the existentialists cut straight to the chase concerning therapy by placing ultimate importance on deep philosophical issues such as:

- ✔ Anxiety
- ✔ Death
- ✔ Guilt
- ✔ Time
- ✔ Transcendence

Why all this morose fascination? Existential therapists, such as Rollo May and Irvin Yalom, shared a philosophical perspective that was deeply dissatisfied with the focus of much of psychoanalysis and other forms of therapy. They believed that our most important issues were ignored, or at the very least indirectly addressed, by forms of therapy such as psychoanalysis and cognitive-behavioral therapy. Specifically, they saw behavioral therapy (see Chapter 20 for more on behavior therapy) as an overly narrow and technical exercise that didn't respect the struggles that all of us face in our lives. They wanted to do therapy with a real person sitting across from the individual, examining his or her real concerns and deepest issues. It seems like they didn't want to be distracted by theories and models that dehumanized therapy, which at its heart is a basic human process.

Existential therapy is more of a philosophical position than a specific technique. It does, however, make some unique contributions to technique, as I discuss later in this chapter. At the center of the philosophy is the assumption that all human beings have a core experience of "I Am." This experience is our basic sense of being alive and striving toward being.

Hanging out with your hang-ups

So we're all striving to realize our truest sense of being, our truest sense of *ontological existence.* Ontology is a branch of philosophy that concerns itself with determining what is real in our universe. I feel real. Hopefully, you feel real, too. If we're both real, we're both able to speak about our sense of ontological existence, our sense of being.

There's always a catch though. If there's going to be being, there has to be not-being. The ultimate not-being experience is death. When we face death, our own or someone else's death, we experience anxiety over the thought of not-being, of not being around anymore.

Existential therapists tend to focus on the differences between a patient's normal or healthy anxiety and what they call *neurotic anxiety.*

✔ *Normal anxiety* comes from striving to be and facing threats to our being. Wait a minute, normal anxiety? Before I started learning about the existential approach, I always thought that anxiety was pretty much a bad thing. It feels pretty bad, and it can get in the way of doing a lot of things.

Healthy anxiety is anxiety that is proportionate to the situation and not out of control. Therefore, healthy anxiety doesn't need to be repressed because it's manageable and realistic. It's also constructive and helpful. If I'm appropriately anxious about my test, I may just sit down and study in order to pass it. My anxiety can motivate me. Many of us can relate to anxiety being at the core of a lot of what we do. "No problem," say the existentialists, as long as your anxiety is working for you, and it's not overblown.

✔ *Neurotic anxiety* has two qualities that work against our realization of being and cut us off from fully engaging the world around us.

- **It's disproportionate to the situation at hand.** Fearing that they may fail, a lot of college students get worked up and anxious about taking big exams. For many people, failing an exam is a big deal, but being anxious about the exam is fine, as long as they don't get carried away. Anxiety becomes a problem when it becomes disproportionate to the situation. If I'm so anxious that I think I'm going to die if I fail, the anxiety has definitely become a problem, and existentially speaking, it's out of whack.

- **It's destructive.** Staying with the exam example, all that anxiety may make students physically ill. If they're sick, they can't study. If they don't study, they fail. Their anxiety was counterproductive. Neurotic anxiety should be tolerated as it comes up, but it should be eliminated to the greatest extent possible. We also tend to repress, or "stuff," our neurotic anxiety into our unconscious in an attempt to cope with it. The anxiety is painful, and when something is painful, a lot of us try to forget it exists.

Guilt is another key existential phenomenon. Guilt is an important concept in our society and, I guess, in most others as well. The existentialists aren't priests who seek to absolve their patients of guilt, but instead, they help their patients focus on issues of guilt as they relate to the full experience of being. There are two types of guilt:

✔ *Normal guilt* arises from two situations:

- **Failing to properly engage in ethical behavior.** This type of guilt comes up when you actually do something wrong according to your own and your social group's ethical and morals standards. Guilt is a normal and healthy emotion.

- **Failing to live up to our own expectations.** I find that this one is often downplayed in psychotherapy. Individuals often talk about letting other people down. A lot of people actually come to therapy because they've let someone down through infidelity, physical abuse, and so on. But what about my own standards for myself? How am I supposed to feel when I let myself down? Guilty!

✔ *Neurotic guilt* is guilt that comes from our fearful fantasies of having done someone harm when we actually didn't. Are you afraid to tell someone what you really think for fear of hurting his or her feelings? That's nice. But, are you afraid that you've hurt someone's feelings even when you're sure that you didn't? That's a *fantasized transgression* — a created or imagined trespass that never occurred.

Being in the here and now

So far, a bunch anxious and guilty people are running around getting in touch with their being. That sounds kind of existential, doesn't it? When I think of the concept of "being," I always think of smoke-filled coffee shops with beatnik poets, sporting goatees, berets, and sunglasses and spouting poetry about the nobility of a cockroach. "They're alive man! Their legs are so short that they can't help but be down to earth. They scurry around with zest and zeal, never worrying about money or pride; they're just looking for their next meal man." Sorry, I couldn't help it, but my little existential poem does illustrate the idea that there's a genuineness in the simplicity of the cockroach. They seem focused on what really matters; to them, it's food. They're not distracted by neurotic guilt or anxiety. They are what the existential therapists call *being-in-the-world*.

Hello, Dali!

There's a famous Salvador Dali painting titled *The Persistence of Time*. A quick story: My wife and I went to Paris, France, to see some paintings. We went to the Salvador Dali Museum to check out this painting and a couple of his other works. When we arrived, it wasn't there! It was in a gallery in St. Petersburg, Florida. We couldn't believe it. St. Petersburg? Come on! Anyway, my fascination with this painting comes from Dali's representation of time using flimsy clocks draped over different objects like the way you drape dirty clothes over the back of a chair. I'm no art critic, but I took that to symbolize the flexibility of time — it's not brittle; it doesn't break; it only bends. Time drapes over everything, and nothing escapes it. Well Mr. Dali, the existentialists would have probably agreed.

Existential therapists try hard to understand the experience of their patients and how they "be-in-the-world." There are three important levels of this being:

- ✔ **Umwelt:** Being among or within one's environment and the external world of objects and things
- ✔ **Mitwelt:** Being within one's social world
- ✔ **Eigenwelt:** Relating to oneself

Being is maximized when we're in touch with each of these levels to a sufficient degree, engaging with each level without the experience of neurotic anxiety or guilt. Remember the cockroach — he ain't guilty man!

Being-in-the-world includes our experience of time. *Time* is an absolute fact in all our lives. It's an existential given. Time goes on whether or not we try to resist it. The key for the existentialists was for each of us to learn to live in the present and the immediate future. We shouldn't waste our time worrying about the past. We should commit to the present, realizing that time only moves us closer to our inevitable deaths and that life is what one makes of it. Make life, or it will make you I guess.

A final important existential issue that serves as background for the actual practice of existential psychotherapy is the concept of *transcendence*. If you weren't depressed before you started reading this chapter, you may be now. All this talk about death, time, anxiety, and guilt isn't much fun. It's not all hopeless though. The existentialists see a way out. Transcendence involves trying to realize our being. It's the act of living one's life without being overly anxious or ill and striving to transcend the past and grow toward the future.

The human imagination and our ability to think abstractly are powerful tools in this cosmic struggle. To "abstract" something is to remove it or extract it. We can take ourselves beyond the limits of our immediate situation with the ability to think of or imagine ourselves as outside of these limits. Our ability to separate ourselves by thinking creatively creates a psychological space of sorts. We can envision possibilities. As long as we're able to imagine alternatives and other possibilities, we can continue to strive toward being. This power is crucial to the existential concept of freedom. It also sounds like hope to me.

In addition to addressing anxiety and guilt, at the center of all existential therapy is the patient's struggle with these four existential issues:

- ✔ Death
- ✔ Freedom
- ✔ Isolation
- ✔ Meaninglessness

Just when you thought you've gotten away from a discussion of *death*, it comes right back. I've often wondered if the existentialists were obsessed with death. In therapy, they emphasize that psychopathology and problems in living are the result of a patient's inability to transcend the idea of death. There's no escaping it. We're conflicted — we want to live, but we know we're going to die. Knowing that I'm going to die may lead to despair. I might think, "If I'm going to die, why should I even try?" Existential therapy helps patients face the fact of death without despair.

After working in jails and prisons, I've come to really cherish one thing — my freedom. Existential psychologists emphasize the importance of the concept of *freedom* in a patient's life. They don't believe that some absolute structure to the universe is waiting to be discovered. We all make up the structure as we go along. For some of us, freedom seems like a burden. Freedom requires that we take responsibility for all our actions, and it means that we've got nobody but ourselves to blame when things go wrong. The good part: We can take full credit when things go right.

Just in case you thought you may catch a break from the existentialists and not have to face every single crappy fact of life, they throw in *isolation* for good measure. A lot of people find shelter from the harshness of the world in companionship. At our core, we realize that we're essentially alone and that we'll die alone. We try to overcome this fact by attempting to *merge* with others. When we seek a merger in the extreme, we engage in disingenuous relating, using other people as a means to our end (ending isolation). When our identities are so dependent on others, we may find ourselves feeling as if we don't exist without the other person. We long for recognition. Get over it! You're alone, and there's nothing you can do about it!

What's the meaning of life? Don't go to an existential psychologist for the answer to this question. Each of us is expected to create our own meanings, to construct something out of this meaningless mass of confusion. When we adaptively and creatively use our wills to build meaning for ourselves, we're on the right track.

Patient: I've wanted to get a new job for while, but I can't seem to find anything.

Therapist: Have you been looking?

Patient: Not really.

Therapist: Then how can you say that you can't find anything when you're not looking? Do you really want another job bad enough to actually look for one?

Patient: I don't know. I think I just want to be treated with more respect at work.

Therapist: Then what you really want is respect, not another job.

Patient: Respect is important.

Therapist: To whom?

Patient: Respect is important to me. I want it.

After the patient becomes aware of what she wants, the therapist helps her remove any obstacles or blocks to action. The therapist also points out that the patient makes decisions every day, even when he or she doesn't realize it. If you're standing in your own way, move over. Here comes the existential express: I'm a lean, mean, existential fact-facing, decision-making machine.

When we start using defense mechanisms to protect us from what can sometimes feel like an abyss of existential truth, we can get into trouble. Sometimes, we can

- ✔ Develop an unconscious sense of being special or omnipotent to ward off the unknown. Irvin Yalom points out that this development may lead to being selfish or even paranoid. I once knew a man who thought he was Jesus Christ. I told him that I had just met Jesus Christ in a previous therapy session with another patient, and I was pretty sure there could be only one. He insisted he was the one. There must have been a lot of emptiness or meaninglessness in this patient's life.

- ✔ Believe in an ultimate "rescuer." Too much indulgence in this kind of thinking can lead to dependency. This is a no-no in existential therapy. It's a cop out and serves as a poor excuse for facing the existential facts. Man, the existentialists won't even let me carry around my almighty teddy bear, Snuggles. Sorry Snuggles, I guess we'll just have to go it alone. The existentialists take all the fun out of everything.

Claiming responsibility

With all this talk about being, you may begin to wonder if the existential therapists ever do anything but philosophize. Existential therapy incorporates core issues into therapy and uses them to guide the focus of the therapist in treatment. Existential therapists

✔ Help their patients to act willfully and responsibly in the face of the existential facts

✔ Listen for existential themes and point them out to patients when they suspect one is lurking underneath some trivial dilemma or psychological symptom

✔ Explore these existential themes and point out the patients' compromised and maladaptive ways of coping with them

✔ Set out to help patients develop more adaptive coping behaviors

✔ Expect patients to create their own lives and worlds through action and choice

✔ Expect patients to exercise their will in making decisions without being too impulsive or compulsive

Acting impulsively and compulsively are not active approaches to living in an existential sense. Active approaches are thoughtful, deliberate, and responsible actions, and active approaches are what existentialists look for. Existentialists emphasize responsible action without the need to defer to someone around us to make our decisions. Because of this, existential therapists can sometimes be frustrating to a patient because the therapist refuses to get into a caregiver-care receiver interaction.

If you have trouble "owning up" to the circumstances of your life and accepting responsibility for them, existential therapy may help. It includes an expectation of owning one's experiences, including feelings, thoughts, and behaviors. One way to demonstrate this ownership is for patients to learn how to say *I*, instead of *you*, when talking about their experiences. Check out this example:

Patient: There are people in your life who you love, and when they hurt you, it sticks with you.

Therapist: I want you to practice saying *I* instead of *you*. For example, instead of saying, "There are people in your life," try saying, "There are people in my life who I love, and when they hurt me, it sticks with me."

Patient: There are people in my life . . .

Therapist: Good. How does that feel?

Patient: It kind of makes you feel sad.

Therapist: It makes me feel sad?

Patient: No, it makes *me* feel sad.

Therapist: You feel sad.

Patient: Yes.

I hope that I haven't painted too bleak of a picture of existential therapy. The truth is that existential therapy is one of the most hopeful therapies out there. It doesn't sound like it at first because it kind of works in reverse. Instead of using hope in external things, such as other people and supernatural forces, it points patients inward, toward themselves, helping them to generate hope from the smallest of actions. With each step we take, we're exercising our hope that the ground will not fall out from under us. It's a leap of faith facilitated through willful action. By taking patients down to the bare bones of existence, the existentialists show them how every thought, feeling, and behavior is an act of will that demonstrates the presence of their being — their striving to exist, survive, and to be.

Chapter 22

Coping with Stress and Illness

. . . .

. . . .

*E*very year around the same time I get sick. It never fails. Come October, I've got a cold. Is it the weather? Is it a cosmic curse? Somewhere along the line I made a connection between my getting sick and stress. When I was in school, it was the stress of midterms. Now, it's the stress of the holidays. Something different stresses out each of us, and some of us can even get physically ill as a result.

Psychologists have worked hard over the years trying to figure out what stresses people out. Within the last 20 years or so, they've started to use their knowledge of human behavior and mental processes to learn more about what makes people sick and how people cope with illness. In this chapter, I introduce the concepts of stress and coping and the growing field of health psychology.

Stressing over Definitions

What is *stress?* When most people talk about stress, they talk about the things or events that stress them out — work, money, bills, kids, bosses, and so on. The western world is a pretty stressed out place. The strains and pace of modern life seem to get to all of us at one time or another. Sometimes, even the gadgets that we get to make our lives easier complicate things. Someone gave me a little hand-held computer to organize my life. I spent more time trying to figure out how to operate the thing than I did organizing my schedule. It seems quicker just to write things down on a calendar or in day planner than it is to mess with the computer. The problem is that even when I owned a day planner I never actually wrote anything in it.

We all have stress. Definitions of stress have ranged from descriptions of bodily reactions to our way of looking at stress. In 1997, Lavallo defined stress as a bodily or mental tension to something that knocks us off balance, either physically or mentally. When we have *equilibrium,* we're maintaining a balance between our worlds and ourselves. Walter Cannon, in 1939, called this concept *homeostasis.* We feel stressed when we're out of homeostatic balance. Basically, stress is change.

Hans Selye gave us one of the most famous theories of stress. His theory was based on something he called the *general adaptation syndrome (GAS).* The idea is that when we're confronted with something that threatens either our physical or mental equilibrium we go through a series of changes:

- ✔ **Alarm stage:** Our initial reaction to whatever is stressing us out, called a *stressor.* Our brains and hormones are activated in order to provide our bodies with the energy we need to respond to the stressor.

- ✔ **Resistance stage:** The activation of the body system best suited to deal with the stressor. If the stressor requires that I run, like if I'm being chased by a pack of wild dogs, my nervous system and hormones make sure that I've got enough blood pumping to my legs to get the job done. Plus, extra energy is provided to my heart so that it can pump the blood faster. It's a beautiful system — what a design!

- ✔ **Exhaustion:** The final stage. If the bodily system activated in the resistance stage gets the job done, our trip down GAS lane ends, but if the stressor continues, we enter this final stage. When we're exhausted, our bodies are no longer able to resist the stress, and they become vulnerable to disease and breakdown.

Our bodies are not the only things at work when we're stressed. Numerous cognitive (thinking) and emotional responses are also going on. Arnold Lazarus stated that during times of stress, we go through a process of emotional analysis. It's kind of like having a little psychologist inside of our heads. We ask ourselves to determine the current significance of the problem and its importance for the future. How does this stress work? We make two important *appraisals,* or evaluations — *primary* and *secondary appraisals.*

In most stressful situations, something important is at stake; otherwise, we wouldn't be stressed about it. The evaluation of "what is at stake" is our primary appraisal of the situation. At this stage, situations are classified into one of three categories:

- ✔ **Threat:** An example of a threatening situation is a situation that requires a response. If I'm standing in line at the grocery store and someone cuts in front of me, I'm not forced to respond. But if a guy grabs me by the shirt and threatens to kick my butt if I don't let him in front of me, I have to respond in one way or another. Like run!

✔ **Harm-loss:** A harm-loss situation might involve getting hurt in some way — physically, mentally, or emotionally. A blow to my pride may be seen as a harm-loss situation.

✔ **Challenge:** I could also look a threatening person straight in the eye and see her threat as a challenge. Instead of seeing the situation in dangerous terms, I might see it as an opportunity to try out those Judo lessons I've been taking.

After I figure out what's at stake, I take stock of the resources that I have available to deal with the situation. This is secondary appraisal. I may take a look at my previous experience with this type of situation. What did I do when this happened before? I also take a look at how I feel about myself. If I see myself as a capable guy, I'm likely to get less stressed out.

Hamilton viewed stress as something more than the actual situation. Hamilton's philosophy was that it all depends on how you look at it. Stress is not a situation. It's a consequence of how a situation and a person's response to that situation interact. If I'm called on to pitch for the final out in the bottom of the ninth inning in the World Series and I come through, I'll likely be less stressed. But what if I blow it? If I give up the winning homerun, you can bet that I'll be feeling some stress, not to mention dreading the unemployment line. If I'm deficient in my coping responses, I'm more likely to feel stressed out.

Stress can also be a product of how much control I think I have over events and situations. Sells proposed that stress arises when people lack an adequate response to a situation, and the consequences of failure are important. Seeing ourselves as having little or no control can have negative psychological and physical consequences.

Are you the "master of your domain?" I remember a cartoon from my childhood called *He-Man,* and He-Man had this phrase that he yelled out when he was getting ready to kick butt, "I have the power!" It would be nice if I could just yell that out and be ready to take on the world, and the bad guys too. In 1982, Mandler defined *mastery* as the thought or perception that things in an individual's environment can be brought under his or her control. Sounds like He-Man to me.

Stressing to the types

So, stress isn't just a situation. It's how we cope, think, and feel about a situation. That explains why some things stress us out and some things don't, and why some of us get stressed out by some things and other people don't. However, some situations are pretty stressful for most people. Some things that most of us find stressful are

✓ **Extreme stressors:** Events that occur rarely and that are extremely stressful, such as natural disasters, human-made disasters (such as an oil spill), war, terrorism, migration, and watching others get hurt

✓ **Developmental and psychosocial stressors:** Events that occur as you grow and change — marriage, childbirth, raising children, caring for a sick person, and being a teenager

✓ **Common stressors:** Things you deal with in daily life — urban living, losing a job, daily hassles (like driving to work), pressure on the job, and household chores

Psychologists Holmes and Rahe created a list of stressful events called the *social readjustment rating scale.* They took different stressful events and assigned a point value to each of them — the higher the point value, the more stressful the event is. Here's the top five:

Event	Point Value
Death of a spouse	100
Divorce	73
Marital separation	65
Jail sentence	63
Death of a close family member	63

If you're wondering what the bottom-five stressful events are, they are (in descending order): change in number of family get-togethers, change in eating habits, vacation, Christmas, and minor violations of the law.

Getting sick of being worried

I've heard people say that they thrive on stress or that they do their best work when they're under pressure. Research shows that this is most likely not true. Stress can have very serious effects on us, and usually, if we work well under stress, we'll do even better when we're not under stress.

As researchers learn more about stress, a psychological and biological phenomenon, the connection between stress and illness, both psychological and physical, has become impossible to deny.

Psychological

One of the most well-known psychological results of exposure to extreme stress is *post-traumatic stress disorder (PTSD).* PTSD can occur when a person is exposed to a life-threatening situation or a situation that might involve serious injury. War, car accidents, plane crashes, rape, and physical assault are all examples of situations that may cause PTSD. The symptoms include emotional numbing, guilt, insomnia, impaired concentration, avoidance of trauma-related events and memories, and excessive physiological arousal (hyperactivity due to fear). Many Vietnam War veterans returned home with PTSD. During World War II, PTSD was called *shellshock.*

Have you ever wondered what it must be like to be a firefighter, police officer, or emergency physician? All the death and destruction that they see every day has to be stressful. According to research, it is. People in very stressful occupations have been found to be at increased risk for *secondary traumatic stress disorder (STSD).* The symptoms of STSD are exactly like those of PTSD, but instead of the sufferers, themselves, facing a life-threatening or harmful stressor, they receive "vicarious exposure" to these stressors. In other words, they're around people who are exposed to life-threatening and harmful situations all the time, and it takes a toll. People who witness an event and feel fear, horror, or helplessness may be at risk for developing STSD.

Physical

Hans Selye looked at the connections between stress, mental problems, difficulties adjusting, physical health problems, and disease. He found that the same things that help us cope with stress sometimes also can lead to disease. When our bodies and minds react to stress, the reactions don't diminish right away. In fact, when Selye performed experiments with stressed out pigeons, he found that a lot of the pigeons died after his stress experiments, even if they "coped" well. He identified several conditions that he called "diseases of adaptation," including peptic ulcers, high blood pressure, heart accidents, and "nervous disturbances."

Based on the work of Selye and others, we've discovered that stress can lead to physical health problems or illness in several ways. An indirect link between stress and physical health problems may involve people who engage in potentially physically harmful behaviors as a means to cope with stress. A lot of people drink alcohol when they're stressed. Drinking alcohol can be harmful to your health, especially if you drink and drive. Another dangerous behavior often associated with stress is increased cigarette smoking. I've heard plenty of patients talk about smoking as a way to relax. But it's so unhealthy!

Another link between stress and physical illness comes from the new and exciting field of *psychoneuroimmunology,* the study of the connection between psychology and the immune system. Researchers have long suspected that there's a connection between the two, and there actually is. High levels of stress and intense emotions have been found to suppress the functioning of our nervous systems. There isn't really a clear-cut diagnosis of all the ins and outs, but the suspicion is that our body's coping reactions to stress cost us in the immune department.

Ever heard of the flight-or-fight response? Walter Cannon showed that exposure to extreme stress causes us to decide whether we're going to take off running or stand our ground and fight. It sounds animalistic, but you can also look at it as a choice between walking away or yelling at someone. Either way, these protective actions require energy. Running from someone can be tiring! So, the brain sends signals to the heart and the hormone system that causes our blood pressure to increase. Our hearts race, we breathe faster, and the sugar levels in our blood increase. When these changes occur, all of the body's vital resources are devoted to the moment. Resources from other areas are used for the immediate purpose of fighting or fleeing.

Back to the immune system. The hormones that kick in when we're in fight-or-flight mode are epinephrine and cortisol. Both of these hormones have been shown to have immunosuppressive effects. If higher levels of epinephrine and cortisol are present in the blood stream, the immune system doesn't work as well. It kind of makes sense, if you think about it. If a bear is chasing you, the last thing on your mind is getting the flu. Forget the flu — you can't get the flu if that bear rips your head off! Save the head, and you can deal with the flu later.

You're probably saying, "Yeah, but I haven't been chased by a bear in at least five years, so why does it seem like I still get sick from stress?" You get sick for the same reason that I used to get sick during every midterm-exam week in college. We live in a stressful time, but it's not the same kind of stress that running from bears every day would produce. Modern stress is typically chronic and low grade. It's always there, constantly gnawing away at our immune systems because our fight-or-flight systems are on medium alert most of the time. So instead of going from no alert (relaxed) to high alert (bear attack), most of us are on medium alert (daily hassles, work, bills, kids, and so on) all the time. It's slowly taking its toll on our immune-system functions.

In addition to the connection between our immune systems and stress, relationships between stress and specific diseases have been found. Strong negative emotions, such as anger, chronic hostility, and anxiety, have been connected to hypertension, ulcers, rheumatoid arthritis, headaches, and asthma.

A final point worth mentioning deals with something called the *Type A personality* — a personality pattern characterized by an aggressive and persistent struggle to achieve more and more in less and less time. These folks are the "real go-getters." They're the corporate executives who build a Fortune 500 company from the bottom up, the millionaire workaholics, and the hyper-competitive college students driven by perfection. They're very impatient, and they view everything as urgent. So what? These people can be very successful, right? Yes, but they can also have a higher risk of suffering from *coronary heart disease* — hardening of the arteries, angina, or heart attacks. Before you quit school and make relaxing walks on the beach your full-time job, remember something. The relationship between Type A personalities and developing coronary heart disease is not one-to-one. The research shows that there's an *increase* in *risk;* developing these health problems is not inevitable.

Risk means that these folks need to take precautions and be aware of contributing factors and warning signs. Read up on coronary heart disease if you're worried (check out *The Healthy Heart For Dummies* by Hungry Minds, Inc.), and if you're really worried, go see your family physician.

Coping Is No Gamble

Stress, stress, stress — we've all got it. So what can we do about it? This question brings me to the concept of *coping* — our reactions to stressful and upsetting situations. Sometimes our coping strategies can make things better (getting healthy from exercising) and sometimes they can make things worse (like blowing our paycheck at a casino). All of us have different ways of coping with stress, some of them good and some of them bad. Even though bad coping skills can lead to problems, not having any coping skills can lead to vulnerability and, sometimes, to more problems than you previously had. Sometimes using bad coping techniques is better than not coping at all.

Don't be a dope; learn to cope

Most psychologists classify coping behaviors into two big categories, *approach processes* and *avoidance processes.* Approach coping is more active and resembles a more take-charge kind of response to stress.

Common approach-coping responses include:

- ✓ **Logical analysis:** Looking at a situation in as realistic terms as possible
- ✓ **Reappraising or reframing:** Looking at a situation from a different perspective and trying to see the positive side of things
- ✓ **Accepting responsibility:** Taking charge of my part in things
- ✓ **Seeking guidance and support:** Asking for help (see the "Everything but the kitchen sink: Resources at your disposal" section later in this chapter)
- ✓ **Problem solving:** Coming up with alternatives, making a choice, and evaluating outcomes
- ✓ **Information gathering:** Collecting additional information about the stressor so that one can more easily cope

Avoidance coping strategies are less active and involve coping in less direct ways. Common avoidance coping strategies are:

- **Denial:** Refusing to admit that a problem exists
- **Avoiding:** Evading possible sources of stress
- **Distraction or seeking alternative rewards:** Trying to get satisfaction elsewhere like watching a funny movie when feeling sad or enjoying recreational activities on the weekend to cope with having a bad job
- **Venting or emotional discharge:** Yelling, getting depressed, worrying
- **Sedation:** Numbing oneself to the stress through drugs, alcohol, sex, eating binges, and so on

Everything but the kitchen sink: Resources at your disposal

Coping is more than just the actions that we take in response to stress. The way we cope also depends on the resources available to us. A billionaire who loses her job may experience a lot less stress than a suddenly unemployed day laborer who makes $30 a day. Our responses to stress are complex reactions that depend on our coping skills, environmental resources, and personal resources. Any life event that a person encounters is influenced by the interaction of the person's ongoing life stressors, social coping resources, demographic characteristics, and personal coping resources. Further, the person's cognitive appraisals of the stressor influence his or her health and well-being in both positive and negative ways. All of these approaches taken together represent an *integrative approach,* which takes into consideration the resources an individual possesses prior to a stressor or stressful event, the event itself, and the appraisal of the event in an attempt to predict the health outcome in light of the stressor.

An individual's ability to resist stress is called *resilience.* Our resilience is the result of the interaction between our *personal* and *social resources* and our coping efforts. Personal coping resources include stable personality traits, beliefs, and approaches to life that help us cope:

- **Self-efficacy:** My belief in myself that I can handle a situation based on my experience
- **Optimism:** Having a positive outlook on the future and expecting positive outcomes
- **Internal locus of control:** My belief that certain things are within, not out of, my control

One type of environmental resource that is helpful in coping is our *social resources.* They aid in coping by providing support, information, and problem solving suggestions. According to Holohan, Moos, and Schaefer, a few good social resources are family, friends, significant others, religious and spiritual organizations, and sometimes even coworkers and supervisors. Other environmental resources include money, shelter, health services, and transportation. These things can make all the difference in the world when we attempt to cope with stress.

Going Beyond Stress: The Psychology of Health

By now the connection between stress, coping, and health problems is pretty clear. But psychologists haven't stopped there. They're attempting to apply their expertise of human behavior and mental processes to the problems of health in general. They're looking for ways to keep people physically well and for ways that people's behavior contributes to illness. These researchers work in the field of *health psychology* — the psychological study of health and illness.

Health psychologists work in all kinds of settings, ranging from universities (conducting research) to clinics and hospitals, which involve the direct care of patients. Their main activities include helping people and families cope with illness and developing programs for engaging in health-related behavior change, maintaining a healthy lifestyle, and prevention.

Preventing

Health psychologists engage in three types of prevention:

- **Primary:** Preventing an illness from occurring in otherwise healthy people before the illness develops. Examples of primary prevention programs are childhood immunization, condom use, and HIV awareness campaigns.

- **Secondary:** Focusing on the early identification and treatment of a developing illness or disease. Secondary prevention programs include breast cancer awareness campaigns and the promotion of self-examinations for testicular cancer.

- **Tertiary:** Helping people cope with already developed diseases and preventing them from getting worse. Tertiary prevention programs include helping people reduce high blood pressure or quit smoking and obesity treatment.

Making health-related changes

Have you ever made a New Year's resolution to start doing something healthy — exercise more often, take a yoga class, eat better, get more rest, wear your seatbelt? Have you ever kept that resolution? Why not? Come on, be honest with yourself: It was harder than you thought, wasn't it? Take a minute to think about what keeps you from doing what's healthy?

This is a common problem with health-related behavior — we don't stick to it. Part of this problem falls under the heading of *compliance* — whether or not we follow through with a physician's recommendations or treatment or our own health-related plans. But what determines whether or not we engage in health-promoting behavior to begin with? Some people make it look so easy. They go to the gym. They eat right. They don't smoke. There are numerous reasons why some of us do more healthy things than others.

For starters, a lot of people won't start or stick with a health-related behavior if substantial barriers are in the way. It's too easy to give up if something or someone makes it hard. I don't go to the gym because it's too expensive. I don't sleep enough because I don't have a nice set of pajamas. Money is a commonly cited barrier to engaging in healthy behavior. Another reason we don't just do it is that the health-related behavior may cut into something more fun or necessary. If I went to the gym, I'd miss my television programs. If I ate right, I'd have to go to the grocery store, and then I'd have to cook, and then I'd never finish any of my other household duties.

Commitment to change is most often brought about when a person believes that he or she can make a difference. A lot of people have a *fatalistic* attitude toward their physical health — the "you go when you go" philosophy. They don't see their behavior as contributing to their health and, therefore, don't bother to change. This mindset is also known as having an *external locus of control* — thinking that control over something rests outside of oneself. Having the belief that the power to change a situation or event resides inside yourself, that it is under your control, is called an *internal locus of control*. When we feel that we can control something, we are more likely to do something about it.

After I've changed, either because of external rewards or because of my belief that I can make a difference, how do I maintain those changes? It's easy to quit smoking for example, but staying smoke free is another story. After I've taken the plunge, I can maintain my commitment to healthy behavior by first, examining the pros and cons of either changing or not changing. This depends highly on having accurate information presented to me in a clear manner. Confusing health messages don't quite do the job.

A number of factors influence our tendencies to listen to and believe a particular source of information. Research on *persuasion* — getting somebody to do something he may not do on his own accord — has supplied psychologists

Information age

Many people have said that we live in the "Information Age," and I'd have to agree that there's a lot of information out there. At times, the world seems to suffer from an information overload. With all of these facts, figures, and opinions floating about, who and what information do we tend to believe? For example, do those stop-smoking ad campaigns really work? Media campaigns usually are only effective when they inform us about something we don't already know. By now, almost everyone knows that smoking is harmful to one's health. We didn't always know about the health risks associated with smoking, and when that information finally became public knowledge, smoking rates dropped. But a lot of people kept smoking, and many people actually picked up the habit. Then again, many people feel that the mainstream media is not trustworthy. I've even heard people say that the idea that smoking causes cancer is bogus.

with much of their knowledge in the area of source believability. Who do we believe? For a message to be persuasive, it must grab our attention, be easy to understand, and be acceptable and worthwhile. We also have to remember it. If we don't remember the message, who cares what it said? Persuasive arguments present both sides of an issue, making the arguments look fair and unbiased. What about those horrible, fear-inducing messages, such as some of the stop-smoking campaigns? They work best when steps toward improvement are mentioned along with the scary stuff.

Decisions to engage or not to engage in healthy behavior are based on many factors, including your beliefs about the behavior and your locus of control. Becker, in 1974, and Rosenthal, in 1988, came up with the *health belief model* to demonstrate the psychological processes we go through when making health-related decisions. The model is based on our beliefs about the following:

- ✔ **Severity:** How bad can the illness or disease get if I don't do something about it?

- ✔ **Susceptibility:** How likely am I to get sick if I don't engage in healthy behavior?

- ✔ **Benefits outweighing costs:** What's in it for me, and is it worth it?

- ✔ **Efficacy:** How effective will my attempts at change be? I don't want to work for nothing.

The answers to these questions play a role in determining the likelihood that we'll do the healthy thing. If I arrive at a high severity-, high susceptibility-, high benefits-over-costs-, and high-efficacy conclusion, the likelihood that I'll choose the healthy option goes up. Otherwise, I may need a real kick in the pants before I select the healthy path.

> ## Working out with Walker
>
> Do we believe celebrities? Usually we do, but only if they're likable, enthusiastic, and perceived to be confident and trustworthy. Who wouldn't trust an exercise machine promoted by Chuck Norris? He's a Texas Ranger, he's the law, and he kicks butt too!

Intervening

After you decide to do something about your unhealthy lifestyle, what can you actually do? When the decision to change has been made, you can do a couple of things to get the ball rolling. Health psychologists or other health professionals can design *interventions* that help you change and maintain that change.

Behavior modification is a powerful method of behavior change. The most basic, yet very powerful, form of behavior modification is to use punishments and rewards for either not engaging or engaging in the target behavior. If I schedule myself to run three times a week at 5:30 p.m. and I don't, I have to clean the kitchen, bathroom, and do the laundry that night. If I comply though, I get to treat myself to a nice dip in the spa. The trick with this technique is to enlist a partner to keep you from cheating on your rewards and punishments. I may decide to go in the spa, even if I don't run, or skip the laundry in the same situation. That's why a partner helps; he or she can keep you honest.

Cognitive change is a process by which I examine the mental messages I give to myself that may prevent me from changing a behavior or maintaining a change. We all have *automatic thoughts* — thoughts that we don't realize automatically go through our minds in situations. I may tell myself or my wife that I really want to run three times a week, but I also may be having the automatic thought, "You'll never do it, you never follow through with anything." Well, thanks for the positive reinforcement. The good news is that automatic thoughts can be replaced with positive self-statements. This process takes a lot of practice and encouragement from other people, but it's usually worth the hard work.

I've only really begun to scratch the surface of health psychology and stress-related issues, but I hope that this chapter provides a good overview of the subject and whets your appetite for more knowledge about living a less stressful and healthier life. Remember: Relax, don't avoid things, and believe in yourself. And reward yourself when you follow through with this advice.

Part VIII
The Part of Tens

The 5th Wave   By Rich Tennant

"I heard it was good to use humor when you're having an argument."

In this part . . .

What's a *For Dummies* book without the Part of Tens? In this part, I first introduce you to a new orientation in psychology called "positive" psychology. The focus here is on psychological *health* instead of the traditional focus on *sickness*. Within this discussion, I provide some practical advice on maintaining your psychological health. After getting you fired up with those positive tips, it's time to go to the movies! In the final chapter, I play Ebert and Roeper as I lay out what I think are ten good psychological flicks.

Chapter 23

Ten Tips for Maintaining Psychological Health

. . . .

In This Chapter

▶ Defining "healthy"

▶ Maintaining relationships

▶ Helping others

▶ Going with the flow

. . . .

*T*here's no magic formula for being a psychologically healthy person. There's no absolute standard. Is being psychologically healthy simply the absence of mental disease or mental illness? If so, a lot of us are healthy. Is the absence of physical disease the same thing as being physically healthy? Some people think that there's more to being healthy than being disease free. Unfortunately, this chapter may create more questions than answers.

Psychology is not necessarily in the business of deciding what we should value as a society or not. A lot of scientists feel that values are beyond the scope of science and that they don't have much to say about the "good life." These scientists feel that values and morals are too subjective and personal and often can not be reduced to scientific analysis Some psychologists however feel that psychological health is as close to a universal value as any. Who doesn't want to be healthy after all? Psychology has learned a lot about human thinking and behavior over the years, and it would be a waste not to try to apply some of that knowledge to our quest for well-being, happiness, and health. I agree that psychologists may be overstepping their bounds when they advocate a particular set of values. But, as a professor of mine once said, "That's an empirical question, isn't it?"

What did he mean by that question? He meant that opinions can be evaluated empirically, and one opinion can be judged with respect to another as long as agreed upon criteria for evaluating the opinions are in place. In other words, we may actually be able to evaluate the "good life" with psychological science as long as we can all agree upon a definition of what the good life is. For example, we may agree that a good life is one in which our needs are met without much effort and we're relatively free to do what we please. Then, we could scientifically evaluate circumstances, behaviors, and thought processes that lead to such conditions. If we can agree upon a standard, we can investigate what contributes to the achievement of that standard.

The standards, however, are a matter of much philosophical and theological debate. Each individual, each culture, and each society may have a very different definition of the good life. Nevertheless, it again comes back to ascertaining a definition. If we can do this, we can investigate what contributes to that particular version of the good life with the methods and tools of science.

Because this chapter is about tips for psychological health, I have to set a standard. So, I define psychological health broadly as *optimal living*. This is a safe position because each of us can tweak the meaning of optimal living to fit our own values. If I'm a devout Christian, my definition of optimal living may be to live as sin free as possible and conduct myself as Christ would have wanted me to. If I'm an anarchist, I may define optimal living as being completely free of all reigns and limitations on my freedom. My use of optimal living in this chapter is a *subjective* view of psychological health. For years, psychologists have studied the concept of *subjective well-being*. This concept refers to my sense of personal well-being and happiness without reference to the views of anyone else. It represents my personal values, and it may or may not be in harmony with others around me.

Some philosophers have argued that it is morally preferable to hold values that correspond with the values of others or, at the very least, to hold values that don't impinge upon or impact the values of others. Subscribing to a value system that doesn't impact the values of others is kind of like having a "different strokes for different folks" philosophy. Another definition of psychological health is perhaps more objective. This definition holds that psychological health centers on behaviors and mental processes that lead to the ability to adjust and function well in one's life. This view can also be subjective to some degree. For example, I may adjust quite well to prison, but this adjustment may involve behaviors that could be considered quite unhealthy in other contexts. But, for most people and societies, the norms for good adjustment and functioning often involve surviving within the typically acceptable rules and boundaries most of us live in, and most of us don't go to prison.

At the very least, psychological health involves being happy. I've never met a person who didn't want to be happy, even if being happy to him meant being miserable. You can't escape the desire to be happy. That reminds me of a joke: If a masochist prefers cold showers, does he take a warm shower instead?

Enough of the philosophical, let's get down to practical suggestions. The following ten tips for maintaining psychological health are not in order of importance. Each of them is as important as the other.

Accept Yourself

A lot of popular psychology and self-help books tell us to "love ourselves." It's not a bad idea. Severe dislike for oneself is often associated with extreme guilt, shame, and depression. Believing in one's abilities and valuing one's uniqueness is not to be underestimated.

Too often, we lead inauthentic lives that are defined by others as we strive for their acceptance. Self-acceptance is a crucial ingredient for motivation and positive emotion, and accepting ourselves even helps us accept others more easily.

Struggle to Overcome; Learn to Let Go

It's an undeniable fact of life that all of us will face challenges and adversity. Being able to effectively cope with these challenges is crucial to maintaining psychological and even physical well-being. Each of us has a variety of skills and techniques that we use to cope with stress and adversity. The best general advice for coping with adversity: Cope actively within situations that you have some measure of control over, and cope passively within situations that you don't have control over. Active coping involves taking actions to improve a situation such as looking for a job when you're fired instead of just saying, "Oh well, I guess I just wasn't meant to have a job."

We have very little control over the death of a loved one. Sometimes we can run ourselves ragged trying to shake our feelings of loss and sadness. But eventually, we have to accept the reality of the situation. Accepting reality when we can not change it is a good example of passive coping. Forgiveness is another good one. In situations that we can control, such as many health-related problems, taking action consistently leads to better outcomes and better psychological functioning.

Stay Connected and Nurture Relationships

Sometimes it seems like our modern lives are lonely lives. Everyone speeds around in their cars, isolated from other people and busy with the details of their own lives. I've often felt like I have to sacrifice productivity at work in order to socialize. I hear people make similar comments all the time, "I just don't have time for friends and family." Here's a tip — make time!

In these times of mega-cities and super-suburbs, it can be hard to stay close to friends and family. The age of the small town is all but gone. Small towns are out there, but most of us don't live in them. Despite these conditions, we can all benefit from working to maintain closer proximity to people who matter to us. The huge growth in cell-phone and Internet use may reflect both our desire to stay connected and our attempt to do so in such a fragmented and fast-paced world.

Having friends and family around is nice, but it's only a good thing if the relationships are good. Some of us can't wait to get as far away from these people as possible. Feeling emotionally connected and supported is just as important, if not more important, than simple proximity. We need intimate relationships that we can count on when times are hard. We need trustworthy romantic partners who value the same things that we value and value them as much as we do.

Some other helpful hints for maintaining good relationships: Practice forgiveness, be tolerant, communicate honestly, express yourself, balance independence with dependence, and act responsibly toward and nurture the values, desires, and feelings, and wishes of others.

Strive for Freedom and Self-Determination

When we feel like the captain of our own ship, we're more interested in life, more excited about life, and more confident. Our motivations are a complex mix of the things we truly want for ourselves and things that we've adopted from significant others over the years.

Feeling as if we have some control over the decisions that affect us is crucial to psychological health. When we're in controlling, punitive, or dominating environments, our sense of importance and freedom is lost. Sometimes we have to adapt to the desires and values of others. When we have to adapt, we can still retain our sense of self-determination if we agree even slightly with what we are adapting to. What if I want to paint my house bright purple, but the city won't let me? Well, if they agree to lavender, I'm more likely to feel less pushed around. It's rarely (if ever) a good thing if we feel like we're being told what to do and we don't agree with the directive.

Find Your Purpose and Work Toward Your Goals

Feeling like life is meaningless is a hallmark of depression. One of the drawbacks of modern society is the sense of alienation that can come from working day in and day out with only the next workday or the next paycheck as a reward.

It's crucial to have goals. Research consistently finds that the process of working toward one's goals is as important as the goals themselves. At times, goals can be too lofty, and we can set ourselves up for disappointment because we can't reach them. This defeats the purpose of setting goals in the first place. That's why realistic goals are helpful.

Find Hope and Maintain Faith

Research has consistently shown that having a deep sense of religious faith can be a protective measure for dealing with loss, illness, and psychological disorders. When things seem dark, it really helps to have a sense of hope and optimism about the future and a belief that our goals will eventually be achieved.

Having a *positivity bias* helps to override fear and keep us motivated. Being biased in this way is kind of like seeing the world through rose-colored glasses. Pessimists may claim that they're more in touch with reality, but a little positive illusion never hurt.

Lend a Helping Hand

We all face challenges in life. When we reach out to others in need, we often get a sense of mastery over our own circumstances, and we certainly foster positive social conditions. Lending a helping hand helps the intended beneficiaries, and it also helps the individuals who offer the assistance. I won't mention that there's a nice tax break in it too.

Find Flow

Professional athletes talk about "being in the groove" when they've had a good game. *Flow* is the experience of feeling totally involved, engrossed, and focused in an activity or experience. Living a happy life is a matter of learning to maximize and control our inner experience so we feel harmoniously engaged in the activity for its own sake.

I once heard a piece of Buddhist wisdom: If you are thinking about resting while sweeping the floor, you are not truly experiencing life as it exists. When you sweep, sweep. When you rest, rest. Find flow!

Enjoy the Beautiful Things in Life

The ability to appreciate beauty is *aesthetics*. There's a lot of negativity and ugliness in the world — wars, disease, violence, and degradation are all around us. Depressing, huh? Being able to appreciate that which is beautiful is a saving grace in a world that's so often unattractive.

The experience of beauty is a personal one and one that no one else can define for us. We may see the beauty in a famous painting or the sun shining through the clouds. When I see a well-executed play in football, it brings tears to my eyes. "That's beautiful man!" Sniff, sniff.

Don't Be Afraid to Change and Stay Flexible

Sun Tzu is a famous Judo master from Japan who wrote a book called *The Art of Peace*. His secret to living a peaceful life was the core principle of Judo: Go with the flow! When we are rigid and inflexible we are more likely to experience resistance and strain ourselves in trying to maintain our posture. When we are flexible and willing to change a behavior that is not working for us we are more adaptable and better adjusted. It takes courage to change our ways, but it is vital for health and well-being. You say you can't teach an old dog new tricks? Who's talking about dogs?

Chapter 24

Ten Great Psychological Movies

So what makes a good psychological movie? The definition of a psychological movie is a film that directly addresses a psychological topic or mental disorder and/or utilizes psychological concepts or a psychological theme as part of the plot.

My ratings of the movies covered here are based on a five-cigar rating system. Sigmund Freud was quite the cigar aficionado, and receiving five cigars would have sounded great to him. For our purposes, five cigars is a great film, and one cigar is a bad psychological film. Each film can earn one cigar for each of the following criteria:

✔ Accurate depiction of a mental disorder

✔ Accurate portrayal of a person suffering from a mental disorder

✔ Accurate depiction of the structure, process, and function of mental health treatment including psychotherapy and medication

✔ Insight into the subjective experience of a person suffering from a mental disorder or other psychological dilemma

✔ Use of psychological principles and knowledge to anticipate, predict, and get inside the mind of the characters in the film is necessary on the part of the viewer

One Flew Over the Cuckoo's Nest

One Flew Over the Cuckoo's Nest was released in 1975 and based on Ken Kesey's book of the same name. The film stars Jack Nicholson as Randle P. McMurphy, a man who is involuntary committed to a mental hospital.

The thing that makes this movie a real contender for the Golden Cigar is the question of whether Nicholson's character is really mentally ill. The film seems to be commenting on the mental health system during the time period within which the movie is set and how the system was used as a means of social control. Is Nicholson's character mentally ill, or is he just a pain in the neck who has a problem with authority? There's no doubt that Jack stands out and bucks the system every chance he gets, but does that make him sick? Maybe he just has a real zest for life.

For the acting, social commentary, and existential dilemma, I give this film five cigars! Definitely check this one out!

A Clockwork Orange

A Clockwork Orange, based on the book by Anthony Burgess, was made in 1971 and stars Malcolm McDowell as Alex DeLarge, a young troublemaker and delinquent. McDowell and his gang of three friends engage in various crimes and shenanigans, such as fighting, vandalism, skipping school, and the like. One night, they steal a car and go for a joy ride. They commit a horrific home invasion, raping a woman and brutally beating her husband. McDowell gets caught.

This is where the psychologically interesting part begins. McDowell is put through a rigorous behavior modification program that utilizes a technique called *aversion training.* After learning takes place, every time McDowell's character is exposed to violence, he becomes violently ill. Therefore, he is compelled to avoid engaging in violence in order to avoid getting sick.

The film seems to pose a number of questions: Do we really want to resort to such tactics in reforming our criminals? Are we doing more harm than good? Is the level of violence in a society a function of a collective aversion to it or more a matter of the strong preying on the weak?

For the macabre nature of the film and its use of behaviorism, not to mention the social commentary on violence in society, I give this film five cigars!

12 Monkeys

12 Monkeys, directed by Terry Gilliam and starring Bruce Willis, Madeleine Stowe, and Brad Pitt, takes place in a post-apocalyptic world in which Bruce is sent back in time to stop whomever spread a virus that destroyed the world.

The psychological crux of *12 Monkeys* is the question, "What is real?" How do we know if someone is really delusional or not? How can we prove that God really does speak to some people? Willis and Stowe develop what looks like a mental disorder known as *folie à deux,* a shared fantasy or delusion by two or more people.

The acting in *12 Monkeys* is great. Brad Pitt's portrayal of a schizophrenic is outstanding. The questioning of reality is a complicated topic, but *12 Monkeys* pulls it off. Five cigars!

Ordinary People

Ordinary People (1980), directed by Robert Redford and starring Timothy Hutton, Jud Hirsch, Donald Sutherland, and Mary Tyler Moore, is about a teenage boy recovering from depression and a suicide attempt following a boating accident that took his older brother's life.

Ordinary People is an excellent story about how complex grief and depression can be and yet how much can be accomplished by taking things slowly and making them simple.

The acting is superb. The depiction of a mental disorder is excellent. Only one problem costs this movie a cigar. Psychiatrists rarely, if ever, do psychotherapy nowadays. Psychologists, social workers, and marriage and family counselors conduct most psychotherapy. Four cigars!

Primal Fear

This film, directed by Gregory Hoblit and starring Richard Gere and Ed Norton, Jr., is another film about reality. But instead of presenting a doctor trying to convince a patient that the patient is ill, this movie is about a patient who tries to convince a doctor that he, the patient, is ill. Say what?

The only thing wrong with this movie is the use of a neuropsychologist as the expert witness in this case. Neuropsychologists do not typically testify in cases involving insanity unless the issue of brain damage is at issue. Dissociative identity disorder is not a typical subject for neuropsychologists. Other than that one flaw, this movie easily deserves four cigars!

What About Bob?

What About Bob?, starring Bill Murray and Richard Dreyfus, is a farcical comedy about the doctor-patient relationship in psychotherapy. This movie is not quite as deep as the previous selections, but it tells the story of mental disorders from a different perspective, that of the therapist.

One of the more serious questions that this movie asks is exactly what does someone with a mental disorder really need? Do they need cold and abstract therapy or just a real connection with a family that helps them get over their fears and feel safe?

What About Bob? belongs on this list because it takes a light-hearted approach to the serious issues of anxiety, professional relationships, and therapist sanity. Listening to people's problems all the time can be stressful. It can take a toll. Therapists need a life of their own where they can get away from their work. Murray is a therapist's worse nightmare, the patient who won't go away. The situation is funny and scary at the same time. But Murray could teach a lot of therapists a lesson — don't forget to address the more mundane aspects of your clients' and patients' lives. Simplicity may be the key. The only problems with the movie are the potential to downplay the seriousness of the type of behavior that Murray's character exhibits and, again, the portrayal of the psychotherapist as a psychiatrist, and M.D. Psychiatrists don't typically do psychotherapy any more.

Despite its shortcomings, and that it's a goofy move, *What About Bob?* deserves four cigars.

Girl, Interrupted

In *Girl, Interrupted,* Winona Ryder plays a depressed and suicidal young woman admitted to a mental hospital. She's reluctant about being there and resists many of the efforts by the staff to help her "get better."

The movie contrasts the characters' lives and afflictions as a way to demonstrate that middle-class suburban angst is small potatoes when compared to other more serous illnesses. At the same time, the film doesn't minimize Ryder's difficulties, but instead it appears to place them in perspective. Developing a new perspective is a turning point for Ryder's character — her life is simply being *interrupted.* She won't let her life end in the institution due to a failure to deal with her problems.

The moral of the story is that Ryder's character was fortunate to have made it out alive, merely taking a detour into mental illness instead of permanent residence. It's a very personal story. It's a story about hope and the harsh reality of some people's lives. Five cigars!

The Silence of the Lambs

This is the movie that made everyone want to go out, join the FBI, and become a *profiler.* Jodie Foster and Anthony Hopkins star in this psychological thriller that gets you inside the mind of a serial killer. Foster's character, Clarise Starling, is an FBI agent who must deal with a famous psychiatrist/serial killer named Hannibal Lector, played by Anthony Hopkins. The movie centers on their interactions and the psychological games they play with each other in order to get what they both want. Hopkins plays doctor with Foster's psyche, while Foster asks Hopkins to look inside and use his self-knowledge to help her catch a serial killer.

The movie's strength does not really lie in its portrayal of a mentally ill psychiatrist, but more in its insight into how the human mind works and how we become who we are. The tragedy of Foster's childhood makes being a profiler her destiny. The serial killer's (Buffalo Bill) quest for transformation into his true self drives his horrendous murders. The real anomaly is Hopkins's character. He seems to represent both the good and the bad aspects of the human psyche. He helps Foster, both as consultant and as healer, but he also demonstrates depravity and demonic insanity through acts of murder. It's as if he is both the giver and the taker of life. His powerful knowledge of the human mind easily turned into a tool for murder.

Hannibal Lector represents what a lot of us fear — those we trust to help us can also hurt us. Five cigars!

Sybil

Sally Field stars in this classic 1970s movie about multiple personality disorder (MPD). Field, playing Sybil, is a reclusive young woman who appears to be shy and quiet, but underneath the surface, a chaotic tangle of personalities swirls out of control. She ends up in the care of a doctor who begins to treat her for multiple personality disorder.

The scenes in which Field and her doctor are in therapy are very dramatic and disturbing. They're intense! Sally Field's performance is very powerful. It's actually pretty hard to watch someone act so strangely. It gets a ten on the "Hair on the Back of My Neck Standing Up" scale. It gives me the willies! As she switches back and forth between personalities, the therapist begins to gain some insight as to how Field could have become so ill.

Field's character was horribly sexually and physically abused as a child. The film presents the professionally popular idea that MPD is the result of the personality splitting off from itself in order to defend the core personality from the reality of the abuse. It does a good job of respecting this notion and stays a true course, not yielding to the temptation to get too "Hollywood."

The strength of *Sybil* rests on three pillars: Sally Field's acting, the emotional intensity of the therapy scenes, and the portrayal of the hypothesized cause of multiple personality disorder. Five cigars!

Psycho

No list of great psychological movies would be complete without Alfred Hitchcock's *Psycho*. Anthony Perkins stars as a depraved psychopath with a strange delusion that involves dressing up like his mother. Perkins's character appears to suffer from a spilt personality in which part of his personality is his mother. How weird is that? The "psycho" in *Psycho* only kills one person in the entire movie, small potatoes by today's standards, but Hitchcock's use of suspense and surprise are superb.

Psycho introduced the American public to the idea of a psychopathic killer, a man with a warped mind. On the outside, Perkins' character is meek and socially awkward, a boy in a man's body. He enjoys the voyeuristic thrill of an occasional peep at his motel customers. The suggestion is that underneath that calm exterior is a deranged killer waiting for his opportunity. But the key psychological component in *Psycho* is Perkins's twisted relationship with his mother. He is the quintessential "momma's boy," unable to go out into the world on his own and enjoy the pleasures that he fantasizes about. Freud would have been proud of this twisted version of Oedipus in which Perkins's mother, rather than the father, is the castrating threat. Perkins's rage appears to be the product of his failure to be the king of his own castle, so to speak.

Psycho is a classic. Don't bother with the remake with Vince Vaughn — go rent the original. Five cigars.

Index

• *G* •

Notes